A Walk on the
Crust of Hell

Jack Markowitz

A WALK ON THE CRUST OF HELL

The Stephen  Greene Press
Brattleboro,   Vermont

FOR THE HEROES
WHO LIVED THESE STORIES

This book has been produced in the United States of America:
designed by R. L. Dothard Associates; composed, printed,
and bound by Colonial Press. It is published by
the Stephen Greene Press, Brattleboro, Vermont 05301.

Library of Congress Catalog Card Number: 73-82747
International Standard Book Number: 0-8289-0186-4

73 74 75 76 77 78 79 9 8 7 6 5 4 3 2 1

Author's Note

THE IDEA for this book did not move in the usual direction from author to publisher, but the other way round. It was conceived by Mr. Stephen Greene and only reached me over a fortunate chain of inquiry linking Messrs. Russel D. Hamilton, associate editor of the Greene Press; William T. Schoyer, a Pittsburgh writer; and Walter F. Toerge, secretary of the Carnegie Hero Fund Commission. Prevented from doing the book himself by the pressure of other business, Will Schoyer generously recommended me. There are many ways of being kind to a newspaperman, but one of them surely is giving him a shot at writing a book on an appealing subject. So I am greatly obliged to the gentlemen named above, not only for the starting signal but for many aids and encouragements along the way.

Large is my debt, too, for the cooperation of those peerless "hero detectives," Messrs. Herbert W. Eyman and Irwin M. Urling; and of Messrs. Stewart McClintic, president of the Carnegie Hero Fund Commission; David B. Oliver, its vice president and manager; and Ronald E. Swartzlander, chief of its field staff. Without access to the Fund's voluminous reports of official investigations of heroic acts, the book obviously would have been impossible. The events told here represent far less

than one percent of the cases the commission has judged worthy
of award since 1904—and of course a much smaller fraction of
all the cases investigated until now. And let me testify that if
there be, in this world of forms, documents and filing cabinets,
any sort of official report worthy of regard as a literary form
unto itself, it must be a Carnegie Hero Fund field report. Some
I have consulted run to a dozen or more legal-sized, single-spaced
pages: great, gray regions of tightly packed words, names, and
numbers—but how the suspense builds and the drama leaps
from those heavily-laden pages of fact after fact after fact!

Additional help for which I am indebted came from Mr. Paul
Chodera; Mr. Don Easterly; Mr. and Mrs. John Hooley; Mrs.
Stanley Long, mother of Dennis Long; Mr. Richard A. Mathie-
son Jr.; Mr. Robert Mentzer; Mr. Rolland D. Sharp, father of
Reta Rena; Mr. and Mrs. Andrew Ulrich, parents of Mike;
Mr. Robert Whitehead; Mr. Joseph C. Wiest; and Drs. Francis
B. Colavita, Joel Goldstein, Martin Greenberg, and Ervin Staub;
Mr. William Meegan; and Mrs. Neysa Hebbard, my copy editor
at the Greene Press. Finally let me thank my wife Middy and
our daughters for granting enough peace and quiet to get the
writing done, yet not so much as to run any risk of spoiling me.

JACK MARKOWITZ

Contents

Caught in a
Grip of Stone

HINCKLEY RESERVATION, twenty miles south of Cleveland, is a unit of that city's Metropolitan Parks System. Its landscape is typical of northeastern Ohio: too gentle to stir any national fame, yet giving a good deal of quiet local pleasure, and at no time more than in the fall. Swimming season is over then, but rowboats still ripple the lake and voices carry across the water with a soft clarity. On weekends thousands of families drive out "to see the leaves." Maple, oak, sour gum, and sassafras glow in every shade of gold and scarlet. When the breeze stirs them, they tremble like butterflies, under towering green nets of Norway pine and spruce. Cars drive slowly along the roads, and ripe walnuts in their green sacs fall on the blacktop with a gentle clunk.

Pleasant as Hinckley is to the eye, the great attraction it offers is Whipps Ledges—giant outcroppings of sandstone and Sharon conglomerate left by the last Ice Age.

Like a pile of giant gray bones the Ledges rear up in places one hundred feet above a wooded ravine. It takes rope and piton, and climbers of experience, to scale their steepest walls of bare stone—yet just a few yards away children and even older folks clamber over cracks and up gentler brushy slopes to the very top.

In the past, some eighty feet up on this tumble of earthbones, like a dark eye in a skull, stared Wild Cat Cave. The name was pure romance; actually its black interior harbored no wild animals of any kind.

On a certain autumn Tuesday, with no weekend crowds to hear him, Morris Baetzold was the cave's only living creature. He had it all to himself for twenty frantic minutes.

The easy way out was not for Morris. With two friends from the Methodist Children's Home of Berea, Ohio, he already had explored the safe part of the cave. Even little children were able to penetrate back to the "room" where (so went the popular legend) runaway slaves had been hidden before the Civil War. This was a space ten feet square and just high enough to allow the three boys—all fifteen years old—to sit up. It gave them a grand crawl of the flesh to snap off the flashlight and to make themselves sit in the utter dark and silence, breathless and oppressive as the grave.

If a boy thought critically about it, he might wonder why any slaves had ever *had* to be hidden this far north, Cleveland being only one good day's hike away. But imagine nights of terror being spent in this very hole!—with no food, the water running low, the whites of the fugitives' eyes glowing in the flicker of candlelight; and filtering in faintly through the stone, the baying of infuriated bloodhounds.

The boys pressed these visions as far as their imaginations could go, and then crept out of the "room" single-file with Morris in the rear. They came to a stone slab on the right which, like a valve, blocked the crossing of the main and a side passage. Thirty-five feet ahead the cave exit shone wide as a door. The first two boys brushed off their jeans and leaped out into the sunlight.

Morris, however, lingered by the fallen slab. It was a massive piece of stone, about six feet square and two feet thick; it must have weighed tons. A thousand, maybe a million years ago, it had cracked out of the cave ceiling—before there ever was a runaway slave, or a State of Ohio, or even such an oddity as a boy from a broken home.

Resting at an angle, the slab offered just two dark triangular openings into the side passage. The tighter of these was fifteen inches on a side, and right down on the cave's floor.

On sudden impulse Morris slithered in there, all five feet eight and 110 pounds of him. He had tried a few feet of the passage before. It intrigued him.

It was pitch dark behind the slab, and chilly—the constant 55 degrees of dead spaces in stone. But the passage was six feet high and a yard wide and Morris could stand in it. Too bad his pals had the flashlight!

Still, he wasn't scared. He wanted to do something strictly on his own. There was, he was convinced, another room down this passage, leading to a second exit: it seemed to him he had heard that somewhere—anyhow he felt sure of it. The thrill of finding it on this trip would be uniquely his. He would inch along in the dark and be drawn into a wash of gray light which would grow brighter as he followed it; and finally he would come upon a beam of gold from the outer daylight and climb it to his own secret exit. *That* was exploring!

And so Morris advanced, his hands carefully feeling along the cold stone walls as he went and his feet gingerly testing forward. It was not until he had made considerable progress that Morris Baetzold, at 11 A.M. on Tuesday, October 5, 1965, understood how much he had dared. By then, though, he was screaming for help.

His absence was discovered by nose-count when his school bus was about to return to the children's home after the outing in the park. There had been three teachers and fifteen students; the census now was one short. "Morris!" they called. Boys ran up

through the trees and onto Whipps Ledges shouting, "Morris!"
Presently a search party returned to Wild Cat Cave. From a
point below and to the left of a massive stone slab the earth
seemed to have acquired the terrified voice of a boy.

"Don't worry, lad, we'll get you out!" teacher William Powell
bellowed into the darkness.

A student with a flashlight squeezed behind the slab. The
passage, it was observed, descended at a 15-degree angle, and its
ceiling sloped down even more sharply. As a result, fifteen feet
below and away from the slab, what started as a corridor
narrowed down to a V-shaped fissure, a mere crack, about four
and a half feet high. It was eighteen inches wide at the top, just
half of that at the floor.

Ten feet in there—into the crack—on the bottom, lay Morris.

Caught in a "V" of stone, he was wedged tightly at his chest
and hips. He had toppled on his side, trapping his right arm
underneath him. His left leg wriggled toward his pals; his face
was out of sight in the far darkness.

He had scratched with his left hand till his nails were broken
and bleeding, but he could not reach any handhold by which to
lift himself. He was as good as paralyzed. Muscles which might
have moved him were all somehow squashed down and neutralized, and the movements he was able to make were squirmingly
ineffective—except to wedge him deeper and tighter into the
unrelenting stone.

Teacher Powell wasn't about to let any other boy squeeze in
there! Someone ran down a quarter-mile to the nearest road and
flagged a park ranger. Within minutes an alarm was alerting
both the police and volunteer firemen in Hinckley village two
miles away.

Fire Chief Paul Chodera and volunteer Bob Whitehead were
among the first at the scene. Whitehead, a tavern keeper in
Hinckley, was twenty-six and wiry enough to worm behind the

slab. But neither he nor any of the other volunteers could get into the tightest part of the fissure. That even a boy could—much less *would*—squeeze in there strained belief. One man muttered, "A kid has to want to get into that kind of mess!"

The best the early volunteers could do was to poke a two-by-four wooden plank along the bottom of the fissure and try to raise the boy on this lever. But Morris was too far down and in. There was no fulcrum, no way to get leverage, though Whitehead and others sweated and grunted in the dim, bruising space behind the slab for some time.

They did, however, push a thin red hose as far in as possible towards Morris. Soon the hiss of compressed oxygen made the air more breathable.

Still, two and a half hours went by and the best help Bob Whitehead could stretch out to Morris was reassuring words. "We'll get you out," he said, "we're working on a lot of things. It's only a matter of time."

When he finally emerged for a break in the mid-afternoon sunlight, Whitehead blinked in amazement. A crowd!

An appeal was pulsing out in widening circles from Hinckley: for strong, small-bodied volunteers to help extract a 15-year-old boy from a cave. This message brought to Whipps Ledges hundreds of individual body types combined, as often as not, with some exotic notion of how best to achieve a rescue. Among the volunteers was at least one dwarf whose girth, however, was as ample as his good will. He was unable to squeeze behind the slab.

The news media picked up the scent. By 5 P.M., as thousands of commuters streamed out of Cleveland and Akron, their car radios told of a boy trapped, by then, for six hours.

That evening, as it happened, Hinckley's garden club ladies were to serve their annual dinner for the police and volunteer firemen. Some of the latter, astonished that "the kid hadn't been got out yet," stared blankly at the empty tables at the dinner and then drove out to Whipps Ledges. Everybody else seemed to be there.

The traffic of feet in the sandy bed of the cave entrance stirred up clouds of dust. It drifted back to the men laboring in the passage and even reached the wretched trapped boy, making him sneeze and cough. Police Chief Ronald Ciammachella finally had to order reporters, cameramen and scores of others getting in the way back—"Back!" They were roped off at fifty feet. Morris's 60-year-old father, with whom he had not lived for some years, was allowed through to shout a few words of encouragement; also a brother, Donald, eighteen.

One skinny fireman was able to stretch far enough in to throw a lasso over Morris's lower left leg. But the boy wasn't wearing a belt and when the others back in the passage started hauling, Morris never moved. Only his pants did. The rope merely pulled on the trouser leg.

As the sunny day darkened into clear, chilly night, coffee and donut wagons appeared. Volunteers' wives brought heavy coats to their men. Fires were lighted, blankets went around shoulders. On the darkening slope little groups talked gravely of the boy's danger.

But for hundreds the vivid fires, the roar of the power generator which illuminated the cave entrance up on the Ledges, the newsmen intoning solemnly to microphones and cameras: all this pulsed with the drama of a nationwide sensation unfolding. People wanted to be part of it. Only the cold of night, which would end with frost whitening the autumn brilliance, finally would drive the curious and the benignly useless back along the shrouded roads to home and TV set.

The struggle in the cave went on. Morris managed to catch a rope-end tossed to his left hand stretched behind him. But as the men hauled on the rope his hand was twisted behind his back and he had no strength to hold it.

Later, firemen extended a steel hook on a long pole. Morris caught the hook and inserted it in the collar of his simulated-leather jacket. When rescuers pulled on a rope attached to the hook, the boy seemed to rise slightly. Then his jacket tore and the hook ripped free, striking a spark off the stone wall.

Morris broke down. "You'll never get me out," he cried. "I'm gonna die here!" And to add to the boy's misery, he at last had to yield to the press of bodily urgencies. Morris Baetzold was as unhappy, as disgusted and ashamed of himself, he thought, as any boy in the history of the world.

Mr. and Mrs. Andrew Ulrich were watching the news on television in their home at North Royalton, a Cleveland suburb. Ulrich was a husky, round-faced man with a broken nose and a grin that almost pinched his eyes shut. He was a tool grinder at an automobile engine plant in the city, and he had eight sons.

Fatherhood was a serious matter with him. Behind his house, on the site of a natural spring, Andy Ulrich and some friends had excavated and dammed not just a swimming pool, but a spacious pond. It was stocked with black bass and some neighbors said the Ulrich boys swam as well as the bass. Disciplined and sure of themselves, these kids might be able to help at the cave, Ulrich thought. His wife wasn't sure. The news reports made great mention of the variety of experts and gear already on hand. "We'd only get in their way," she said. And her husband agreed this made sense.

In fact, by then a Cleveland mining company was preparing to bring up a thirty-six-inch drilling rig. This could gouge a shaft twenty-five feet down from the top of the Ledges to a point somewhere in front of the trapped boy. But it would be used only as a last resort. Mysterious stresses web through a rock structure: hit one nerve of weakness and tons of rock might collapse.

The mining men urged that a trained cave rescue team be summoned from the National Speleological Society in Washington. Fire Chief Chodera got on the phone and by 3 A.M., famed spelunker William Karas and his crew arrived by Air Force jet with a splendid assortment of ropes, straps and clamps . . . but no one skinny enough to reach Morris and hook the lad up.

A nurse from Akron tried. Five feet two and eighty-five pounds, with ropes slung to her belt, she strained to within two feet of the boy—and then dissolved in claustrophobic panic. She had to be pulled out.

It was a maddening situation. In actual walking distance this boy was no farther than sixty feet from the mouth of the cave! And so much help was on hand. There was a volunteer welder, able to fabricate any sort of metal hook or tool ordered; several carpenters rigging up devices of wood; a doctor from the town; the muscle power of any number of men; and cave experts who had pulled spelunkers and miners out of dozens of deeper, more complicated scrapes. If only this boy had fallen with his head toward, rather than away from, his rescuers. Or if he had more than one hand free. Or a belt on. Or even clothing sturdy enough to hold a hook. Somehow these disabilities and mischances had to be overcome.

"I guess we considered—at least talked about—a hundred different schemes during the night," Deputy Fire Chief Bob Mentzer recalls. Some were wildly impractical: to try to force the rock walls apart with jacks; to rig up the hardware of an overhead garage door and pick the boy up and out like a haunch of beef. There wasn't even a way to get food or drink to Morris. It was a disspiriting night, whose only comfort came in the brief periods the exhausted boy dozed off.

Next morning at 6:30 Andrew Ulrich was leaving home for work. He turned his car radio to the news. The boy in the cave was still trapped. Eighteen hours! It was like a slap in Ulrich's face.

Could his boys help? The second and fourth eldest, Michael, fifteen, and Gerald, twelve, were both small, sturdy fellows. Abruptly Ulrich pulled his car alongside a phone booth and reported off work.

An hour later he and his boys were clambering up to the cave at Whipps Ledges.

The "circus atmosphere," as he saw it—all the cameras, vehicles and crowds in what looked like almost a festive mood—repelled him. Quietly he asked to see someone in charge, but he was possibly the four or five hundredth man to ask that and for an hour or more no one paid much attention to him.

Some thought already had been given to using younger volunteers, but the authorities quailed at the risks. What was to keep an inexperienced kid from also getting trapped? But a certain modest firmness about Ulrich and his sons impressed the firemen and spelunker Karas. There was no bluff about these people. And if the father himself was volunteering the boys, well . . .

The choice fell on Gerald, the younger. First Andrew Ulrich had to sign a release of liability. Not too pleasant that. With an expression of distaste he scratched his name.

Gerry Ulrich, a blond, cheerful boy, stood four feet eleven in his shoes and weighed eighty-two pounds. With two ropes running from straps around his chest and waist, he crept into the passage. His father, too chunky to get around the stone slab, watched from an opening, biting his lip.

Gerry made unprecedented progress. Able to stand nearly upright in the fissure, he got to within six inches of the trapped boy's foot. Morris's spirits leaped. "Is there anything I can do to help?" he begged. "Just tell me."

Then something happened which Gerry Ulrich, even years later, was at a loss to explain.

He could not bring himself to lean down.

The boy blubbering on the floor, miserable and filthy in that dim, suffocating enclosure, looked like a snarled, smothering, foul-smelling fish. Nauseated, suddenly gasping for air, Gerry cried to be pulled out. Disgustedly the firemen hauled him back. That's what came of using a kid! But Andrew Ulrich gathered his boy up in a bear hug and held him tight till he grew calm again.

Andy wasn't daunted. "Why don't you try the other guy?" he said.

The "other guy" didn't talk much. Some might have said that Michael Victor Ulrich was taciturn to the point of being withdrawn. Blond and intense, with pale blue eyes, he studied what was happening with his lips drawn to a tight line above a small, firm chin. He had had some First Aid training as an Eagle Scout. Normally 135 pounds, he would have been husky for his five feet seven, if he had not with schoolboy grit trained down to 120. This was to prepare for wrestling at the Catholic high school where he was a tenth grade student.

While Bill Karas was briefing him, Mike took off his jacket to reduce his bulk. That left him in a cotton shirt, trousers, shoes and socks. He had on a strong belt. To this, at his left side, a rope was tied. A nylon strap went around his chest and another rope trailed from that, under his left arm. But that wasn't all. Mike stowed a nylon strap and a metal clamp in his left trouser pocket. And one more strap went inside his shirt. He held the two long ropes that trailed back from him in his left hand, to keep them up out of the way. Plenty of hardware—now if he could keep it all straight and still move!

He started into the fissure. Two feet in, the ceiling drew so low and the side walls so tight, he could neither stand nor stoop. So he began easing himself down toward his right side by pushing both hands against one wall and arching his back against the other. While changing handholds as he lowered himself, he would take a deep breath and lock himself in place between the walls.

The boy's self-control and patience impressed the men peering in after him. He finally worked himself down parallel to the floor of the fissure, his head lower than his feet, his right hand down—down at all times!—for support. He would *dive* in on top of Morris, but he wasn't going to rest on that squeezed floor, not for a minute. It was vital to stay out of that vise.

He progressed by emptying his lungs and simultaneously heaving himself up and ahead with his right hand—an inch, two inches at a time—then, with another deep breath, locking himself in place between the walls. Then heave and lock again. It was a weird kind of "swim," and torturously slow. At times, laying down the trailing ropes, he could find skimpy holds with his left hand, briefly taking some weight off his right. At no point was the fissure sufficiently wide to let him bring either hand between his body and the black, pressing walls.

It took Mike ten minutes to move eight feet. But at last he was looking down on Morris Baetzold's ankles.

From back in the passage men poked battery lamps into the fissure as far and as high as they could. There was no real help for it, though: Mike's position inevitably blocked most of the light. He would have to work on Morris in his own shadow.

It must be stressed that he could not use his right hand. That was needed strictly for support. He could only use his left, and that only by reaching over and past his own face and head. Still, little by little he was able to work Morris's sodden trousers down, down, past the boy's knees.

Then Mike drew one of the straps Bill Karas had given him from his pocket and awkwardly passed the strap around Morris's left leg, three inches above the knee. Now the hard part: slipping the end of the strap through the buckle with just one hand. But he did it. And then he tightened the strap, not too snugly yet, on Morris's leg.

He still had to fasten a hauling rope to that strap.

All the while he talked to Morris. "It's only a matter of time and you'll be out," Mike said, unconsciously giving echo to words

Morris had heard again and again for nearly twenty-four hours.

Back in the passage the men were breathlessly silent, too tense to realize how close and fetid the air had become, or how crowded the passage with grimy, weary bodies. Mike wiped the sweat from his eyes and dried his left hand on his shirt. Then he unhooked one rope from himself and passed about twelve inches of it through the strap above Morris's knee. Another tricky task: knotting the rope one-handed. Somehow he managed that, too, and then, as the final step, tightened the strap itself as Karas had told him to.

For the first time in a full day, something concrete had been achieved—one tight strap around Morris Baetzold's knee, and a rope to pull on it.

That was that. It had taken Mike another ten minutes to work on Morris. His supporting right hand had put in plenty of service already and felt as though pierced by a swarm of hot and cold needles. But it had to stand up for another ten minutes of retreat from the fissure, a reverse "swim," coming out backwards. And it did.

"Good boy, good boy, you little son of a gun!" the men in the wider part of the passage were saying as he came out. It was good to be slapped on the back by grown men, to be accepted as one of them; it was worth the needles in his hand. Mike did have to be helped to his feet, though. He was that cramped.

The men in the passage wasted no time. A crewman of Karas's picked up the rope from Morris's leg and leaned into the crack as far as a man could. He put the rope up across his shoulder—to provide some lift—and the others started hauling from behind him.

Morris Baetzold budged. Two inches. And no more!

They weren't *raising* the boy, that was the trouble. He had to be lifted up—UP—not just dragged in the bed of the fissure. If anything, he would wedge tighter. There had to be some way of getting elevation!

Bill Karas, looking almost ashamed, walked over to Mike Ulrich resting beside the stone slab. The kid was still massaging his arm. It must feel plenty cramped, Karas guessed. But look here, if Mike took a few minutes more to rest, did he think he could . . . ?

That was enough for Andy Ulrich. He had to step outside. Some prayers deserve saying in fresh air. After the suffocating suspense of the cave, daylight came as a shock. There was sunshine out there, blue sky, trees stirred by the wind! And people: hundreds of them among the brilliant foliage and the tumbled boulders of the slope, gazing up at the cave, waiting to cheer a life saved (or would they—depressing thought—be as morbidly satisfied by a life lost?).

How could it be that one life merited so much attention? Every week a thousand die on the roads and others unnumbered in hospitals, by illness, natural disaster, old age. These, however, are too many and past help. The heart cannot absorb such numbers; it stiffens to them. But one life on the razor's edge, able to fall either way, draws on the nerves of each of us. Every man knows that he will sway in that balance one day; that though he be in bed, with doctors the struggling would-be rescuers, the ultimate fall will be his alone. He must wrestle it with death as one—*the* one. The life in peril is always his.

Back on top of Morris Baetzold's ankle, Mike Ulrich now knew better what had to be done.

First he opened the strap on Morris's left thigh. Hauling on the rope had slid it down to the knee. Then Mike circled the strap around *both* of Morris's legs, three inches above the knees. The pulling rope stayed attached.

The critical question was whether there was something, some sort of projection, that could give the hauling rope some *lift*. With his left hand, Mike felt up along the rough rock wall. He put his hand up, over, across. Yes! There was an outcropping. No bigger than a fist, but it might do.

Mike pulled out the strap he had stowed in his shirt and with his left hand—and his *teeth*—he worked the strap's end through the buckle and drew it to an 8-inch loop.

This he hung on the projecting rock.

Now he took the metal clamp from his trouser pocket. It was shaped like a letter C. This he connected from the loop around the rock to the hauling rope. It would act as a pulley, providing an almost straight-up force on Morris's legs.

Mike's return squirm took another ten minutes. Once again he couldn't stand without help. He limped over beside the stone slab to stretch out.

The tension in the passage was all but unbearable. The men who would haul on the rope couldn't seem to get the sweat off their hands. They rubbed their pant legs. Should they give the rope a real jerk—or pull easy? "Easy, easy," Karas cautioned. And they started pulling. Nobody breathed. The rope tightened up over the leg of the C-clamp, tightened, tightened some more . . .

Suddenly Morris Baetzold's hips swung up out of the wedge of rock.

"It's working," he cried, "it's working!"

He was able to pull his right arm out from under his body. He could use both hands! The men kept pulling till Morris's bare legs were almost up even with the loop around the projecting rock.

But something was wrong. Only the bottom part of his body was moving. He was still wedged at the chest. It was as if his breastbone were hinged in the stone.

Bill Karas swore aloud. He stamped angrily around the passage. Still stuck! And he looked down at the game boy resting by the stone slab. How could anyone ask him to volunteer even once more?

On his third trip into the fissure, Mike Ulrich once again worked with his left hand and teeth and made a slip loop in a second long rope. He pushed this loop out across Morris's free left hand and head. Then with groaning difficulty the trapped, exhausted boy inserted his newly-freed right arm up through the circle of rope and worked it down on his torso just below the shoulders.

Mike removed the C-clamp from the rope to Morris's legs and transferred it to the new rope at the shoulders. Object: to dislodge the upper part of Morris's body.

Once more Mike checked and tightened the other ropes and straps, he hoped for the last time. And then he made one more—this time, agonizing—return trip out of the fissure.

He had thought of switching to left-hand support, right-hand work. But he had considerable apprehension about sinking and getting wedged in the narrow bottom himself, and no matter how much punishment it took, he simply trusted his right hand more. And it did get him out of there. But the way it felt after his third mission, he wondered if a fourth wouldn't be just physically impossible.

This time the rescue team was taking no chances. Karas put every chip he had on the table. Through a hose extended on a long pole, a gallon of a slippery glycerine solution was dumped on Morris. Volunteer Curtis Peck, of Akron, then shoved a narrow greased board under the boy. They'd *lubricate* him out of there!

The men met resistance as they started hauling on the rope to Morris Baetzold's shoulders. "Pull," said Bill Karas, "pull!" And if anyone could have seen Andy Ulrich's tense face as he stood helpless outside the slab, his lips might have been read mouthing the word, "Please!"

Morris groaned as his chest and back scraped stone, but there was more joy than pain in it. He swung upward. His chest was free!

No time to cheer yet. More timbers were stuffed in under the greased board beneath Morris. These would keep his body from sagging while being drawn out. At all costs he had to be kept suspended where the fissure was a foot or more wide. And slowly, carefully, the men, no longer tired, pulled on the ropes and on the greased board.

It was 1:30 P.M., Wednesday, October 6, 1965, when Morris Baetzold, cramped, skinned, a great black bruise on his left cheek, and staring vacantly in shock, was brought again into the sunlight. Cameras and microphones floated at him out of a dazzling sky which hurt his eyes; police struggled and shouted to hold people away from his stretcher, while cheer after cheer rose up, gathered more throats and swelled to become a chorus sung from the eternal stones of Whipps Ledges which had clutched him for twenty-six and a half hours.

Six years later; another sunny October day; and a reporter went searching for the life that had been saved. Morris Baetzold recovered quickly in a hospital, but he left the Methodist Children's Home a year later and went to Boys Town, Nebraska. Later he was known to have held, briefly, a series of menial jobs in the Cleveland area. A friendly chaplain at the Home hadn't heard from him in some time. Possibly he would get in touch again, possibly not. That was how it was sometimes with boys from the Home.

At Hinckley Reservation the usual Sunday crowd was clambering over Whipps Ledges. But no one seemed to have heard of a place called Wild Cat Cave. Then the reporter spied a man pointing out to his wife a hole in the rocks about the size of a door. "Would that be where the rescue was a few years ago?" "That's it," said the man. A few feet in from the mouth, the cave ended in a solid wall. Within twenty-four hours of the rescue, on police orders, it had been dynamited and sealed forever.

Driving up to a comfortable ranch home in North Royalton,

Ohio, the reporter smiled at what seemed a horde of boys washing not one but several cars in the driveway. Mr. and Mrs. Andrew Ulrich, after all, are parents of eight sons.

Little Gerry, who approached but could not help Morris Baetzold, had grown to a handsome six-footer. Mike Ulrich, newly home from a tour of duty in Germany with the Army, was planning marriage. Embellished now with a small goatee, he was still spare and tough, but no more talkative. "There was too much hassle about it. It happened a long time ago," he said.

And it was all he would say.

His genial parents suggested, apologetically, that the front-page fame which had come to Mike at fifteen, the Boy Scout and press awards and honors from community groups, had pleased him at first, but ultimately repelled him. To be called "Mike the hero" by jocular classmates was less desirable than it sounds. In short it had all been "too much hassle," and Mike Ulrich would just as soon never speak of it again.

He had never even shown his fiancée what, for one of another temperament, would have been a prized possession. His mother had to dig it out dusty from behind a shelf full of knick-knacks and school mementoes.

It was a bronze medal three inches in diameter. On one side it bore the likeness of Andrew Carnegie and the words, Carnegie Hero Fund, Established April 15th, 1904; and on the reverse, a motto beginning, "Greater love hath no man than this. . . ."

Six Dead,
How Many Heroes?

A PATCH OF ASPHALT in the street, not bulging so high as to cause a car going over it to bump, marks the location of death. Standing on it, Irwin M. Urling checks his watch—it is a minute or two before ten in the morning—and looks at his shadow in the street. It slants forward and somewhat to the left. "I'm looking north," says Urling, and he makes a note of it.

He is a portly man of sixty-two in a rumpled gray suit, worn shoes, a raincoat, and a battered hat whose wide brim has been out of style for most of a generation. But Urling's duties do not call for elegance and the hat has done him good service against sun and rain. If anything, the rumpled look serves him better. People are less on guard with him. They talk more.

Urling stands easily: heels together, shoulders relaxed, belly comfortably extended. He is concentrating. There is a kind of heavy dignity, not quite officiousness, in the way he, taking his time, occupies the middle of the street. If a car came, he would give way, but slowly, so as not to blur the mental fix he is carefully trying to achieve.

Now he has it. A few stately paces to the curb and, feet together, he lifts a folded sheet of paper up close, very close, to his straining eyes. With a ballpoint pen Urling draws a few lines, a crude map (he will refine it later) of the intersection of Lowrie and Gardner Streets in the Troy Hill section of Pittsburgh, Pennsylvania. One corner he labels "school," and the others, "store," "gas station," and "funeral home." He draws a tiny rectangle in Lowrie for the underground vault twenty feet west of Gardner and six feet away from the north curb, where, on November 17, 1971, six employees of a local gas company met a swift, suffocating death.

Urling makes careful notes knowing that his employers want everything definitely located—his employers being the Carnegie Hero Fund Commission, for which agency he and five other special agents earn their living by traveling the continent in search of the truth about reported acts of civilian heroism.

"We live in an heroic age," Andrew Carnegie wrote in a Deed of Trust to the commission he founded in 1904. In retirement at age sixty-eight the little Scot was as energetically giving away his millions as he had earlier been accumulating them. His shining causes were education and peace. It exasperated him that military courage, necessarily spreading death and ruin, should monopolize public glory and the emulation of youth. The worst sort of example! Why not equal, yes, greater honor to those who *save* life at risk of their own?—and aid to the widows and orphans of these unsung?

The heroic deaths of two rescuers in a 1904 coal mine disaster were the direct spur to Carnegie's creation of a "hero fund." But the idea of honoring, and more important, of financially aiding, heroes of peace had been turning over in the philanthropist's mind for a considerable time.

"I have long felt," he wrote, "that the heroes and those dependent upon them should be freed from pecuniary cares resulting from their heroism, and, as a fund for this purpose, I have transferred to the Commission five million dollars of First

Collateral Five Per Cent Bonds of the United States Steel Corporation, the proceeds to be used as follows. . . ."

More than 53,000 acts of rescue have been reported to the commission in the seven decades since, and it has made over 6,000 awards for heroism. That is a greater number by far than the total of Congressional Medals of Honor bestowed over the same period in the nation's wars, though the essential high qualification is the same: an act "above and beyond the call of duty."

From the very first, the commission realized it could not depend on news accounts or hearsay but would have to perform its own painstaking investigation of reports of heroic deeds.

"This is going to be a hard case to establish," Irwin Urling says to himself, frowning at the asphalt patch on Lowrie Street. His most obvious difficulty is that the six men are dead. Which of the six were would-be rescuers and which only victims? Further it can never be known for certain whether those who tried to rescue others realized the risks they were taking. And this is of the essence. Blunderers who absently trip into death cannot be Carnegie award heroes. Yet one fifth of all the Carnegie awards since 1904, some 1,200, have been made posthumously. For the commission and its investigators death is a hindrance, but not an insurmountable obstacle.

Urling has been investigating rescues for a quarter of a century. He completes an average of fifty cases per year. From these he then submits perhaps thirty-five for an award, and the commission may approve thirty-one. The final decision is not his.

That is made in a comfortable, but hardly lavish, suite on the 19th floor of an office building in downtown Pittsburgh. The commission always has sat in the city where Carnegie made his fortune. Its membership has turned over many times since 1904; but its spirit and style are virtually unaltered (though time, prudent stewardship, and the growth of the United States economy have increased the fund's endowment to about $14,000,000). The commission still consists of twenty men of a certain standing in the city of steel: business executives, lawyers, physicians, other professionals. Every two months they gather around a long table in a carpeted room, away from the stress of the events they must judge, with even the noises of the city muted far below. They consult official reports prepared for their eyes alone, gravely discuss questions of risk and mysteries of motive; and decide whether at such a time and place, such a man, woman, or child has performed a deed of the sort their founder had in mind.

If so, some weeks later, the hero or his next of kin will receive a medal, three inches in diameter, most often cast in bronze, with an engraved inscription concisely describing the deed. Approximately ten percent of the heroes honored over the years have received medals in silver for special valor. Nineteen gold medals have been awarded, but many years have passed since any individual won one. The commission nowadays reserves gold for those rare occasions when great numbers of people, entire communities, are caught up in a spirit of mutual help. Thus, a specially mounted gold medal went to the doctors, mine officials, and numerous volunteers who, toiling for nine days in constant danger, at last rescued 99 of 174 coal miners trapped below ground in October, 1958 at Springhill, Nova Scotia.

It is only by coincidence that Irwin Urling happens to be on a case in the commission's headquarters city. The field embraced by the fund, as Carnegie laid it out, is the United States, Canada, Newfoundland, "and the waters thereof." A map of this territory hangs on the wall of the Chief Special Agent's office at the commission's headquarters. Movable pins mark the locations where field agents happen to be working at any given date, where there are widows and pensioners to be visited, and where cases are pending for investigation.

Urling's "pin" is home, he having just returned from Texas,

where, among other cases, he investigated the rescue of workers from a flaming oil rig in the Gulf of Mexico by sportsmen in a fishing boat. Field agents normally are on the road ten to eleven months of the year. Pittsburgh hears from them in bundles of meticulously detailed reports: a private news service on splendid human moments.

Urling has done his homework on the Troy Hill case. From correspondence and newspaper files he has copied names and addresses of everyone supposedly involved. He knows the rough outline of what happened. Gas was leaking into a manhole in Lowrie Street. One man was pulled out, but two were overcome still down there. Four others jumped in to save them. And all six died.

The first name on the investigator's list is that of the woman who gave the alarm.

Mrs. Helen Flack operates the Hilltop Confectionery on the corner. After the sunny street, the store's interior seems dark, and it takes a moment for the eyes to solve a maze of candy and magazine racks, grocery shelves, a luncheon counter, and pinball machines. Urling removes his hat respectfully but he is in no hurry to identify himself. He takes a seat at the counter.

A young woman in blue jeans brings his cup of coffee. He asks, "Would you be Mrs. Flack?"

She is a blonde with steel-rimmed glasses. Her shirttails are out and her lower lip has a saucy curl. "Miss Flack," she says, "I don't want to be Missus."

"You will be," Urling easily remarks.

"Not me," she says, but her smile is a sign that the contrary view does not offend her.

Urling had hoped to see *Missus* Flack, he explains, to talk over the gas accident of the previous autumn.

"My mother saw everything that happened," Miss Flack quickly volunteers, and Urling is immediately alert. In a case where six direct participants are dead, someone who "saw everything" could be an invaluable witness. Unfortunately, he is told, Mrs. Flack has left the premises on business and will not be back till afternoon.

The investigator sighs. Normally he would have telephoned to make certain she would be there. (He almost never *writes* ahead, however. Too much notice that a Carnegie agent is en route can distort the case. Witnesses and rescuers might "rehearse" and invent details they do not actually recall.)

"I got here when it was over," says Miss Flack, running on. "I talked to the widows. Some of them came up the same day. They had to see where it happened. One night we heard a man crying over the hole in the street. My mother went out and put her arm around his shoulder and tried to lift him up. She said, 'Look, you can't keep on like this. You're not going to be any good to your family.' "

"Well," says Urling, getting up, "I must certainly come back and talk to your mother."

An hour later in the fire station corridor he is interviewing Joseph E. Meier, a lanky, solemn fireman, aged thirty-seven.

"We got a call there was a man in a hole," Meier is saying. "When we got there, there was six of them in the hole. From what I understand, they were working and one got sick and came up, and some went down to get their buddies."

This testimony is after the fact, of course. Urling merely listens with his head cocked to one side, his pen and note paper motionless in his hands behind his back. "Could you smell gas?" he inquires.

"Oh yeah," says the fireman, smiling at the seeming naiveté of this. From Urling's point of view, however, if gas could *not* be smelled, it could reflect on whether the would-be rescuers knew the risks they were taking. "We had to use 'air-packs' to go down in there," says Meier. "I helped pass two bodies up."

"How much space was down there?"

Spreading his arms, the fireman suggests an area about six feet square and eight feet deep.

"How were the men lying?"

"Every which way," says Meier. He holds out two fingers of his left hand, crosses them with two of his right. "In a pile."

"Were any of them 'tied in'? Any ropes to pull them out in an emergency?"

Meier shakes his head. "I couldn't see any."

This discussion has been useful to the Carnegie agent, but the official fire department report is a must. That is in the hands of Battalion Chief C. P. Harris, who is away at a meeting and will not be back for an hour. Thus, it is a convenient time for lunch.

At the restaurant Urling studies the menu by cocking his spectacles on his brow and passing the bill of fare slowly three inches before the pupil of his right eye. His hair is white except for a few remnants of the wheat of youth, but his voice is as resonant as that of a man twenty years younger, and there is craftiness and humor in his myopic glance.

If asked what ails his eyes, "everything," he admits, cheerfully rattling off a half-dozen afflictions of which the most commonly known is astigmatism. He sees reasonably well at a distance but close work is a strain. He once edited a suburban newspaper, until a doctor warned him he would have to quit reading copy or go blind. Now, instead of recording too many notes that he would have trouble reading, he forces himself, in interviews, to listen with great concentration. "My memory usually gives it back to me," he says.

Back at the fire station, in Battalion Chief Harris's office, there are piles of forms stacked up on the desk and even on the cot where Harris might catch a nap.

"The curse of the day," Urling remarks, "is paperwork."

The chief accepts this sympathy with a solemn smile. He is a dark, powerfully built man with a tattoo on his forearm. The walls of his office are decorated with framed photographs of his sons in football uniform.

"The call came in at 2:53 P.M.," the chief says, referring to his official report. An "extremely dangerous gas condition" was the radio phrase. The first victim was being brought to the surface as Harris arrived at the scene. Gas was shooting out of the manhole with such force that dust and rust were whirled fifteen feet in the air. "It looked like a damned tornado," says the chief.

He and some of his men jumped into the hole with masks on. They stuffed a man's jacket and some wet cloths into the six-inch main from which the gas was pouring, and finally forced a metal seal into place, stopping the flow.

Meanwhile, other firemen on the street were trying to resuscitate the victims by mouth-to-mouth respiration. The chief joined in this effort. "There was no response," he says. Natural gas, methane, is not a "poison gas." But it suffocates by replacing the oxygen in a person's lungs. Harris remembers rust in the eyes of the dead men staring up at him as he tried to breathe life into their gaping mouths. And there was rust caked in the backs of their throats.

"Shouldn't they have been wearing life lines down there?" Urling asks.

"Life lines are one thing," says the chief, "but they didn't have a mask! I know why, all right. Because you can't tell people what you want to say through a mask, never mind safety! Utilities are always doing jackass things like that—changing equipment 'on the fly,' they call it."

"On the fly?"

"Yes, instead of shutting off the gas in the neighborhood first—that way they'd have to notify every home—they leave the gas on, remove the old valve, and shove in the new one real quick. 'On the fly.' They do it all the time."

Harris angrily pulls off his glasses. "In this case," he says, "the negligence was very evident to me."

Irwin Urling blows the air from his cheeks. Establishing negligence or culpability is not any part of his function. He is looking for the admirable, not the guilty, deed. But now the question of fault inevitably is going to shadow his work on this case, creating reticences where there are more than enough complications already and more than enough men silent.

Urling has calls to make. A nearby YMCA offers as convenient a phone booth as any. First, the gas company. It is cooperative. It arranges to have him meet the few surviving members of the Troy Hill manhole crew. But they are out on a job and will not return to the maintenance division shop till four o'clock in the afternoon. That is still two hours away.

Has he time to meet a widow?

The widows of all the rescuers in the incident will have to be visited personally. The Hero Fund is not only, or even primarily, an agency for dispensing medals. Carnegie made it quite clear that, if financial need could be demonstrated, heroes and their dependents "should not suffer pecuniarily."

Thus, over the decades the commission has paid more than $8,000,000 in pensions to injured heroes and in monthly "contributions to the livelihood" of heroes' widows, until they remarry. Another $1,000,000 has gone to further the education of awardees or their orphaned children; and nearly $3,000,000 in outright grants to heroes in need.

These are not "rewards." It was Carnegie's view that true heroism could not be "stimulated" by hope of gain. In fact, persons who earn their living by protecting life—e.g., police and firemen—usually are ineligible for Carnegie awards. So, too, are most members of the armed forces and those rescuers impelled by the spurs of kinship, like the father who rushes into a burning house for his own child. The fund exists for the selfless volunteer.

With his spectacles again up and his head bent close over the telephone book, Urling is noting the home phone numbers of the six dead men: the crew's boss, plus William Letzkus, Albert Zeleny, Raymond Grundler (the only one who was unmarried), Donald DeVine, and Monroe Coleman.

The latter two, so far as Urling knows, were the pair in the pit: victims rather than heroes; the others went in after them. The commission can do nothing for victims' families. So for them Urling needs only to "fill in some blanks," as he puts it; confirm the victims' names, addresses, ages, marital status. He will go to some lengths to do this without the painful necessity of visiting their homes, if he can avoid it. In the case of one of the victims, with a few phone calls and some patient waiting on the line, he is able to coax sufficient information from a funeral home.

It is not unusual for him to encounter people who get exasperated at the amount of detail his reports require. But usually his plea, "I have to fill in the blank somehow," works. Anything but force a man to leave a form blank empty!

Classes are out at the high school across the intersection when Urling returns to Mrs. Helen Flack's Hilltop Confectionery. Gray and plump in her loose housedress, the lady exudes an air of gruff maternity with the teenagers who fill her shop. Her voice is a husky whisper—from the cigarette in her fingers, or from years of yelling at kids, who knows? "I bought this pop," says a boy, holding out a dime to her without the two cents for the bottle deposit. "I'm gonna drink it here," he says. She smiles and chucks him under the chin, saying, "If you don't, I'll get ya tomorra."

But she is unable to confirm that she "saw everything" to Urling. She remembers a man running into her store crying, "Three of our guys are down in the hole! Call the rescue squad!" And she did. A minute later someone brought in a fellow who was still alive. She gave him a glass of ginger ale. But that was as close as she got to the accident. When she looked outside and saw firemen trying to revive, mouth to mouth, the dead men in the street, she felt woozy herself and didn't want to get any closer.

"They worked and worked on them for hours," she says but instantly withdraws the exaggeration, ". . . oh, not for hours but quite a while. There was nothing they could do."

No, she didn't know any of the victims. They had been working outside her store just that one day. A few of them had come in for a snack at one time or another. One nice fellow—she believed it was DeVine—had a cup of tea about 2:45, not ten minutes before the accident, and a lady who happened to be in the store at the time remarked that she would be afraid to work with gas all the time. DeVine smiled, she recalls. "What's to be afraid of a little gas?" he said.

"A few nights later," Mrs. Flack continues, "I heard crying outside. I went out and found this man kneeling by the spot. I said, 'Come on now, you don't want to do that.' 'You don't understand,' he says, 'he was my father.' He named one of them, I forget which. 'He was my father.' "

And Mrs. Flack, remembering this, has tears in her eyes.

Driving toward the maintenance depot of the gas company en route to meet surviving members of the ill-fated gas crew, Urling recalls that this is not the first industrial case he has investigated in which the failure to employ fundamental safety equipment has caused what he calls "needless" death. "I've known 'em to die while life jackets and masks were sitting on the back of a pickup truck six feet away," he says to the driver.

In the tool room of the maintenance depot he catches up, at last, with a true eyewitness. Edward J. Klingensmith, thirty-one, is a friendly, red-haired man who wears his work pants slung low on his hips and his white cap at a jaunty angle. He is a welder. He was about to enter the manhole in Lowrie Street when the gas started pouring out.

The job had looked routine enough: changing a worn valve in a six-inch main. The main itself had been turned off. The gas that figured in the accident was a so-called "back flow" from the neighborhood lines off the main.

In the manhole stood DeVine, Coleman, and John J. Ladasky. At street level, handing equipment into the hole, were Letzkus, Zeleny, Grundler, Herman Ranallo, Klingensmith, and the supervisor of the crew.

The latter had telephoned one of his own superiors at the gas company, and the decision had been made to change the valve "on the fly"—that is, as the fire chief had told Urling, to remove the old one and replace it with a new one immediately, within a few seconds.

DeVine and Coleman, Klingensmith tells him, unbolted the old valve. Ladasky was standing ready to slip the new one into place. But when he tried to work it into position, for some reason the fit wasn't right. Gas from the back-flow began escaping. Up on the street, the boss ordered the men in the manhole to stuff the line with a wad of wet rags, which were thrown into the pit. This was done; yet enough gas escaped that Ladasky's knees suddenly buckled. DeVine and Coleman caught him before he fell. "Get Ladasky out of here!" shouted DeVine, a 23-year-veteran of the gas company. He and Coleman hauled Ladasky over to the ladder; Ray Grundler came part way down to help him up, and Ranallo and Klingensmith hoisted him to street level. Unnoticed in the confusion, the wad of wet rags slipped out of the gas pipe and fell to the floor of the manhole.

"I took Ladasky over to the side of the building to walk him around," says Klingensmith. "You could see he was overcome with gas. By then you could smell a lot of gas."

And by then DeVine and Coleman had collapsed in the bottom of the pit—and Letzkus, Zeleny, and the boss, one after another, were jumping in after them to try to get them out.

Klingensmith distinctly saw two men enter the pit, but he was not sure which two they were.

"Why did they jump in the hole without masks?" asks Urling.

"I guess they thought they could hold their breath," says Klingensmith. "It was awful quick though. I yelled after the superintendent. There was no answer."

Ray Grundler whipped off a light sweater he was wearing, wrapped it around his face like a mask and desperately seized a rope. Klingensmith saw him too late. "Ray Grundler came running with the rope," he says. "He was going down in the hole. Me and another guy grabbed him—and then he just keeled over into the hole. We had him by the arm. He fell right out of our hands."

It is four o'clock and the maintenance crews are coming back from their various jobs out on the division. They are big men, most of them, with strong, grimy faces; they wear Levis and hard hats, sweat shirts, and mud-caked boots. They stamp into the depot from the parking lot joshing each other. They don't pay much attention to the portly gent in the gray, rumpled suit standing in the middle of the floor with his note paper behind his back. Through the open door, Urling watches the trucks as they pull in. He is looking for two more men, but one especially. Ladasky has the key to it, he feels sure.

Someone in the lot is pointing him out to two men who have just arrived in their truck. He walks out as they approach and introduces himself.

John Ladasky is an "m and s" man, meaning that his job involves maintenance and service. He is thirty but looks younger, with straight black hair and a boyish face that turns instantly solemn when he learns that Urling has come to talk about "the case." He was the only man actually in the pit to survive: one out of seven. And he still can speak of the incident only in the awestruck tone of one who, for reasons he cannot fathom, has been somehow singled out by fate.

After the first unsuccessful attempt to replace the valve, he had, he says, at the boss's orders stuffed the gas line with rags. Then, as he was removing this plug of rags, to try again to install the new valve, he passed out. "It gets into your system," he says. "You get kind of dizzy." He opened his eyes to see Ray Grundler on the ladder extending a hand to him. "He came down to help me, and Coleman and DeVine got me up on the ladder."

The story is taken up by Ladasky's companion, Herman Ranallo, fifty-five, a wiry man in a red cap and with a stubble of beard. "I helped pull Ladasky out and then I ran into the store to tell the lady to call the fire department. Grundler went back in the hole to help the others out—he went in twice. And I saw the supervisor jump in. There was four in the hole when I went in the store. When I came out, there was six in."

Urling asks, "Weren't there any life lines or masks that could have been used?"

Ladasky and Ranallo look at each other and shake their heads. "I didn't see any." "Me neither."

The case, with its many implications, has rather shocked the agent of the Carnegie Hero Fund. He is sorting it out in his mind as he drives home through the long shadows of late afternoon.

He had thought DeVine and Coleman, the two men in the pit, to be only victims. Might they also now be heroes? There is corroborated testimony that they both helped Ladasky from the pit, certainly saving his life. Yes, but did they think he was just momentarily overcome and themselves in no imminent danger? Or were they giving him a place on the ladder at the hazard, fully comprehended, of their own lives? Heroism—or just a helping hand? That would take thinking about.

Grundler seems clear enough. He went into the pit once for Ladasky, and a second time to try to get a line to the other men down there. He meant to save life, not much doubt of that.

But Zeleny and Letzkus: less clear. They were seen entering

the pit, at best, out of the corner of someone's eye. None of their words at the scene are recorded. Can it be fairly inferred that they intended to perform rescues? There were several moments when desperate men were literally jumping into the pit, taking a risk that they could hold their breaths long enough to save a buddy—and yet no one precisely saw what they were about. A heroic moment—perhaps—while everyone was looking the other way!

And the crew's supervisor: the hardest case of all. No question but that he courageously entered the pit to try to help his men out—and gave up his life for their sake. But he was the supervisor! Would they have been down there at all, if not for his decision? And where were the masks, the life lines? Were they not his responsibility? Or was he himself the victim of lax company procedures? An ordinary man may be such a victim, but a hero: would he not insist on safer procedures for his men no matter what?

The Carnegie fund is adamant on this point. One who causes peril to others can be no hero. No matter that he tries later to attempt a rescue, even if at the loss of his own life.

"This will be a hard case to establish," Urling had thought at the beginning of the day. He now realizes that for all his experience he hadn't known the half of it.

In the commission's own city some men will be declared heroes, perhaps with financial aid to their kin. Other men, just as dead, equally brave, no less precious to their own, will get nothing. Such an uneven division of praise and hard cash will create as much bitterness as joy and pride.

And yet to walk away from the case would be unthinkable. Carnegie could not have made his instructions clearer: the survivors of heroes "should not suffer pecuniarily." But it's equally clear that the seemingly pleasant chore of dispensing praise and a rich man's money also can be a burden and wearisome; for it at times requires the stern withholding of praise and money even when they may be passionately and pathetically anticipated.

There is only one way in which the twenty men in the carpeted office will be able to defend their decision in their own city: if they are supported by an investigation of the facts as fair and as air-tight as human ingenuity can make it.

Urling must study the gas company's own official reports and review its safety procedures. He must check out the coroner's findings in the case and probably get back to witnesses Klingensmith, Ranallo, and Ladasky with more questions. And there are still all those widows to see.

It has been a long day. Tired, the Carnegie investigator slouches in his car seat. But then it occurs to him that perhaps there is a just design in the fact that he—the most experienced man—is the one agent back in Pittsburgh and available for this complex assignment. His confidence in his skills returns again. The loose ends will somehow be tied, the questions answered and the report blanks filled.

———

Based on the facts as told in Six Dead, How Many Heroes?, *Monroe Coleman, Donald DeVine, Raymond Grundler, William Letzkus and Albert Zeleny were awarded bronze Carnegie Hero Award medals—all posthumously.*

Above Ceiling, Below Zero

AT 7:20 P.M. on Tuesday, May 17, 1960, Link Luckett's helicopter was laid up at the airport in Anchorage, Alaska, its innards on the hangar floor. Luckett was waiting for a replacement part to be shipped up from California. Until it arrived, he would earn nothing on his contract to ferry men and equipment to a pipeline construction project in Cook Inlet, the broad arm of the sea west of the city. He could only wipe parts and wait.

At practically the same moment, 120 miles north, four men driven by other urgencies were achieving triumph. With short steps in the snow and panting breath that blew about their hooded faces, they came to the summit of Mount McKinley.

All North America lay below them. At 20,320 feet their victory took light from the sun, but not warmth. The temperature was 30 degrees below zero. Ten miles to the west Mount Foraker glistened above a collar of clouds. Eastward, towns and villages, winding roads and the glint of rivers spread out under density beyond density of blue for 200 miles: a vast pool bounded at the misty rim of the world by other mountains—Hayes, Sanford, and Blackburn—piercing huge and white into an immaculate sky.

The four climbers said little. They preferred not to muddy the moment with too many words. But they shook hands and slapped backs and grinned through their snowglasses; tight, effortful grins in the pinching air.

They were John S. Day, fifty-one, the expedition's leader, a cattle rancher from Oregon; Peter K. Schoening, thirty-three, chemical engineer of Seattle; and twin brothers Louis and James Whittaker, thirty-one, who operated a sporting goods store in Redmond, Washington.

More than triumph was in their smiles. The spirit that drives men up mountains had played a prank this trip. Another climbing party stood on the peak: four men from Anchorage had preceded them by just a few minutes. "It's a crowded mountain," somebody joked.

In good humor the two groups congratulated and photographed each other, shapeless as bears in their parkas. But the Anchorage climbers were preoccupied. Their leader, 40-year-old Helga Bading, a woman, had fallen ill from oxygen deficiency. She lay in a tent at the group's high camp more than 3,000 feet below; they had to get back to her.

But Day's party could linger another quarter hour on the summit. Here and there, poking from the ice, shaft markers left by previous parties shivered and whined in the wind. Otherwise there was stillness, magnificent and forbidding. No man could stay long on that celestial island above all struggle. But each hated to leave, for then it would be over. And only by another total muster of will and strength on some other peak could each possess such a moment again. And when might that be? There could not be too many McKinleys in a man's life.

Reluctantly, they roped up and set off down the summit ridge. In motion, joined as they were by sturdy line, they resembled a kind of elongated bug on eight legs; this physical unity, in fact, expressed the only way men could hope to prevail in so challenging an environment.

The upper reaches of Mount McKinley suggest a camel's spine, if a camel can be imagined cloaked in ice. The hump is the mountain's summit, with a ridge coming down to the base of the camel's neck and rising from there to the head, which is a secondary peak lower than the hump.

It was down the "hump ridge" that John Day's party now trudged, moving a mile and a half northward as they descended a vertical 2,300 feet. At 10 P.M. the men arrived without incident at the "base of the neck," this being the top of Denali Pass, which divides the mountain's head from its hump. The men rested on the windy ridgeline of the pass before attempting to descend further.

Despite what their wristwatches said, the sun still blazed in the southwest. May in Alaska spreads daylight with a lavish hand, twenty-two hours of it each day, with the other two hours a dense blue twilight rather than darkness.

Denali Pass is a great sliding board of ice falling from the western side of the summit ridge. A hundred yards wide, mostly smooth but roughened in spots by the wind, the slope hangs for half its length like a sheet out to dry, then it scoops outward at 25 degrees—still steep enough!—to the ice field known as Peters Glacier a thousand feet below.

Day's party strung themselves out laterally at intervals of forty feet at the top of the pass and started down. As one man descended, the others would dig in with ice axes and crampons and haul the ropes taut. Then the lead man would root and someone else would advance downward a few yards. It was slow work but that was how it should be done, and in spite of fatigue each climber took pride in the style and the progress of it.

All went well during the first, steeper half of the descent. Though still 600 feet above the foot of the pass, Pete Schoening, who was in the lead, had nearly reached the gentler portion of the slope. High camp, with its tents, stove, and hot food, lay only a half hour away.

But then someone relaxed his caution, as climbers put it, "that one little bit."

One of the Whittakers slipped. The sudden heave on the line peeled the others off the ice like a strand of ivy from a wall. Down they rolled, a sliding, tumbling confusion of rope, axes, arms, and legs, with the slope rushing past, as one put it later, "like a freight train two inches from your face."

Each man clawed desperately for a grip on the ice. John Day, after 200 feet of fall, found himself tumbled up onto his feet for one solid moment. He jammed his crampons hard into the slope, but the lash of others on the line slammed him over again at once and he heard a clear snap of bone as head-first he plunged on. The wild fall continued for another 300 feet.

Then, having flogged its challengers sufficiently, Denali Pass seemed to lose interest in them. They rolled to rest 100 feet above the base of the pass.

Pete Schoening had suffered a brain concussion: he had tumbled most of the way down blacked out. Lou Whittaker's ears also rang from a knock on the head, but he was conscious and on his feet immediately; as was his brother Jim, who had been only bruised. The two of them unroped and scrambled over to Schoening just as he regained his senses and wobbled to his feet. "I'm all right," he said, telling an unwitting whopper. As he rubbed his hands absently over the stubble of beard on his jutting chin, it was clear that Pete Schoening was not all right. He was a badly dazed man. The Whittakers insisted that he sit down. Then they crunched across the sloping ice to their expedition leader, John Day, who lay motionless, but whose head was likely the clearest of the lot.

"I think," he said, "my right leg is broken."

He had, in fact, a compound fracture of the right ankle—and something amiss in the left foot, too.

And nearly 7,000 feet of vertical descent, over miles of glaciers, crevasses, and perilous slopes, lay between him and the "base camp" on a broad ice field at 10,500 feet—the nearest spot a light plane could land to fly an injured man out.

The Anchorage party by now had left the base of Denali Pass and were about a half mile away working along Peters Glacier to their own high camp. Alerted by the falling men's cries, they stared back as Day and his mates had gone twisting down the towering wall of the pass.

Questions and answers, shouted, flew clearly along the frozen fastness. Learning that Day had broken a leg, the Anchorage men parleyed and decided that three of them should push on to their own camp, where, of course, Helga Bading also lay ill. It was high time to get some help up here!

Soon, back at their high camp, the scrape of a hand-cranked generator was warming up a radio with line-of-sight communication to the base camp on Kahiltna Glacier, miles to the northwest and far, far below.

The faint signal of that radio would stir up, in the days ahead, one of the most extensive mountain rescue efforts in history.

Meanwhile, however, it was necessary to secure the continued existence of John Day through the night. Carefully the Whittakers slid their leader into a sleeping bag. Then they axed out a level niche in the slope and erected a crude fence of axes and pack boards to keep Day from rolling off. He assured them he would be snug.

It was past midnight now. The cold blue ocean of twilight had rolled in over them, up and over the slopes of McKinley, whose heights glistened in the blue twilight under the moon. Slowly the Whittakers dragged themselves down toward their high camp with the still dazed Pete Schoening in tow.

On their way down they met Paul B. Crews of the Anchorage party going up. Back up! An architectural engineer, Crews, forty-three, had a collapsed tent on his back. When he reached John Day, he cut a slit in the tent bottom, slipped it over the injured man, and erected it. Later the Anchorage team's Rodman Wilson, a physician, went up to Day with an aluminum splint and medicine to lighten the pain which had begun to throb in the cattleman's leg.

Next morning, Wednesday, at about nine came the first sign that the radio SOS had got through. An Air Force plane roared overhead to check the climbers' position. At noon, bush pilot Don Sheldon, who had a contract with both parties, flew his Supercub over from the two base camps and dropped radio batteries and medical supplies. Late in the afternoon two additional tents, a stove and fuel, a stretcher, C-rations, and tanks of oxygen for Mrs. Bading rained down from an Air Force plane.

Meanwhile, in Anchorage and as far away as Washington and Oregon, volunteer climbers—who ultimately would number fifty men—were being enlisted to fly to the village of Talkeetna, forty miles south of Mount McKinley, and from there to the base camps at 10,500 feet. In teams of six or seven they would then begin the trek of two or three days to the high camps: of necessity slowly, in order to accustom themselves to exertion in the rarefied atmosphere.

It seemed clear that the injured would need many hands to help them down—and on the ground. No plane could hope to land on the lofty washboard of Peters Glacier. At least no plane ever *had* landed, and taken off again, from so high as 17,100 feet.

Nevertheless, helicopters would be needed and Link Luckett, grounded in Anchorage, hankered to volunteer. His wife and three children at home, the fellows warming their hands around coffee cups at the airport, everybody, it seemed, was excited about the trouble up at McKinley. And yet there was his helicopter in surgery. Luckett decided he'd just wait all night, if he had to, for the part to show up!

On Peters Glacier, meanwhile, the Whittakers and Schoening

had erected the two tents which had been dropped to them about 100 yards below John Day's eyrie on the slope of Denali. Schoening's head had not yet cleared. His eyes were swollen, too. He climbed into a sleeping bag and promptly lapsed into a long snooze, unthinkingly leaving his left hand outside the bag.

The hand had no glove on it.

During the night the temperature sank to 15 below zero.

Schoening woke with a start. It was 5 A.M. Thursday. For the first time since his fall his senses were clear. Clear enough to feel something awfully wrong with his left hand.

It was frostbitten.

At nearly the same moment Link Luckett's replacement part arrived at Anchorage by air cargo. With a helicopter serviceman Luckett at once set about making his plane flyable again. If the engineers who had chartered his ferry service would allow it, he would get right on up to McKinley.

For those on the mountain Thursday passed as a day of precious little progress. Mrs. Bading's condition grew worse. Dr. Wilson now judged it absolutely critical to get her off the mountain. But there was no way of knowing, and none of finding out, how far away the ground rescue teams still were. The radio buzzed uselessly through long hours of static, as gusty winds rattled the tents.

Day's comrades, at least, were able to ease his condition by getting him off Denali and down by stretcher to the new tents on the glacier below. It was a slow, tortuous effort, requiring frequent pauses in the thin air, and with Pete Schoening able to lend just one hand to the task.

Finally, all together again in the tents, the group heard the drone of an approaching plane. There it was, a silver speck soaring above the enormous slopes. But it was fixed-wing; what could it accomplish? Reconnaissance? *Their* position already was known. The real question was where the *rescuers* were!

In fact, pilot William Stevenson and Air Force Sergeant Robert Elliott had been dispatched to find out just that—that and no more. They reported strings of men toiling up the slopes at around 12,000 feet. But then, for unknown reasons, Stevenson and Elliott extended their flight.

Mystified, the men in the high tents watched as the light craft made a pass over Peters Glacier. Suddenly the plane jerked out of control. It crashed on the ice and exploded in flames. The horrified onlookers had no chance to reach it before both men in the cockpit burned to death.

The Anchorage party had reached a decision. If Mrs. Bading had to wait for the rescue party, she would die. Thus it was decided that Paul Crews and Charles Metzger would start carrying her down at first light Friday. Dr. Wilson and Andrew Broughli would keep pumping this information out by radio, praying someone would hear it.

Below the high camps, a half-mile down vertically, Peters Glacier flowed out into the larger Kahiltna ice field. At 14,500 feet Kahiltna offered a stretch of fairly smooth ice a mile long and a half-mile wide. No plane ever had landed there, but one might, and this chance seemed better than no chance.

To get there was something else. A portion of the Peters slope plunged at 76 degrees, making it a very tricky descent even if there had not been a helpless woman lashed to a stretcher between Metzger and Crews. They did have one vital assist: a previous expedition had left fixed ropes at some of the tougher spots on the slope. These certainly would be needed.

Link Luckett was airborne again! With a decent night's sleep and permission to take another day off from his contract, he lifted from the Anchorage airport, waved to his repairman below, then made a wide, climbing circle out across the blue expanse of Cook Inlet. It was a splendid day. To the north, Alaska's broad Susitna Valley pointed Luckett directly toward the village of

Talkeetna an hour away. Lifting over the horizon beyond it, he could see the immense white shoulders of McKinley.

Link loved his plane. It still had a pile of money owing on its $60,000 price tag, but it was starting to earn him about $12,000 a year as head of his own company. What he loved it for most was its responsiveness. To him, the subtle growls of its engine and rotors and the ease or resistance its control stick offered his hand were like honest speech. What he asked of this plane, and it said yes to, it would deliver.

Link Luckett—his name really was Link, not short for Lincoln or anything fancier—was a native of Arkansas. The flying bug had bitten him early. He had learned to pilot a plane as a teenager and had knocked about North and South America for years, flying for gas and oil prospecting teams. He was only thirty-two but, having lost all his hair, looked indeterminately older. Five feet eleven and 170 pounds, he had a piercing gaze and solemnly sculpted features.

The message about Mrs. Bading's being brought down had reached Talkeetna and volunteer Luckett was immediately dispatched to the mountain's 14,500-foot-high ice field to get her.

A fact which nobody had asked Luckett for—and which he kept to himself—was that he never before had flown his bird over 6,000 feet! Sure, he had taken one like it 11,000 feet above the Gulf of Mexico once; and the papers that came with this plane put its maximum ceiling in black and white at 16,200 feet, though its cruising and hovering ceilings were of course a good deal lower. But Luckett judged these numbers all too conservative: engineers' numbers!

They varied, after all, with the weight of the ship, which was 2,700 pounds fueled, fully loaded, and manned. Link could not do anything about his own 170 pounds. But there were lots of gewgaws along twenty-eight feet of helicopter body that could be lived without.

Doors, for instance. So he removed both doors as a margin of safe lifting power for the added weight of the sick woman he'd be taking aboard.

Rising from Talkeetna, his open plexiglas cabin spooned in wind. The blasts poured and swirled around him but he was dressed for anything: long underwear, wool socks, fur-lined cap and boots, flannel shirt, heavy trousers, a flight suit over them, and an eiderdown parka over that. Fur gloves, over another pair of silk gloves, kept his hands warm on the control stick.

Talkeetna shrank to an insignificant patch on the green plain behind him. Ahead loomed the Alaska Range, an army of mountains with McKinley as the towering commander. More and more of its bulk, as Luckett flew nearer, appeared to flood up from some endless internal supply, as though the whole earth sought to be mountain.

Moving over that massive body, Luckett's plane seemed a mere gnat, with a tiny whir at its tail and another on its skinny back. But it could fly! The currents which flowed invisibly along the mountain flanks seemed to give the plane an extra dash of buoyancy. An hour out of Talkeetna Luckett had no trouble setting down on Kahiltna Glacier: 14,500 feet.

But what an anti-climax! Another plane already was there.

Bush pilot Sheldon, the pilot for both climbing parties, also had gotten the message about Crews's and Metzger's descent with Mrs. Bading and had decided to go get her in his fixed-wing craft. A communications foul-up had caused Luckett to waste his flight. In fact, both pilots watched without amusement as yet *another* plane came down on Kahiltna! Three of them! However, it was Sheldon who flew Mrs. Bading out: first come, first served.

Link Luckett's gaze was already wandering up along the tremendous walls of ice and rock eastward toward the top of Peters Glacier. Out of sight up there somewhere lay John Day with a broken leg. From his briefing at Talkeetna, Link had obtained a fair idea of Day's position.

All of a sudden the decision was made: he was going to go get John Day!

But first the adventurer had to make peace with the planner. To begin with, Link decided he would need an exploratory flight to test his craft in higher altitudes and to survey possible landing sites and special problems. He re-entered his helicopter and removed the face mask from the oxygen supply unit: he didn't want it masking his vision. He stuck the bare oxygen hose in his mouth, gripping it between his teeth. Then he took off.

If he rode the updrafts with care and respect, using them to increase his plane's buoyancy, who knew what this little baby could do? He climbed northward, swimming up into the wind, feeling for invisible currents. They were there, all right! He turned slowly eastward in a long upward bank, raised by updrafts pouring against the mountain wall; higher and higher he climbed, a bubble on the atmosphere—up over the Anchorage party's high camp, then the Day camp, then over the new tents on the glacier's high shelf where men were waving to him.

He flew the length of the glacier. It was about half a mile long and 1,000 feet wide; not smooth, though, nor level. Rippling shadows indicated considerable ridging and corduroying of the surface, and the whole mass of ice sloped upward some 200 feet toward the south, ending in a bowl of jagged rock ridges. Luckett's brain clicked all these details into place, including the wreckage of a plane that he thought must have crashed long ago (he had not heard of Stevenson's and Elliott's fatal wreck; no one had).

Yes, he reckoned; he could land there—but just. Could he, though, take off again out of that bucket of ice cubes, with his rotors slicing the skimpy air at 17,200 feet and with the weight of one more man aboard? It would be better to test out how much more his plane could do before it told him, "No more."

The men below had to be thinking that here was another dead pilot—because Luckett now took his ship *higher!*

Nobody knew better than he how risky this was. The plane climbed with a drunken lurch of sluggishness. But it still talked to him. It would not pull any surprises. He had gotten it up over 18,000, nearly to 19,000 when, at last, the controls quit responding. At once he eased the ship into descent. Very well, he finally had found the craft's true ceiling and his own ceiling. He waved as he flew over the Day party's tents, and then dropped all the way down to the party's base camp at 10,500 feet. He felt a tremendous cutting edge of excitement.

But the seasoned pilot made it cut on a dense reserve of patience. He already had decided another preliminary flight was needed. First, he would want to drop the Day party a radio, so they could send a last-minute check on weather before the rescue flight. And he would want a marked landing area—with the injured man close by on a stretcher, ready to go.

He summoned his helicopter serviceman from Anchorage. He needed help stripping the plane down further. But one item of weight had to go back *on*. The right door. With both doors off, the wind blasting through the cabin had hindered free operation of the controls.

At 2 P.M. the serviceman was landed with his tools at the 10,500-foot level. He and Link pulled out the helicopter's seat cushions. It didn't have to be a *comfortable* flight.

They drained all but twelve gallons from the gasoline tank, sufficient for about thirty-five minutes' flight.

They decided, too, that after the engine was started, the battery might as well go! It weighed twenty-eight pounds.

If, up on the glacier, the engine stalled . . . well, he had just better not let it stall.

And so Luckett flew on up the mountain again, a feather on the updrafts; and up over the high shelf of Peters Glacier to the bowl of ice at its upper end. He dropped a smoke bomb to test the wind direction, made a three-quarter circle, and 200 feet from the tents set his ship down.

At once the Whittakers and two of the Anchorage men started toward the plane. They had Day on a stretcher.

Luckett shocked them. He was waving them back!

Dropping the oxygen tube from his mouth, he stepped down from his cabin and ran across the ice with the radio he wanted the climbers to have. The thin air dizzied him. He fell to his hands and knees. As the men approached, he thrust the radio at them and told them, between gasps, to lay out a marked landing area about 100 feet square where the ice looked least rough. "I'll be back," he said.

And then under the sweep and blast of the moving rotors, he staggered up into the helicopter cabin again, and got the oxygen tube back between his teeth. There, that was better. And now, head clear, he gave his plane the throttle. The helicopter's skids bounced down the sloping, rough ice for 100 yards before the rotors bit on air solid enough to give him buoyancy.

Once airborne, he flew back down to 10,500 feet.

He had his plane rechecked and fueled to just ten gallons; this would be enough. Luckett and his repairman figured the weight down to a skeleton 2,143 pounds.

Link was as ready now as he was going to be. But when he tried to make radio contact with the glacier, there was nothing. A layer of cloud had settled in over the base camp. It hung at about 13,000 feet. McKinley had not, after all, entered into a contract to provide continued good flying weather. Link waited several hours but the cloud refused to go away, and he determined he was going to fly at 9 P.M., cover or no cover.

He took one more try at the radio, however, and it worked. Day's men told him the wind up above was just 4 to 6 miles per hour out of the southeast; the temperature 10 below zero, and that a landing area was marked off with bits of camp gear.

So now the payoff flight!

As he soared up through the cloud—it proved only 300 feet thick—into the brilliant high sky beyond, Link Luckett recalled that in the past he had taken many men on and off mountains; but never a helpless man, never anyone needing rescue. No one was paying him to do this, and if he stalled up there on those eaves of ice, 1,000 feet above the engineered ceiling of his ship, he would never get started again without a battery. His plane would be $60,000 worth of hardware that all the climbers on earth couldn't bring down in a stretcher. As a businessman, he was taking what any accountant clearly would condemn as an "unacceptable risk"—not to mention his life.

Even now—he glanced at the altimeter—at just 15,500 feet, his plane's response to the controls had all of a sudden lost its usual snap. Everything about flying in these altitudes was fickle and quirky. He let himself drift away from the mountain whose enormous bulk loomed nearly a mile higher. Where were those good updrafts? He pulled the fur gloves over his silk pair off. Whatever the cold, he wanted optimum feel of the controls. Slowly but now a bit more steadily his plane mounted eastward; the wind came in under him, swelling like the surf toward the shore, lifting, lifting—and up, over the shelf of Peters Glacier. Then there below were the men with the stretcher by the tents.

Down went a smoke-bomb for wind direction, and Luckett flew south over the strip of ice to the bowl at its upper end. With the sun lower now, the pressure folds along the head of the glacier were strongly visible. Some of those ruts were two and a half feet deep and a foot wide. It was a good thing he had had them mark a landing area, a squared patch 300 feet from the tents. Down went a second smoke-bomb for a final wind check, and Link set down.

The Whittakers, Crews and Wilson already were hustling over the ice from the tents with John Day on a stretcher. Luckett stayed in his cabin. Not for an instant was he going to leave the throttle which kept the rotors roaring. The heel of his boot beat impatiently on the floor. He bit on his oxygen hose. Hurry up, he wanted to shout. But the thin air forced the stretcher bearers to move with agonizing slowness. At last they made it under the whipping rotor and opened the passenger door of the cabin.

With some difficulty they lifted John Day onto the cushionless seat and maneuvered his damaged legs to a more or less restful position on the floor. The helicopter was now 170 pounds heavier, and every second gulped fuel.

The Whittakers were asking Luckett something he couldn't hear under the roar of the rotor. Did these guys want to talk now, too! He glared at them. Could he come back, they were shouting, for Pete Schoening? Pete who? . . . Fellow with a frozen hand . . . doubted he'd have a chance getting down by foot.

Luckett nodded. "But later," he snapped, pulling the oxygen tube out of his mouth. "Need a rest first."

He waved them away; they slammed the cabin door and moved off.

Link gave the copter some throttle as he glanced around. Now what was that! Dead ahead: a staff used to mark the landing area. It might foul his take-off. Once again he pulled the oxygen pipe from his mouth. "Move that!" he yelled with a gesture toward the staff. Somebody got it out of the way and got out of the way himself as the chopper came sledding down the ice.

The skids of a helicopter are not engineered to function like the runners on a sleigh; but that's what they were doing. With a biting noise, *chuk . . . chuk . . . tuk,* they rattled metallically on the ice flutes, bouncing, jarring, spitting sprays of chopped ice.

It felt as though this sort of punishment must surely shake loose every bolt in the plane. Nor was it that the ship got *up* exactly; more that the slope dropped away. The skids were five feet off, then eight feet—enough! Link eased her out above the dropping ice on the left; and behind them, as if removed by freight elevator, the glacier slowly sank away.

He turned to John Day beside him and grinned. They were up. Son of a gun if they weren't up! And with a margin of safety.

They landed at base camp with a full two and a half gallons of fuel left. Day was transferred to Don Sheldon's plane for the flight down to Talkeetna, thence to a hospital in Anchorage and the arts of the bone-menders.

Link Luckett suddenly felt held together with wires and chewing gum. He powerfully needed to unwind and he figured his chopper rated a thorough service check. He gave himself the luxury of adding fuel—more than enough: let her get drunk on it!—then floated her down to Talkeetna for some rest for the both of them.

It was near midnight when he landed, but newspapers and radio stations in Alaska and down across the "lower 48" states were crying for the story, and the little village was swarming with reporters and photographers. They kept at him till 3 A.M.—it was now Saturday—and after getting his plane checked and oiled, he somehow wasn't tired anymore, though he hadn't really shut his eyes. So he flew back to the Day party base camp on the mountain. He landed at 5 A.M.

And now McKinley had stopped kidding. There had been a change in the weather. Clouds hid the upper elevations. Gusty winds flapped the tents of the base camp. A snowstorm was coming. It could almost be smelled on the air.

Luckett decided to get up to Pete Schoening at once—before the weather got worse. Ten gallons of fuel had served before; it would be enough now. He drained the 30-gallon tank to that level, hopped aboard and started the engine. Out again went the battery's twenty-eight pounds. The rotor's strong vibrations flowed through his flesh like a massage.

His ship hadn't lost any of its guts. But puffs of wind rocked it hard now like the first searching jabs of a boxer. He climbed up through the dirty cloud and pierced its top layer at 15,500 feet.

Good: the coming storm hadn't yet risen this high. Luckett's course over to the head of Peters Glacier was familiar now. And there were the climbers beside their tents waving at him. It was as if this were getting routine—and he mustn't let it get routine, not ever! That's when the mountain would get him.

He dropped a smoke-bomb over the landing area. The wind was okay, but he hated to set down there: there would be all that "sledding" again before he'd be airborne. Better a place closer to the edge, where he could just lean her over into the air for buoyancy. He touched down at a spot, didn't like it. Another. No. He landed and took off again three or four times.

And then he just flew away!

The men in the tents must have thought he was crazy. But he had over-explored for the amount of fuel he had brought. And now, swearing at himself, he felt compelled to drop back down to 10,500 feet for more gas before attempting the rescue of Schoening.

Once more the tank was filled to ten gallons, and once more the helicopter rose through the thickening clouds, a summer dragonfly—out of season—with its glistening whirs of wing lifting it up across the enormous black and white crags of Mount McKinley.

As it turned out, the spot from which Luckett had removed John Day was indeed the optimum landing site. It was 8 A.M. when he put down on the glacier. Visibility was clear, but it was 30 degrees below zero, and Link's ship, with its rotors never stopping, vibrated in wind gusts of 10 to 30 miles per hour.

Pete Schoening walked from his tent to the plane and was able to climb into the seat under his own power. Just in case they had any ideas, Luckett told the Whittakers he would not be back for them. They obviously were mobile enough to climb down. The weather was kicking up; Link felt tired and tense with no sleep in more than twenty-four hours, and how many sevens could a man expect to roll in a row?

The Whittakers nodded, waved him good luck and moved away.

Schoening, Link noticed with some disapproval, was a bigger man than John Day, perhaps five pounds or more heavier, therefore tougher to get off the ground. But time was wasting. He gave his ship more throttle, asking this one more favor from her. The rotors roared louder but she was tired, loaded with tons of inertia. She got up on her toes and leaned northwest, leaned a little more, and then stumbled and bounced along for ten feet, twenty-five feet, her skids bouncing *chuk-tuk* on the ice flutes for 150 feet, until finally she bounced up—it was no more than a bounce—and was airborne just enough for Link to ease her off over the falling-away slope of the glacier.

He descended quickly. She was starting to tell him bad news. The engine was growling and suddenly let out several tremendous backfires that practically stopped Link's heart. But as she sank lower, down through the gray pool of clouds, the plane seemed to drink in strength, and she swam smoothly across the lower slopes, though the wind was now blasting up sprays of snow. The tents of base camp emerged from the gloom, tiny gray trapezoids with men jumping up and down beside them.

Link set his plane down. There was the good crunch of snow under the skids. Solid. Engine off. Rest.

Men were running from the tents toward the plane; Pete Schoening was slapping him on the back with his good hand, and Link Luckett realized his own hands in the thin silk gloves felt frozen. Fortunately, they just felt that way.

Schoening spent a week in the hospital and left the tips of three fingers there. John Day was hospitalized two months. He was left with a limp that lasted quite a while, but eventually he mended. In spite of her close brush with death, Mrs. Bading fully recovered. All the other Day and Anchorage climbers still at the high camps managed to get down to the base camps without incident. There they met advance rescue parties.

But the blizzard which had been building roared over McKinley that very afternoon. It pinned climbers and rescuers alike in the tents at 10,500 and 14,500 feet, forcing them to remain four more days till the storm abated. Luckett's last flight had come off just in time.

He and his plane were off the mountain by the time the storm hit. He touched down at Talkeetna and took off again for Anchorage, beating the storm home. A vast gray was spreading down the Susitna Valley. Ahead stretched the broad sheet of Cook Inlet and, to the left of it, his city and airport and home.

He thought about those climbers. Broken legs, frozen hands, oxygen sickness, and what for? To play the game of courage. Well, it wasn't for him. No being a hero for old Link. That struck him funny. And so tired he could hardly see straight, Link Luckett started laughing.

Based on the facts as told in Above Ceiling, Below Zero, *Link Luckett was subsequently awarded the silver Carnegie Hero Award medal.*

Man Catchers

THE BRITISH TANKER *Chelwood Beacon* carried 30,000 tons of crude oil. A sheath of steel 665 feet long, riding 33 feet deep in the water, she bellied through the sea with a massive, murmuring grace; until, having lost her channel, she ceased to be a ship and became a plow.

It happened in mid-winter. A nor'easter was blowing, one of those tantrums of weather the Atlantic now and then hurls at its American coasts. There is a shift from the normal winds, the good and reasonable westerlies, out toward the north and east. From there, instead of moderating the surf, they abet and goad it. Tongues of wind lick in between the seas, pushing them up higher and higher—fifteen feet and more from trough to crest—and blow them like black sails at the beaches.

In such a storm, on January 23, 1966, *Chelwood Beacon* was beating north off New Jersey, blindly feeling her way toward Lower New York Bay. The temperature was freezing, the winds 40 to 50 miles per hour. Curtains of snow whirled about the ship, masking any landmarks ashore. She could make way only by faith in the tolling buoys which jounced in the water to mark the channel. Unknown to her, they beckoned to no safe harbor—the storm had blown and washed the buoys westward.

She struck ground in twenty-five feet of water, two miles off

Sandy Hook, New Jersey. Her belly sawed on hard sand. Inexorably she was bullied about to east and then southeast, slewing around so that she came to rest almost stern forward and broadside to the heavy seas. Though her flat decks stood ten feet above water, waves up to twenty feet swept across them. Only her bridge, amidships, reared over the foam like a rock.

A split rock, though. She was leaking at a gash 265 feet from her bow. Captain Peter H. Jones at once ordered all fires extinguished. As a battery powered radio emitted appeals for help, oil fumes wafted sickeningly through the ship.

Aboard with Jones were ten other Englishmen, chiefly officers, an American pilot, and thirty-nine crewmen, all non-Europeans. Engine room helpers were Arabs from Yemen; the deckhands and stewards, Malayans and East Indians. Under the fury of the storm, several of the seamen panicked. The impossibility of getting lifeboats away, the cold and dark, the stench of oil, the rising tumult of wind and waves, snapped all ties of discipline. In a sudden raid the ship's liquor stores were looted, and soon the men became even less manageable.

Three Coast Guard vessels arrived. But with wind and surf conditions worsening, the officer in charge judged it wisest to await the arrival of another cutter which had the gear and crew best qualified for rescue work. It was some miles down the coast on another mission.

But *Chelwood Beacon*'s cry had reached other ears, too. Captain Robert J. W. Carl Jr., forty-one, was a member of the grandly named United New York Sandy Hook Pilots' Benevolent Association. He was a friend of the pilot aboard the *Beacon* and, although he knew his friend was blameless in view of the wandering buoys and invisible shore, to Captain Carl, the honor of all pilots seemed at stake.

And so, in the howling darkness, like relatives come to a bedside, two more vessels gathered in the lee of the stricken *Chelwood Beacon*. One was Carl's "pilot standingship" *New Jersey,*

163 feet long and roomy enough to shelter the tanker's entire crew, *provided* that *New Jersey*'s smaller companion, the pilot boat *Narrows,* could pluck them off.

Narrows' usual duty was merely to taxi individual pilots to and from the big ships navigating New York Harbor; accordingly, she was spare in design. There was just a small square wheelhouse standing in the middle of her open deck and a metal railing running around the deck. She was forty-seven feet long and thirteen feet in the beam. A necklace of automobile tires hung on the bows as a bumper. At the helm stood John C. Punger Jr., twenty-five, and Robert A. Deane, twenty-six, both apprentice pilots and sons of pilots.

For them this was not a duty trip. They had volunteered for Captain Carl's daring plan.

"Don't," the Coast Guard warned in a parley by radio: "wait for the proper rescue vessel to get here."

Captain Jones on *Chelwood Beacon* not unnaturally expressed a different view. If only his most frantic seamen could be taken off, he said, he and the rest would try to manage aboard. The last thing a skipper wants to do is abandon ship. More than sentimental considerations are involved: a deserted ship is fair game for any salvager daring enough to drag her to port. With 30,000 tons of oil aboard, there would be no lack of candidates.

Leaking oil had spread a black smear 600 feet wide along the tanker's starboard—now leeward—side. This had its uses: it partially smoothed the frothiness of the water. It was a time to be grateful for small favors. Not only were massive seas pounding landward over the *Beacon*'s decks, but the ebbtide was flowing. And a third, coastwise, current also was running three miles an hour from north to south. A fine witches' brew altogether!

Outvoted, the Coast Guard boats drew off a bit and stood by, disapproving but ready to spring back in if needed. Steady on the left, as near as he prudently could, Bob Carl held the *New Jersey* about 100 yards from the tanker.

John Punger, feeding power slowly, eased the *Narrows* forward. It was noon, but a forbidding, howling noon, filled with torn ribbons of snow. The tanker loomed ahead like a low, black fort with walls 600 feet long, intermittently turned to waterfalls as the seas rolled over her. Only the bridge stood tall, though at an angle, splitting the seas and serving somewhat as a windbreak for the approaching pilot boat.

A rope ladder with wooden rungs was suspended over the side of the tanker. A shivering crewman, lightly clad against the possibility—maybe the likelihood!—of being spilled in the ocean, crept out on the ladder. Two ship's officers both held and hustled him. Like a fly on a dancing web, he clung to the ladder as the *Narrows* came pumping up toward him.

And so began again the drama of life reaching for life, this time with men's soft bodies hung between the steel jaws of ships.

On a narrow shelf of slippery outboard off the tossing bow of the little boat stood Bob Deane. He clutched the metal railing with his left hand and was reaching out and up with his right. At the helm John Punger was fighting a half-dozen battles at once: seas that punched him off, the tide egging him forward, coastal current dragging him sideways, spray smearing the wheelhouse windows, and others he was too busy to think about. He coaxed the *Narrows* on, easing and backing, then urging her up again into the wind and onto the lift of the seas, going with the punches and the smart of the gale. With her auto-tire bumper she could take a fair bump, but Lord!—let her not wash too high on the tanker's side and get hung up. She would knife back stern first into the seas.

Bob Deane on the forward rail was trying to mesh the rise and fall of the sea, the wicked side feints, and ins and outs, with the actions of his reaching arm. He wished he could have rooted into the deck through his boot soles, but he could only hang onto the railing with one hand, while above and ahead of him dangled the crewman on the tanker's ladder. Oily spray kept spitting Deane in the face: furiously he sleeved it off.

Closer now came *Narrows*. Closer. Deane was timing it, the fall, the rise of the boat. Down she went under the ladder . . . up . . . a bit too far . . . again dowwn and . . . uuppp . . .

Now!

Deane hooked out. He closed, he embraced—and tore the man off the ladder, clutching him in his right arm as the sea dropped the *Narrows* down and away.

They had him!—a trembling little Arab whose name they never caught but who was soon clutching the railing with both hands and scrambling back to the shelter of the wheelhouse.

Sixteen times in the next hour the man-catching feat was repeated.

Repetition didn't make it much easier. So terrified were some of the crewmen that, instead of letting go of the ladder, they resisted and nearly snapped Bob Deane off the *Narrows'* bow. On two occasions the little boat fell back before he quite had hold of his man; only the clutch of the tanker's officers kept the fellow from being washed away. Eventually a technique was worked out. When Deane had a fair grip on his quarry's waist, he would shout, "Let go!" Those on the tanker would heave the man loose. No second tries. But it worked.

The *Narrows'* little wheelhouse, just ten feet by five feet, became so crammed with shivering humanity, Punger could hardly manage the helm. And Deane in the bow was cold to the marrow, soaked, and utterly bushed. Punger asked by radio if they couldn't change places, but Captain Carl on the *New Jersey* said no; among the apprentices John had the keenest skill at the helm.

However, they did transfer the seventeen rescued men to the *New Jersey*, and another volunteer, Robert D. B. Rice, relieved the much exposed Deane. In the next forty-five minutes, Rice, in the bow of the *Narrows,* racked up a notable score: twenty-two catches, no misses.

In all, thirty-nine crewmen were plucked from the tanker and later brought safely to land.

The nor'easter wasn't yet worn out but three young pilot apprentices certainly were. With earlier duty that morning Punger had spent a total of seven continuous hours at the wheel of *Narrows.* But, undaunted, he and his mates were fit for duty again the next day.

So, too, in a sense was *Chelwood Beacon.* With skipper Jones and other officers remaining aboard, she did not break up after all, but lived to the next high tide. Tugs were able to haul her off the bottom and maneuver her to port, and she later was repaired at a cost of $4 million and returned to service.   □

ANOTHER STORM, another season, another sea. This time the victim was that ugliest of ducklings, a scow. She hadn't even a name, only a number—143—this grimy hired girl, sweeper of harbors in Lake Michigan.

She was 130 feet long, with a dingy metal shed of an engine house at one end of the deck, a crane at the other, and at the four corners vertical "spuds," metal legs that lowered to the lake bottom to steady her as she dredged. Day's labor done, she'd pick up her spuds which stuck up out of her like stripped tree trunks, and her 100-foot crane boom would be put to rest in a cradle on the engine house roof at the other end of the deck.

Thus dressed to travel, behind her tug, Scow No. 143 on May 25, 1961, was heading for home before a storm.

Lake Michigan in a gale forgets it is only a lake. Gusts 60

miles an hour, and driving needles of rain, can and do whip the surface to instant, almost incredible ferocity. Twenty-foot waves are not unknown, nor sudden plunges to the chill and darkness of winter, never mind that the calendar says May.

Aboard Scow No. 143, machinery groaned and cables whipped and twanged, as the lake washed over her decks. Soaked and shivering, the five crewmen soon realized they were in the worst storm they had ever seen. The waves hammered the metal sides of their engine house like battering rams. Then a big one smashed right through the windows. The floor was awash waist-deep, till the rise to the next swell flushed the water out the gaping door. There was nothing for the men to do but climb up to a four-foot storage shelf that ran the width of the engine house above a row of lockers; and huddle there while succeeding waves crashed in under them.

But worse was yet to come. The towline to the tug snapped and Scow No. 143 was on her own, with no power to exert against the storm slugging its way toward the end of the harbor at Michigan City, Indiana.

The crests were sweeping clear over the stone seawall, seven feet high, that rimmed the harbor. There seemed no way the scow could avoid crashing. But one of her vertical spuds jigged loose and stabbed down into the lake bottom. It bent—but held. And on that one twisted leg the scow came to rest, 150 feet from the seawall. Her deck listed twenty-five degrees; the crane threatened to topple off at any moment, and if it did, it would claw away the engine house shed, too.

She was just 150 feet from land—but how to get her crew away?

The space was too confined to operate a rescue boat in such a storm. One crest could lift a small boat onto the seawall and crack it like an eggshell. A helicopter? Unthinkable in the 50-mile winds. The same for trying to extend a fire ladder out from land. After many nervous minutes the Coast Guard did attempt to shoot a line out by gun; the wind just blew it down short.

Other ideas were soon discarded. There seemed to be only one way: if a heavy crane with a 150-foot boom could be mounted on the seawall. That might work but a telephone survey of all construction firms in the area failed to turn up a boom long enough. To summon one from a distance, in this storm, might involve fatal delay. The best any nearby firm could offer was a 110-foot boom. Forty feet short. But maybe it could swing a line out by means of an iron wrecking ball. At least that would get a line out to the men!

An experienced foreman, Theodore E. Smith, thirty-six, took charge of volunteer construction crews that set to work on the plan. With the storm getting worse, and all the work having to be done out of doors, it took several hours to assemble the 110-foot boom, to transport it to the harbor—and to bulldoze a ramp for the crane over the soggy ground before the seawall.

Meanwhile, the scow's crewmen hadn't been seen for hours.

Floodlights had been set up on shore but towering billows of spray threw back their glare. Behind that misty curtain the scow was but dimly visible, its gaping windows and doors gushing water. It took practically an act of faith to believe the crew was still alive out there, not washed overboard.

The wrecking ball idea worried volunteer Kenneth L. Hanke. The more he thought about it, the less he liked it. Hanke was an ironworker superintendent, a brawny man of forty-three with a round face and a fringe of sandy hair. He knew how little control could be exerted on a wrecking ball in high winds. The swinging sphere of iron might overturn the scow, or kick the crane right off its slanted deck, or even bust into the men out there—and who could be sure where they were?

Hanke had a safer plan; at least it was safer for the men on the scow, though not for him nor for foreman Ted Smith. But Smith agreed to it. And, after the usual official fuss, so did the authorities.

Thus, well after midnight, in heavy clothes and life jackets, and trailing lines which extended back to shore (and which would not have helped a bit, had they fallen into the murderous churn below) Ken Hanke and Ted Smith began climbing out on the bare metal struts of the boom extending horizontally from the seawall.

It would not be a wrecking ball swinging a line to the scow, but their own bodies.

Their progress was slow and punishing. A crane boom is not for working on easily, even in fine weather. Now it swayed and vibrated in the gale. Its angular iron members were slippery to the feet, cold to touch. Wind and spray tore at the two men as they crept forward out into the raging dark in their bulky jackets and lines, one on each side of the boom, hand by hand, foot by foot. They were tired when they reached the end of the boom, 110 feet out, yet their effort had only begun.

From a hook on his belt, Hanke drew a coil of rope a half-inch thick and 100 feet long. To the end of this he attached a metal cable-splicing device, as a weight. It weighed about two pounds. He meant to pitch the rope across the gap of forty feet and hook onto the cables of the scow's crane.

Smith lashed a cord around Hanke's waist and took a tight grip on his belt to brace him for the rope toss. Hanke's first cast carried far enough, but the weight at the rope's end failed to engage the scow. He hauled the line back and recoiled it for another throw.

Once more he pitched rope and weight out through the storm. Another failure. Then another . . .

Hanke lost count of the attempts.

An hour passed. And still with dogged persistence, he tried to snare the scow, while Ted Smith held fast to his belt and both of them were buffeted by constant wind and spray. Hanke simply would not give up. It was his plan and it would work.

At last, about 3:30 A.M., he got the metal weight to spin around a cable on the scow. He tugged at the rope. It held.

At a signal the crane operator slowly raised the boom with Hanke and Smith riding on the far end of it, until it angled some forty feet above the crests of the breaking waves. The rope Hanke had thrown now swung down in an arc to about ten feet above the waves, then upward to the caught cable atop the scow's crane.

Ken Hanke already was bone tired in his legs and arms. He was cold and drenched. It was 3:30 in the morning and he hadn't slept. He had accomplished a lot just getting a rope to the scow. But from this point, could he ask someone else to take the risk that he had put in being?

So, with one hand, then the other, he transferred his 180 pounds—not to mention his bulky clothing—from the boom to the suspended spanning rope. It took his weight. So far so good. He crossed his ankles over the rope and lowered himself hand over hand down toward the churning blackness below. He descended slowly, never without the fear that when he reached the low point and his weight shifted to that part of the rope depending from the scow cables, it might tear loose.

But at the bottom, ten feet over the water, the rope still held.

Now, though, he faced a climb to the scow's crane house roof—fifteen feet up-rope! With growing numbness in his hands and hampered by heavy, wet attire and by that useless lifeline trailing back to shore, he started struggling up the rope hand over hand. People on shore gasped as they saw, by the misty glare of the floodlights, that Hanke's legs dropped from the rope and hung dangling almost in the water. Desperately he inched upward, minute after struggling minute. It seemed that his cramped fingers couldn't possibly tighten on the rope even one more time. With a supreme effort he kicked out and up toward a projection on the crane house roof, gained a purchase, held it, worked himself closer, and climbed on.

After twenty minutes on a half-inch rope—he was across!

He rested motionless for a while on the wet, tilting roof to regain his wind and strength. Somewhat refreshed, the first thing he did was pull 100 feet of the useless lifeline into his lap and cut it off. He coiled it for use in moving about the scow.

Now he let himself down into the crane house. Nobody there. Not good. Then he started for the engine house at the other end of the scow. The only way to get there was on the scow's own horizontal boom. It hung twelve feet above the deck, which was almost constantly awash. Crouching on the metal bracing, Hanke gripped the boom's load cable. And cautiously, with the waves crashing in under him, he crept along the boom to its resting cradle on the engine house roof.

From there he shouted into the shed but got no response. Still, the gale was howling so loud he wasn't satisfied that he was heard. He lowered himself from the roof by his rope and clung to it as he waded around the listing deck to the engine house door.

Inside was a streaming shambles of wrecked gear, floating work clothes and smashed lockers. Again Hanke called, but the wind was like a hand in front of him, shoving his voice back into his throat. He poked his head in directly under the storage shelf where, ten hours before—an eternity before!—five helpless men had climbed to escape the raging flood.

Still no answer. Empty. All his effort for nothing!

Ken Hanke by now was so tired he thought it safest to creep back the length of the scow *inside* the framework of the boom. When he reached the crane house roof he called out to Ted Smith, still riding the end of the land boom, that all the scow crewmen were gone. Then, exhausted, he lay down on the roof.

Smith relayed the tragic report to shore. After so much tension, so much prayerful waiting, the news broke like one of the lake's horrendous waves. Relatives of the crewmen broke down.

Frustrated rescuers, construction workers, employers and by-standers raged and grieved.

Then someone saw a man on the scow waving.

The crew of No. 143 had spent a hellish night. Cold, soaked and miserable—and having heard nothing but the wind—they decided to see what, if anything, was being done to rescue them. Lashed to a length of rope, engineer Ambrose J. Meagher climbed down off the shelf and struggled out on the streaming deck and around the engine house where he saw a rope left behind by Hanke.

Though he had not seen Hanke prostrate on the crane house roof across the ship, elated, Meagher fought his way back to inform the others that a rescue was apparently afoot. Crane operator Herschel A. Benell then came down from the shelf for his own look; it was Benell who was spotted from shore.

The report that at least one man was alive on the scow was shouted out to Ted Smith, and he relayed the word to Hanke. The latter at once found new energy to crawl back through the scow's boom and discover not one but all five men alive and not unwilling to go home.

Hanke fashioned a rope sling and hauled the crewmen one at a time up into the framework of the boom twelve feet above the deck. The men were Meagher, Benell, Ludwig J. Bednar, John J. Sweeney, and Nicholas M. Grbich. A wave hurled Bednar against a projecting winch, injuring his back; but with the aid of the others, he also was raised up into the boom and through its open framework to the crane house at the other end of the scow.

Meanwhile, Ted Smith, who by then had been two hours exposed on the end of the land boom, climbed back to shore to obtain a Coast Guard breeches buoy—a contraption of straps and pulleys in which a man can be hauled along a rope strung between ships. With this in hand, Smith again climbed out on the boom. He attached the breeches buoy and the boom's load cable and hook to the spanning rope over which Hanke had reached the scow. Thus, Hanke was able to haul on the rope and draw all this gear to the crane house roof.

He rigged up the breeches buoy, aided Bednar into it, then payed his rope out gradually as the land crane swung the injured man across the churning harbor to shore. With Hanke's rope still attached, it was no problem to haul the breeches buoy back to the scow for the rest of the men.

Bednar was seven weeks in the hospital; his four shipmates were discharged in three days. Ted Smith and Ken Hanke were numbed, chilled, and tired, but back on their regular jobs the next day.

Across the smeary gray light of a stormy morning, Hanke was the last man to ride over to land by breeches buoy. The cheer that greeted him was one cry the gale could not drown out.

Based on the facts as told in the two stories related in Man Catchers, *a silver Carnegie Hero Award was won by Kenneth L. Hanke and bronze medals by Robert A. Deane, John C. Punger, Jr., Robert D. B. Rice, and Theodore E. Smith.*

"I Am With You, Officer!"

THE PULSE of the most experienced police officer races when a light flashes on at a street callbox. It can mean anything from a distressed kitten to riot and insurrection. When Patrolman Philip A. Siegel picked up the phone, the message was: "Burglary in progress. Gift shop. Third Avenue and 174th Street." That was less than a block away. Siegel set off with long, quick strides of his six-foot-two, 195-pound frame.

Two youths were hustling out of the shop as he approached. They saw him as he saw them. Instinctively they opted for the fifty-fifty chance, dashing off in opposite directions under the tracks of the elevated trains. For a large man of forty-four, Siegel was a pretty fair sprinter. He chased one of the boys and caught him. A routine piece of police action, the sort of disorderly trivia that precinct blotters in every city are filled with—if it had ended there.

It was 9 P.M., May 22, 1965, Saturday night in the Bronx ghetto: a neighborhood where the architectural basic is the storefront tenement, block after grimy brick block, festooned with fire escapes, clotheslines, and overflowing rubbish cans; but alive, bulging, teeming with people, people of all sizes, shapes and ages, almost all poor and nearly all black, with a scattering of Puerto Ricans.

The evening was mild, a respite, in those hovels, between the equal miseries of winter freeze and summer swelter. The balminess of the coming night, its message of something sweet and exciting seemed to draw people toward the air. At open windows fat women leaned on their elbows and gossiped with neighbors or gazed down to the street, where children played, young folks strolled, and men sat about in shirtsleeves, joshing and playing cards in open halls, on front stoops and rickety chairs drawn out on the sidewalks.

Suddenly Patrolman Siegel charged into the scene, shouting, and grabbing at someone. There was a brief struggle; a black boy caught. Hundreds of bystanders saw it—many already resentful of the functions of a white peace officer in their black neighborhood.

No sooner had Patrolman Siegel made his capture than he was surrounded by a gang of blacks, about eight of them, all in their late teens or early twenties. They accosted him with hearty, bold cajolery. "Whaddaya want him for? Wha'd he do? He didn't do nothin'." From this they escalated to demands. "C'mon, let him go. Look, there ain't nothin' on him."

It wasn't a novel experience for a ghetto cop. Setting his jaw, Siegel's face became an expressionless wall. Nothing could insult that wall, or move it. Ignore them, he told himself; just take the kid in to the precinct.

Then the situation radically changed. Siegel found himself flat on the sidewalk. Someone had punched him from behind. His prisoner was hot-footing it north to 174th Street. The officer scrambled to his feet. It was sheer futility to bother with the gang around him. He drew his gun, fired it in the air, and yelled to the fleeing boy to stop. But the youth scooted around the corner of 174th, with Siegel in hot pursuit, the gang following *him*, and a growing herd of the curious trailing behind.

The chase went on for a block in the deepening dusk, past men who detached themselves casually from chairs and front stoops, past shouting youngsters, baby carriages, women in open windows and the blare of music from indoor radios. At the corner of 174th and Bathgate Avenue, Siegel again collared the boy.

But now it was fox and hounds, and sympathy rode with the fox.

"Let 'im go, let 'im go!" members of the crowd were chanting. By the time the officer doggedly moved to handcuff the boy at least 100 persons had gathered, with the gang of eight who first had accosted Siegel forming an inner ring.

A tall youth stepped forward. Emboldened by the crowd, he said, "Let that boy go." He was brandishing a Coca-Cola bottle by its neck. "You gonna give us that boy," he said.

In as firm a voice as he could muster, Phil Siegel replied, "He's in police custody." The skin of his face felt tight and hot, yet he had the awful feeling that he looked pale. "He goes with me," he said.

Down crashed the Coke bottle on the back of his hand. His handcuffs fell with a clatter of metal to the sidewalk. The prisoner darted out across the street. The crowd roared as Siegel snatched up the cuffs, drew his gun, fired another shot in the air and again took up the chase.

What the crowd was demonstrating, however briefly and subconsciously, was a surge of desire that on this night and in these streets, the law must wait upon its approval. For once! And look at the law: one white-faced fellow in uniform. They'd show *him* who was boss!

On his side, Phil Siegel's reactions were no less instinctive. To yield was twice unthinkable: to let a criminal suspect go, and to let the whim of a mob have mastery over the law. Not a chance!

He ran out between the parked cars and across Bathgate Avenue to the opposite sidewalk, where once more, and for the third time, he caught his prisoner. This at a spot just a few feet

from the front of the small grocery and confectionery store of
Enrique A. Negron.

No other police cars or officers had appeared. But certainly
they must soon. This lent an urgency, an imminence, to whatever
was going to happen. The street was jammed with people now,
close to 200, some perched up on car bumpers and hoods for a
better look, and the bolder filtering through the parked autos to
the sidewalk.

As Siegel again tried to handcuff the boy, the crowd surged
toward him. Bitter words were shouted, taunting, vile words, a
reservoir of ghetto frustrations unsluiced.

"Keep back now," Siegel warned. But the crowd—and
especially his eight original tormentors—jeered at his effort to
put authority in one voice against 200. He drew his gun.

The mob became furious. "Gonna shoot people?" some
demanded. "Who you gonna shoot?" They advanced on him,
and the sheer press of bodies forced him to give ground. One of
the gang close to him, darting in from behind, snatched the
nightstick out of his pocket and held it aloft like a trophy. Cheers
went up.

The officer still held his suspect with one hand, but he
holstered his revolver to free the other. Step by step he was being
forced back to the building wall. One youth feinted in from the
side, reaching for the loosely-holstered gun. The crowd was
closing in on him like the jaws of a vise. A milk crate suddenly
crashed beside him. Fists started flying. Patrolman Philip Siegel,
agent of the laws of the State and of the City of New York, was
getting a beating.

But over the tumult the officer heard one solitary cry carrying
shrill and clear:

"I am with you, Officer!"

Enrique Almestica Negron was standing at the counter of his
store with his wife and two customers as the mob swept by. He
ran to his front door. A friendly man with a round, placid face,

and a native of Puerto Rico, Negron had served as a seaman before becoming a grocer. Three times in his fifty-five years he had broken up ferocious fights. And though not a big man—five feet five, a pudgy 160 pounds—he had once successfully stepped in as peacemaker between two sailors battling with knives.

Now what he saw outside filled him with indignation. This was not a victimized populace rising up against its "oppressor"; no, just the age-old howling of a mob for blood. To the little Puerto Rican storekeeper, there was no ambiguity about the situation, no mystery who, at this point, was the persecuted minority.

"Leave him alone!" he shouted. "He's only doing his duty." No one paid any attention.

Negron hesitated on his doorstep just long enough to observe the motions one youth was making toward the officer's gun. In another second he'd have it! The storekeeper picked up the first object that came to hand. It was an empty milk crate standing on its side in the store entrance as a makeshift chair.

With a roar Negron hurled the crate with all his strength at the youth going for Siegel's gun. It hit the boy. And then, caught up in his own anger, Negron threw himself out into the melee with a passionate cry toward the policeman whom he knew only by sight:

"I am with you, Officer!"

He heaved himself upon the gang of eight mauling Siegel. Grabbing one youth by the shoulder, he turned him and drove a fist straight to his jaw, knocking him down. Then he leaped astride the fellow and beat at his face and head with both fists. Another member of the gang peeled away from the officer and jumped on Negron's back. Punching and shoving, he dragged the storekeeper off the fallen man.

Someone struck Negron hard, unusually hard, in the back. The little battler was stung by the sharp pain but he was unstoppable. He lashed out with both fists at any living flesh that came within range. Patrolman Siegel also was kicking and punching to good effect, though he did, at last, lose hold of his prisoner. The lad scampered away through the crowd.

Now, finally, sirens could be heard approaching.

As though by signal, the gang that had attacked Siegel melted into the surrounding mass and away. Others in the mob drifted off. By the time police cars screeched into view with reinforcements the melee was over.

Patrolman Siegel had suffered some bad moments but, in physical terms, only minor bruises. Eight against one might have done permanent damage; eight against two evened the odds.

However, Enrique Negron's wife and friends immediately noticed the storekeeper's shirt was wet with blood—and from a wound inflicted by no fist. It was a small round hole under the right shoulder blade. What Negron had felt as a stinging punch in the back was the three inch penetration of an ice pick.

Luckily the blade had struck no vital organs. A week in the hospital at the expense of a grateful city healed the wound completely.

Another wound did not heal.

Though Negron's bravery earned him the plaudits of press, police and citizen's groups, it lost him his neighbors. "Cop lover," people called him, and worse. They boycotted his store. After a few months, he was forced to put it up for sale, receiving $400 for the inventory. And, later, he went back to work as a seaman.

"If I had it to do over again, I'd do it," he told a news reporter. "It's the way I am. I don't like to see nobody abused. They'll have to kill me to keep me from stopping and helping someone." ☐

THE AMERICAN DREAM had a fresh gloss on it for Primitivo Garcia. Twenty-three years old, intelligent and ambitious, three months after emigrating from Mexico he had begun evening classes in English and history at a high school in Kansas City, Missouri, to prepare himself for United States citizenship.

He was earning $72 a week as a stock clerk. His younger brother, Alfredo, twenty-one, was a bottler at a soda plant. Together they supported their widowed mother and a teen-age sister. They had bought a car and also a small house, on which the brothers shared the payments. There seemed no reason to suspect that life in the United States would be anything but rewarding in proportion to the effort expended by the good sons of Mrs. Gregoria Garcia.

On November 15, 1967, the brothers emerged from English class at Westport High School at 9 P.M. It was dark out, but street lamps threw a dim glow into the small park across Oak Street from the school. About fifteen black youths were loitering there. A few of them yelled derisive remarks at the two "schoolboys," not neglecting to stress that their own circle of friends would be unlikely to include persons from the land of Montezuma. Primitivo Garcia usually paid no attention to ethnic slurs, but one youth went so far as to dash across the street and take a slap at him. Primitivo struck back and the aggressor retreated to his pals.

About that time the Garcias's English teacher, Mrs. Margaret R. Kindermann, came down the steps of the school. Twenty-five and pretty, she was expecting her first baby in about four months. Two of the gang members sidled toward her from across the street. They made obscene remarks and purposely jostled her. Then one tore her purse away and dashed over to the park with it.

Mrs. Kindermann had too much spunk to just let that happen. She ran after the boy. "Take the money but give me back the bag . . . !" she said.

But the gang was not taking any schoolmistress's advice at this point. The two thieves and three or four others suddenly turned on the young woman. They threw her face down to the sidewalk. At this, the rest of the gang, numbering about ten, took to their heels. Mrs. Kindermann felt her coat and dress being lifted, hands tugging at her underclothing. One boy (she couldn't see him) must have known better; she heard a voice urging the others to "let's go, let's go," and then helplessly, "Lady, I can't do nothing."

But the Garcia brothers heard her cries.

They had walked about twenty-five yards north to the corner of Oak and 39th Streets. Mrs. Kindermann was Primitivo's teacher. He often had told her how much he appreciated the help she was giving him. And now he ran back, roaring at the gang—alas, mostly in Spanish—to leave the lady alone. Twice he called to his brother Alfredo to quit following him, to get away, because the gang might have weapons.

Primitivo seized one of the boys huddling over the woman and violently hurled him off. That youth and the others at once turned their fury on Garcia himself. They punched and cursed at him. Mrs. Kindermann for the moment was forgotten. The one gang member who seemed to have misgivings helped her up, thrust her purse in her hands and said, "Run!"

Though skinned and bruised, the schoolteacher was otherwise unharmed. She ran across Oak Street to the steps leading up to the school door, calling in Spanish as she retreated: "Alfredo, 'Tivo, run!"

As soon as he saw his teacher reach relative safety, Primitivo began to back away slowly across the street. Alfredo, on his orders, was already across. However, two youths kept after Primitivo, swinging wildly and sputtering furious obscenities at his Mexican origin. One boy suddenly drew something from a coat pocket.

Primitivo cried: "Run, Alfredo. They have a gun!"

The younger Garcia had reached the corner of a retaining wall at the school steps. His brother was fifteen feet behind him.

"I'll shoot you!" the gunman screamed.

Alfredo turned to see his brother stop and face around squarely at his assailants.

Then the boy with the gun fired three shots.

The third bullet struck Primitivo Garcia in the abdomen. He doubled over, crying out in pain. All the gang members immediately fled. The two brothers and their teacher were left alone.

Mrs. Kindermann ran up the steps, but the school door already was locked. Primitivo, assisted by his brother, sat down on the steps, and held himself where the blood was flowing. "They have shot me, they have shot me," he kept repeating. The teacher meanwhile ran around to another school door, which she found open, and phoned for police and medical assistance.

Garcia was taken to a hospital. The bullet had lodged in his pancreas.

Three youths subsequently were arrested. The gunman said he hadn't meant to shoot, merely to scare, Garcia.

An outraged community took the young Mexican to its heart. Two housewives started a fund to pay his medical expenses; a bank agreed to act as trustee. Donations flowed in from civic groups, postal workers, the city's crime commission, students at Westport High School, and hundreds of individual givers. A billboard advertised: "Primitivo Garcia Did Not Hesitate. Join the Fund at the People's Bank."

There were two dozen volunteers for blood donations. "We never had a response like this," observed a blood bank technician.

The cash donations totaled $15,000, which, as it turned out, became the nucleus of a trust fund for the young Mexican's heirs. Two weeks after the shooting, in spite of the most intense medical and surgical efforts, Primitivo Garcia died. □

OTHER DANGERS of the urban life call for other ways of "getting involved." Edward M. Susino, thirty-six, was seated in his parked car near a Bronx public housing project the morning of June 23, 1962. He heard women and children screaming, saw them pointing at a 10-story apartment building where a window was open on the sixth floor about fifty-five feet above the ground.

What Susino saw made him spring out of his car and dash 150 feet along the sidewalk. A bench stood in front of a metal fence three feet high. He put one foot on the seat of the bench, the other on its back and leaped over the fence and a double row of hedges five feet wide to a lawn. He ran another fifty feet across the grass till he stood directly under Bradford W. Simms.

Otherwise, all that stood directly under Bradford W. Simms was empty space.

Bradford was six years old. He was a black boy three and a half feet tall. Alone in his family's apartment on the sixth floor, he had been playing at a window and—now he was hanging outside it!

He was hanging in a remarkably twisted way, too, with his back to the building wall and his hands locked over his shoulder around a metal frame.

"Hold on, boy!" Ed Susino shouted up to him, hoping that someone inside the apartment might still pull the lad back in.

The apartment building had casement windows—the type which swing outward on a vertical axis like doors. A number of other residents, alarmed at the commotion, had opened their windows. At least two of these stood out on lower floors like knife edges, directly under the hanging boy.

"Shut those windows! He'll hit them," Susino yelled to the women looking out. They complied—and not a moment too soon!

With a cry Bradford lost his hold.

His body made a half somersault as he came off the building wall, forty-eight pounds of boy in coveralls—head first.

Susino instinctively extended his arms out and up. He meant to catch the child like a football. Bradford's shoulder hit his wrist and the back of the boy's head struck Susino in the face just below the left eye. He closed his arms and the force of the plummeting boy—equivalent after so much acceleration to about 500 pounds—drove him to his knees and then sprawling. The impact was so sharp, it tore the crystal and movement out of his watch, leaving him with just a strap and an empty case.

But he almost completely broke the boy's fall. Save for a severe shaking up and a fright, the boy was unhurt. Susino's forearm, knees, and cheek were bruised; his left eye wore a shiner for a week.

Asked later why he did it, he explained only that he had two children himself and figured any man who was a father would have wanted to try to save the boy.

It was only as he was getting himself together on the ground that machinist Ed Susino, who, after all, knew what it was to work to close tolerances, realized that he had missed death by only about two inches. Bradford's skull had come that close to striking his own squarely on top.

———

Based on the facts as told in the three segments of "I Am With You, Officer!", *bronze Carnegie Hero Award medals were won by Enrique A. Negron, Primitivo Garcia and Edward Susino. Primitivo Garcia's was awarded posthumously.*

High Water,
Fast Water

 IVE MEN HUDDLED in the cold and drizzle on the
roof of Economy Auto Sales, Inc. in Logan, West Virginia. All
through the night they had listened to the cries of old people
from down the street. Not that the street itself at that point could
precisely be said to exist anymore. It was under nine feet of
water. Island Creek and the Guyandot River were in flood, as
was the Ohio to which they flowed on the northwest. The drain
of the continent was backed up.

It was March 12, 1963, and river towns like Logan were
sinking in the embrace of a restless, brownish ooze of many arms
and fingers. It turned hills into islands, lapped across gardens,
floated chairs, pillows and breadboxes out of open doors, covered
the bulging eyes of dogs chained by habit in their yards, and here
and there against the ceilings of submerged bedrooms pinched off
a human life.

The men at Economy Auto Sales were in no imminent danger.
That night they had stowed books, records, car batteries and
tools on the second floor of the building, and then found their
exit cut off by rising water. The better to attract attention, they
broke out of a dormer window and crawled onto the roof with an

77

automobile tire tube as life preserver, just in case. Neither moon nor stars were visible. The temperature dropped to the low 40's; the slow cold rain seemed to drill clear to the bones. Shivering, waiting for light, each man judged himself fit bait for pneumonia. And all the time the flood slid by in the darkness like an immense sewer, sucking and slurping, while the wind carried voices of old people calling for help.

At dawn an electrical equipment dealer named William H. Neal brought his 15-foot outboard motorboat to the men on the roof. But they urged him on toward some ramshackle dwellings nearer to Island Creek. The cries coming from there indicated a much more serious situation than their own.

Neal piloted on down the "street." This was the Negro section of town and weirdly altered by the flood. One-story frame houses, flimsily built on timber pilings eighteen inches off the ground, sunken nearly to the eaves, resembled chicken coops, practically all roof. The sky was low and dirty. It barely offered light; only a dead gray wash which gave color to nothing but glinted from the numberless tiny punctures the rain kept adding to the flood. Bill Neal's motor buzzed along the row of inundated dwellings. Neal would not have been surprised to see one house, or all, lift from their pilings and go drifting down the dark tide of the Guyandot. The water, it seemed, was going to get everything anyhow. Yet before this day was over, Neal and Edwin Pauley, an employee, would remove 187 persons from flooded buildings.

It was not hard to trace the cries now. They came from the house at the end of the row, where Charlie Smith, seventy-five, a retired coal miner, lived with his wife, Estella, fifty-eight. With the Smiths was a friend, Oliver Dillard, forty, who was nearly blind. Visiting the night before, he had been stranded by the flood.

Neal circled the house in his boat. The water had gone higher than the top of every window and door. Only the roof stood above the surface. Voices issued from underneath the roof as from a nailed coffin. Indeed, it was possible to hold a shouted conversation through the roof. The three inside simply had no way out. Neal said he would have to come back with more help.

From the men at Economy Auto Sales, he obtained an axe, a tire tube—and two volunteers.

They were Charles H. Stover, forty, unemployed, and Stewart Miller, nineteen, a carnival worker. Neither worked at the auto agency but had pitched in to help move the valuables up away from the flood. Though a man of some strength, Stover was a disabled veteran of World War II and subject to frequent crushing headaches. A father of three children, he had suffered three shrapnel wounds in Germany and a silver plate now served in place of a section of his skull.

On their return to the house of the trapped people, Stover, Miller and Neal took turns with the axe hacking a hole three feet square in the porch roof. Fifteen inches under the roof was the porch ceiling: they chopped a hole through that, too. Then Stover, wearing a life jacket, lowered himself into the chilly water, its temperature being about 45 degrees.

Directly before him was the submerged window from the porch into the house. The figure of a man was plastered against the glass on the inside. It was blind Ollie Dillard. He had raised the lower sash, so that he could stand on the sill, and he was straining to keep his face above the rising water inside the house.

Stover shouted to him through the wall to move aside. Then, holding the porch roof timbers for support, Stover kicked the window completely in, glass and sashes both. This opened a hole five feet high and two and a half feet wide into the house, with its top about three inches underwater.

Stover then reached inside and took the sightless Negro by the hand. He talked him into holding his breath and ducking down and out through the window. Then with Neal and Miller lifting from above, and Stover pushing from below, Dillard was drawn up to the porch roof.

The sound of Charlie and Estella Smith's voices placed them at the other end of the house. Could the Smiths work themselves over to the point where their friend had been pulled out?

Dillard doubted it. It was a four-room house and the doorway between the front and back rooms was already most probably under water. Beyond that, Charlie Smith was a feeble old man and his wife a sick woman, wasted with tuberculosis. How they—and how he, Ollie Dillard—had lasted even this long was a miracle, just a miracle!

Stover and Miller determined to swim into the house after the old couple. They took off their life jackets, which were an encumbrance under the circumstances, and stripped down to their undershorts.

Descending through the hole in the porch roof, they pushed the tire tube in through the submerged window and let it bob up inside the living room. Then they followed in after it and surfaced—into glaring light!

A bare electric bulb was still burning in the ceiling, and with the rising water just fifteen inches from the top of the room. The electrical wiring was all at ceiling level, evidently. But from the moment Stover saw the light, the thought haunted him that if the water should reach the power source, he and Miller might be instantly electrocuted.

Yet as much threat as the light represented "on," how much worse if it went out! Total darkness in this mess! The water's surface was cluttered with debris: pillows and bowls, articles of clothing, furniture. It seemed all too imminent that the house itself might begin to float, leave its pilings, and roll over, dragging everyone to their deaths.

Stover pushed various objects out of his path and swam toward the opposite wall of the room, with Miller following. They felt underwater for the door into the next room, the room from which the groans were coming. Miller pushed the tire tube under water and up into the other room and then followed it, Stover right behind. There, too, a ceiling light was burning.

In a far corner past the glare of the naked bulb they could make out the gaunt features of Estella Smith. She was keeping her head above water by standing on a submerged object of some sort. "Help him first," she said.

In another corner Charlie Smith had just about given up. Having survived by what seemed nothing more than the continuation of seventy-five years of habit, the old coal digger was too weak to grasp the inner tube Stover and Miller held out to him. They had to drape his arm over it, with Miller clasping his wrist under water to hold it on.

"Hang on, we're coming back," Stover called to Estella Smith.

Pushing the debris aside again, the two men floated her husband ten feet back to the submerged door. Still holding Smith's wrist, Miller ducked and came up in the next room. Stover told Smith to take a breath. As he did, Stover pressed him down through the doorway and up to Miller. Then Stover followed.

By now the water was within a foot of the ceiling. The two rescuers pushed through the debris and hauled the old man the twelve feet across the flooded room to the window. Once again they submerged Smith as before, got him outside under the porch roof and then hoisted him up onto it. The men placed a life jacket on the old coal miner and helped him into the boat.

During the five minutes on the roof, Stover and Miller rubbed their bodies and swung their arms to warm themselves. They had labored in the cold water about ten minutes to get Charlie Smith out, and had not exactly emerged into tropical sunshine. Dawn's grayness had lightened scarcely at all; the rain had abated some but the breeze stung their wet skins. All around for hundreds of yards spread a streaming desolation of muddy waters. There was no time to waste. The flood was rising an inch every three or four minutes.

Back into the window and past the floating debris and the eerie ceiling light swam Stover and Miller; and through the submerged door to the far bedroom where Mrs. Smith still hung on. She was just strong enough to lock her thin arm over the tire tube. The woman weighed only 95 pounds.

The space between water and ceiling had narrowed by now to just nine inches. Stover and Miller couldn't get their chins out of the water without bumping their heads. A splash of water hissed off the hot bulb. The entire top of the room seemed choked with floating objects and their own bodies.

"Hurry, hurry!" someone above the roof was calling to them. As though they needed the advice! They ducked and kicked through the submerged door. Stover was starting to feel numb with cold and exertion. It was harder to push the junk out of the way. Other objects kept floating at him.

And the light!—it was flickering. They reached the window. Mrs. Smith was coughing and gasping. One last gulp of air inside the room, then down—the three of them clutching, struggling past a murky glimpse of window frame, then out . . . out . . . through the hacked hole in the porch roof and back under the gray, dirty, beautiful, blessed sky above!

Later the flood rose two more feet and completely inundated the empty dwelling of Charlie and Estella Smith. □

"PATTI, PATTI!"

As she stepped from her house, Mrs. John Leibel heard children frantically calling the name "Patti" at the far end of the back yard. Alarmed, she hurried over to them and looked down. A concrete irrigation channel ran through her property and Patricia Hunter, who was ten, had been swimming with other neighborhood children in the clear, cold water. Why, oh why, did the kids do that!

The current became too strong here. The channel dipped, and its converging walls spooned the flow to a whirlpool as it entered a culvert which tunneled under Golf Course Road. The culvert looked awfully full of water to Mrs. Leibel: nearly six feet of water, leaving but a few inches of air space under the arch.

She climbed up onto the road. It was forty-five feet across. The girl should have been swept along underneath to the other side in a few seconds. Children were always riding through from one end to the other when the water was lower. But Patti Hunter's inflated tire tube was sucked against the culvert entrance, while she herself had not yet come out the other side. She was stuck down there!—held by something in that black tunnel of racing water.

Mrs. Leibel began to shout for help.

Her voice sounded so small. It seemed outmatched by the cries of insects and birds and the roar of a tractor some distance off. She would never be heard, she thought, as she stood screaming on the road under what residents of her state like to call "the big sky." The nearest town was Hamilton, a mile away. The nearest man was Joe Kochis, 250 yards away. It was 4:30 P.M., Saturday, July 13, 1968.

At work in his fields Joseph L. Kochis, forty, was making every hour of his off-day count. He was a technician at the U.S. Department of Health, Education and Welfare's Rocky Mountain Laboratory, in Hamilton. But he also farmed part-time and, for him, that was why there were long warm Saturdays in July. The sun was riding a glossy sky over the sawteeth of the Bitterroot Mountains ten miles to the west and a mile high. Soon the mountain wall would lay a deep blue shadow down across the fertile Montana valley where explorers Lewis and Clark long ago foresaw a populace of contented husbandmen—like Joe Kochis.

Kochis was driving his tractor when he noticed his neighbor Mrs. Leibel gesticulating wildly out on the road. Was she yelling at him? He flicked off the engine and cocked an ear. What he heard made him leap down and start running, his high leather boots chopping the soft clods of earth.

His oldest daughter, Janet, fourteen, was chatting with a friend inside the screen door of the house. When she saw her father running across the fields—running like *that*—she knew something was amiss. "What's wrong, Dad?" she called from the porch. But Kochis never broke stride. Janet and her chum, Joy Ayers, took up the chase.

When Joe Kochis reached the road, he saw the children huddled over the irrigation ditch and Mrs. Leibel, up on the road, pointing frantically down to where the water funneled into the culvert.

Kochis, who was clad in shirt, trousers, and heavy boots, was winded from his long run. He barely gave himself time to register the fact that the child in peril was not one of *his*—he had four—before he took a flying jump out into the irrigation channel.

Its bed lay eight and a half feet below field level, and at this point the channel was twenty feet wide. Kochis landed in water three feet deep and waded forward, the current lengthening and speeding his stride. The water was sweet, cool, and pearly, a gift to the valley from springs in the Bitterroots.

But the culvert was only six feet in diameter: to squeeze a 20-foot channel into it, the walls had to converge and the bottom slope sharply down. This created a vortex, as in the drain of a tub of water—what Kochis felt as a forcible downward pull, almost like suction. He took a gulp of air, and the water, now suddenly five and a half feet deep, hauled him into the gushing dark of the culvert.

He was hurled twelve feet forward—to a dead stop.

There was a barricade of debris blocking the tunnel. It felt—and Kochis, in the dark, could only sense it by feel—like a mad fence of boards, tree limbs, wire, cans, bottles, pieces of packing crates. He sensed something else also, softer, squirming, gasping, submerged at times, but struggling with the screen of junk against which the flow of water was pressing both of them. No wonder Patti Hunter had not yet emerged from the culvert!

There was no hope of trying to haul the girl *back* against that current. Kochis took a breath in the air space under the tunnel ceiling and submerged himself. With both hands he tugged at the debris, trying to pull it apart. It wouldn't budge. He kicked desperately at it with his feet and legs and finally felt a little "give." Then he dug into the loosening point with both hands. He ripped a few pieces of junk free and managed to create a gap—a window—perhaps ten inches square.

The girl still was twisting and squirming between his chest and the barrier. He took her by one arm, thrust her down into the hole he had opened in the clogging—and let her go.

She shot away down-current, free.

Now he had to get himself out.

He took a breath and resubmerged. His aim was to widen the window in the debris. But clear as the water was, in that darkness he might as well have been working in tar. Absolutely blind, he could feel no way to enlarge the opening. And Joe Kochis, at 170 pounds, was not about to try to thread a needle under water with his body. There was just one way out.

And that was back. Against the current.

First he took a few deep breaths, then he pushed down into the rushing water and began swimming with every ounce of power he had. His progress was wickedly slow. For every three feet of gain he lost two. But he felt there *was* gain. He knew it was only twelve feet to the great outdoors and that Joseph L. Kochis was not going to allow himself to drown for lack of the will to move twelve feet—against anything!

There was a blur of light before him. He reached out, caught his hand on a solid concrete edge: it was the portal to the culvert. He pulled himself forward, thrashing his legs against the current, pulled some more—and got his other hand out on the portal. A wall of water seemed to be trying to force itself through his chest. He thrust himself out through the avalanche and the roar of the suction into the light, and then clung like a wet leaf to the outer wall till he regained strength and breath enough to climb out of the ditch.

Downstream, Patti Hunter was helped from the water, and after a night in the hospital, was all right.

Joe Kochis had a bump on his head (though he couldn't remember banging it during his two-minutes' struggle in the culvert) but he was up on his tractor in dry clothes before the hour was out. The Saturday sun was still high enough to get some more plowing done. □

LESLIE D. HUESCHER had spent twelve hours up a tree. The Two Medicine River was nine feet deep beneath him, in flood. Drowned cattle, deer, and horses rolled past along with sections of wrecked buildings and entire trees. At times masses of debris would clog in a riverside cottonwood—like the one Les Huescher was uncomfortably in—and simply tear it out by the roots, dragging it irresistibly down the current of destruction.

On high bluffs to the north and south people stood in the rain with their eyes on Les Huescher in his tree. What they knew and he didn't was that an old irrigation dam fifteen miles upstream was crumbling. If it collapsed, as seemed likely, a massive slug of water would come foaming down the Two Medicine on top of the flood already ravaging the valley.

It had been raining four days when Huescher awoke before light on Monday, June 8, 1964. He was forty-one, a hand on the Merle Magee ranch south of Browning, Montana. He looked out a window and saw three feet of water streaming across lower areas of the ranch. Cattle were bellowing in the corral.

Huescher threw on trousers, hip boots and a raincoat and waded down to release the animals to higher ground. But by then the current was rising so fast he couldn't get back. He climbed into a tree in a grove of cottonwoods to rest. Then he had to climb higher. His refuge was fourteen feet tall and it wasn't too long before he needed every bit of that height.

After daybreak, when people could see the spot he was in, several attempts were made to reach him. Two men in a rubber raft tried to fight the current by pulling on a rope they tied from tree to tree. But they lost their hold and, flailing uselessly with their paddles, were driven 100 yards downstream to a side channel of quieter water, from which they were able to pull out to dry ground.

In another try a 14-foot aluminum boat was nearly swamped.

A skin diver hoped to reach Huescher with a rope, figuring that the crowd of people ashore could haul him out with it. But the fellow managed to swim just 100 feet in the current before *he* had to get up a tree—where he stayed a considerable time before hazarding the swim back to safe ground.

Archers tried to shoot lines to Huescher: they fell far short. Certainly he was a case for helicopter rescue, but engine trouble had disabled the only such craft in the vicinity.

So Les Huescher shivered in his tree from before dawn to late afternoon. It was a gray, raw day. The temperature never went above the 40's. How tough it was to get comfortable in the branches of a tree! Before his eyes a buck deer and a horse, two of the strongest swimmers in the animal world, tried to work their way out of the current and perished. What he didn't see but could guess was that the flood that day in Two Medicine valley was taking the lives of forty men, women and children.

It didn't seem possible that a man within easy view of other men might not be reachable with help, but now it looked as though that might just be the case.

A few minutes after four o'clock the dam went.

The news reached officers on the bluff by radio. Huescher, 150 yards away, was mercifully out of voice range. Not that there would have been any sense calling to him that he had just an hour to live; that soon he would hear at first faintly but growing to thunder, a windy, washy murmur, something with the far snap of timber in it, then, dark and vast—the coming wall of water.

But two men were determined not to let that happen.

Lee R. VandenBerg had arrived late on the bluff. He was an inspector for the U.S. Border Patrol at the Montana-Canada line. At thirty-six years and 185 pounds, he seemed the picture of uncomplicated outdoors strength, square-jawed and even square-haired: his crew cut was trimmed flat on top. A former Navy frogman, he made scuba diving a hobby and he had come prepared in his wet suit.

One glance at the speed and spread of the flood waters showed him how useless any try at a swimming rescue would be. Still, that 14-foot aluminum boat with its ten horsepower outboard motor was available. The boat had failed before, but Lee VandenBerg asked for a volunteer to make another stab at a rescue with him.

Henry F. Cobell at once stepped forward—again. "Bud" Cobell had gone along on the earlier boat attempt and nearly taken a fatal dunking. He was twenty-three, a member of the Blackfeet Indian tribe and a police officer on their reservation, within whose boundaries most of the flooded valley lay. Cobell's police duties didn't include rescuing ranch hands from trees, no more than Lee VandenBerg's did.

The two strangers who were about to risk their lives for a third stranger shook hands and climbed down the bluff to the boat. But not before VandenBerg pressed some personal effects into a bystander's hands with a request that they be passed on to his wife and two sons, aged twelve and fourteen, if anything happened to him.

They shoved the boat out into navigable water and jumped in. VandenBerg started the motor and Cobell took a seat in the bow. Their only "rescue equipment" was a 100-foot length of rope and an inflated tire tube. It never left their thoughts that the water had a long head start on them: the dam had burst twenty minutes before. How long it would take the released backup to sweep down the gorges of the Two Medicine no one knew for sure. The general guess was an hour. But it could be less, much less.

Even so, to try to hurry this boat ride might be just as deadly.

Starting upstream of their man, VandenBerg carefully eased the boat 150 feet along the flood fringe, then angled out through the drowned grove of cottonwoods where the projecting tree tops seemed to have a moderating effect on the current. In this manner he groped about 200 feet closer to the man in the tree, but he was still 100 feet away when the boat poked its nose out into open water.

The current rammed it like a train. The boat was hurled out of control fifty feet downstream in spite of its own opposing motor power. Then it was thrown into a wash of less turbulent water where, once again, the rudder answered to VandenBerg's hand. He couldn't let down his guard with that current for an instant.

While Bud Cobell shoved debris away with an oar, Lee brought the boat about and threaded it back upstream between trees that offered some deterrent to the flood's force. He managed to work her alongside a tree just twenty feet from Huescher's.

Close enough. "Get hold of the tree," VandenBerg said to Cobell. The younger man stood up and embraced the trunk in both arms, till Lee could knot a 12-foot mooring line around it.

At this timely juncture the motor conked out. But fortunately VandenBerg got it started again immediately. Then he took the 100-foot length of rope he had brought along and threw one end of it out toward Les Huescher in the tree twenty feet away. He missed. He coiled the rope for another throw—and again the motor died.

The two rescuers looked at each other but said nothing as Lee pulled on the starting cord. Each had the same thought: a more reliable motor would be a considerable comfort out here. With the motor on, at least, there would not be that awful urge to listen for that other roar upstream to the west.

The second throw of the rope Huescher caught.

At VandenBerg's suggestion, the ranch hand stripped down to his jeans—his boots and raincoat would cause too much drag in the water. Then he tied the rope around his chest. At his end Lee wrapped the rope once around the mooring tree and then around his waist and several times around his wrist.

All this trussing proved foresighted when Huescher lowered himself into the frigid water. The current at once dragged him; without the rope turn around the tree, Lee VandenBerg might have been plucked straight out of his boat. As it was, he had to struggle to inch Huescher closer against the fierce strength of the river. Hand over hand he pulled the man in, while Bud Cobell kept hugging the anchor tree to try to steady the boat. With VandenBerg's help, Huescher at last lifted a leg over the gunwale and was wrestled into the boat.

None of the three heard the cheers that went up from the distant bluff.

Meanwhile, the motor had died a third time, and the rise and pull of the flood waters had knotted the mooring line too tightly around the tree to untie. VandenBerg was not prepared now to waste a single extra moment; the crest from the damburst could be down on them at any time. He cut the line with a knife—happily, he had brought one along—and he felt with profound thankfulness the pesky motor as it kicked over again. Then he piloted the boat obliquely upstream through threads of less turbulent current among the cottonwoods.

They were just fifty feet from where the flood lapped on terra firma near some ranch buildings when, with a loud twang, the boat's motor was wrenched partly off its transom. The propeller blades had hung up on a submerged strand of barbed-wire fence.

VandenBerg acted fast. He jumped up, threw his weight on top of the motor, and twisted it back on its transom. This action somehow freed it from the fence, but VandenBerg held it physically in position after that.

Nearer shore, he leaped out into waist deep water, as did Cobell; they hauled the boat in and assisted Huescher up to higher, dry ground.

Fifteen minutes later the unpent waters of the dam swept down on the ranch in a wall over ten feet high and half a mile wide, uprooting trees and demolishing buildings in one tremendous smash of destruction.

Based on the facts as told in the three stories recounted in High Water, Fast Water, *silver Carnegie Hero Award medals were won by Stewart Miller and Charles H. Stover, and bronze medals by Joseph L. Kochis, Henry F. Cobell and Lee R. VandenBerg.*

A Girl Named
Reta Rena

RETA RENA SHARP'S TEACHER smiled as she read the school theme the girl had written about herself. The bluntness of the child! Such candor was delightful, but as she corrected points of grammar with her pen, the teacher found herself mentally filling in some qualities that no 12-year-old could or would be able to put down: things like intelligence, friendliness, an air of sturdiness that touchingly preceded any sign of physical maturity; a face not beautiful but pert, with shrewd, amused eyes set wide under her bangs, and a square chin that jutted when she smiled like a little tough guy's. Enjoy honesty like this while you can, thought the teacher as she read; you won't get it from grownups.

MYSELF

by Reta Sharp

I have black negro hair. I am not a negro and I wear pants all the time when I ain't at Sunday School or Church. My eyes are blue. I have little ears and a bad cold. I ran my hand through the washing machine and broke my hand. My hands are big as the littlest book in the world. As I said on up in the page that I had black hair and it is short. I am about four feet eight inches tall.

My teeth are little in the back and big in the front. Half of them are rotten. The two big teeth in front are black up at the gums. I wear size four and a half in shoes. My shirt is size 10. My socks is size five. My nose bleeds all the time even if I start to blow it, it starts to bleeding. My legs are 3 feet long. I wear a shirt with pockets in it if I have one that will fit me. My hair is about five inches long. I have a one inch little finger, a two inch next to the littlest finger. My ears stay dirty all the time.

Reta Rena Sharp lived at Floral, Arkansas, a village seventy-five miles northeast of Little Rock. Her father, Rolland D. Sharp, was a bookkeeper for a trucking company. Her mother, Betty, worked at a dairy. They married as teen-agers and had two boys and a girl before Reta was born in 1957.

Reta attended seventh grade at a school a quarter-mile walk down a country dirt road from her home. It was a consolidated school serving 200 elementary and high school students for miles around—or about twice the population of the crossroads village.

There being a shortage of children to play with in Floral it was prudent for a girl to learn both boys' and girls' games; but Reta was something of a tomboy anyway. She liked to play baseball with the boys and she was on the Junior Girls basketball team at Floral School.

The afternoon of Saturday, January 24, 1970, was sunny and clear after a long frost. Ice in the ruts of the country road had melted and was glistening in puddles that squished under the car as Reta and her mother drove down to market in the village.

While Mrs. Sharp shopped, the girl strolled out in search of a playmate. On the nearby school grounds, alone, was Anthony A. Cousins. Reta knew him as she knew all the kids in Floral. He was ten but just about the same height as Reta, a little chubbier though, a boy with a sunny nature and a moon face. They were dressed practically alike, both in blue jeans and waist-length jackets, except that Tony wore loafers and Reta was in tennis shoes.

"What should we do?"

"What do *you* want to do?"

"Well, let's go see the pond."

A man-made pond, used for watering farm animals, lay about 600 yards north of the school. The children had been over every inch of the ground many times. In summer they could walk right up to the horses and cows endlessly twitching their tails at flies as they grazed. In winter the youngsters often had seen the muddy water frozen solid, a floor of ice 170 feet long and 140 feet wide, surrounded by gaunt trees and brush. The pond was fed by springs and emptied, at its southeast corner, by a rivulet which in dry seasons merely sopped into the nearby fields.

On this day Reta and Tony could cross the outlet stream on foot, so solidly was it still frozen; though underneath they could see and hear the pearly trickle of its flow. The two children walked up the east bank, and Tony flicked a stone onto the pond. It skittered and spun over the smooth ice, carrying a lot farther than he had expected, with nothing to stop it.

This was fun. The boy and the girl skated a number of objects onto the ice: stones, pieces of wood board, twigs, and a few empty cans that littered the bank. Some would bounce and slide nearly all the way across.

That, they discovered after awhile, was the object of the game: sliding the objects all the way across the ice. Things which stopped halfway were losers. Things which bounced on the ice and didn't really slide well were losers, too.

When they had pretty well cleaned the bank of good things to throw, Tony walked out on the pond to retrieve some. It seemed solid enough, and he would not go too far toward the middle, where he knew it must be weaker. He was not unaware of the peril of thin ice.

But thirty feet from the bank, without so much as a warning crack, the ice suddenly opened under him like a trap door and he splashed into a hole about four feet square. His face bobbed up immediately and he grabbed the edge of the ice crust, which was about an inch and a half thick. But there was nothing under him. The depth at that point was eight feet. He was floating in a void with only a shelf of ice to cling to and the coldness of the water stabbing through his clothes. The breath went out of him. He whooped and gasped with the cold.

Tony Cousins could not swim and Reta knew that. In a little town children know what each other can and cannot do. Reta's father had taught her to swim and like everything athletic she did it well. But she had had nothing that anyone could call water rescue training.

Now she walked out onto the pond. She was careful but she didn't waste any time. She slid her feet along and moved her weight gradually. The ice felt strong enough right out to the lip where Tony Cousins was clinging. She leaned over, took both his hands and tried to haul him out. This, of course, added weight to the shelf she was standing on. The edge gave way and she fell in, too.

Tony was helpless. Except for the pain he was feeling, it was as though he had turned to a block of ice himself. He heard Reta gasping behind his back. She had both arms around him and was trying to lift and push him up onto the ice crust. But she might as well have been trying to put him on a mountain. His body wouldn't move. He felt the greatest longing to see people, hundreds of people, come running through the bleak trees along the banks to see what was happening and help. But it seemed there was no one else in the world.

And then Tony felt Reta sinking beside him.

Her hands moved down his legs. All of a sudden there was a force under his feet, lifting him, pushing him up from below. She had submerged till her own feet were on the mud bottom of the pond and, forming a stirrup with her hands, she was boosting him up.

He hooked a knee onto the ice and wriggled out on his belly. It held!—the crust under him was solid enough to hold. He inched away from the hole about two feet. He lay there, afraid to get off his belly, almost afraid to breathe.

Reta's face emerged from the water beside him. Now he was going to help her, too. Her face scared him. She hardly looked like the same girl. Her lips were blue. He could hear the clicking of her teeth. Her features seemed tense with a fear beyond his imagining. He put his hands out toward her. She said nothing. Then she just slipped below the surface.

Tony waited for her to come up again. He stared at the spot where the brown water had closed over her head. He hoped she was submerging to get a good spring off the bottom, enough to carry her up onto the ice. He said to himself: "Come up, Reta, come up." There was no motion in the water.

It took him a moment to comprehend. Then with a cry he got up and ran across the ice to the bank and kept running in his dripping clothes through the trees and over the fields about 500 yards to the nearest farmhouse.

The men who came found that the ice cracked under their weight only eight feet from the bank. They had to get a boat and break it into the ice. With a makeshift grappling hook, a pick attached to a rope, dragging down in the murky water, they caught onto the collar of Reta Sharp's jacket.

Tony Cousins was able to give a fairly clear picture of what happened that day to the police and others who came. But he became a quieter boy after that, subject to depression. Everyone said it was because of what had happened and his elders made it a tactful rule not to mention Reta Rena Sharp when Tony was near.

Classes at Floral School were dismissed the day of Reta's funeral and almost the entire village attended.

Speaking of Reta later, her father said, "She never was idle, always on the move or doing something. She always had something to say to everyone she met, old and young people alike.

"When she was ten years old," he continued, "her baby brother was stillborn. We were looking forward to a new baby very much. I was grieved beyond words and she stayed with me all during the funeral and comforted me and shared the grief with me in a way that would seem beyond her understanding at her age. She seemed to understand other people's feelings very much and was willing to share their grief and happiness."

———————

Based on the facts as told in A Girl Named Reta Rena, *a bronze Carnegie Hero Award medal was awarded to Reta Rena Sharp posthumously.*

The Nagging Doubt

THE URGE TO GO FISHING came upon John Hooley as he planted shrubs in his garden late on the pleasant Sunday afternoon of June 4, 1967. Not that the urge needed much encouragement. To throw a line into water infested by finned edibles was a recreation that Hooley in his fifty-three years seldom had found the will to resist.

What surprised him was that he should specifically desire to fish Tomer's Lake. This artificial pond lay only a few miles from his home in Jeannette, Pennsylvania. But he had once nearly wrecked his car turning across a three-lane highway into the entrance of the place. The bad traffic situation ruined his day and he had not returned. Now all of a sudden it had to be Tomer's Lake and nowhere else!

This time, though, he'd be more careful. He planned to drive ahead to the next intersection and turn there, then turn again and come back to the lake without darting in front of opposing cars. It gave him a particular satisfaction to make this simple, safe plan.

He said good-bye to his wife and enjoyed a pacific sense of freedom as he drove through the rolling green countryside of western Pennsylvania, past homes and small farms that looked bright and well kept in the late afternoon sun. It was good that his son and daughter were grown up and on their own and that Pop could take off like this for a few hours of sport. Yes, if a fellow did his job, kept his health, middle age had its compensations. In fact, life had done all right by factory worker John Hooley, despite only eight grades of schooling and having had to start young in the coal mines. His Slovak father, born Hula, had helplessly seen the name changed to "something more American" by a jovial immigration officer at Ellis Island. And now, in two generations, John Hooley's own boy, the immigrant's grandson, was doing well as a young executive in the international operations of a major corporation.

A handsome man with steel gray hair and a strong jaw, Hooley smiled as he drove east on the William Penn Highway a mile out of the town of Delmont. There on the left lay the pond, its four acres reflecting the sky—and not *completely* walled around by fishermen.

And for once the busy highway was clear of cars ahead and behind him. With all his worrying, he could safely cut directly across the opposing lanes. Of little breaks like that no life could have enough. Thus, John Hooley saved a mile or two of extra driving and also—what would ring down on him later, in retrospect, like the hammer of fate—a few absolutely vital minutes. In this and in his unpredictable choice of Tomer's Lake he would come to feel that his steps were mysteriously but purposefully guided that day.

He bought a one-day fishing license and a pack of cigarettes, and since the pond was more crowded with booted men and lines on the near bank, he drove across a low earthen dam to a sand and gravel beach on the far side. He was hauling fishing gear out of his trunk when he heard the cries.

"They're drowning! Somebody please, they're drowning!"

Hooley gaped. A hundred yards away, up on the bank of a

smaller, higher pond used for carp fishing, a girl of about fifteen was screaming and gesturing. A few men were fishing much closer to her than Hooley was, but they were not moving.

The girl was Patricia Tomer. Her father owned the lake, but was on the other side taking care of his duties. The girl had been calling for help, in fact, for several minutes but the stolid anglers near her evidently had decided it was a teen-age prank and that they were not going to make fools of themselves puffing up to the higher pond only to have a bunch of kids get the laugh on them. The more the girl yelled, the more it seemed a prank.

The terror in her voice sounded worthy of investigation to John Hooley, however. He began running, legging it fairly fast for a man his age and size, nearly six feet and 210 pounds, over the beach and up a steep, weedy bank to the upper pond. He was winded when he reached the Tomer girl, who was hysterically pointing out at the water.

Twenty-five feet from the bank, face down, floated her cousin Samuel Stephenson, fourteen, and near him in a sort of bobbing human triangle the girl's little brother, Robert Tomer, eight, and another boy whose identity in all the confusion never was established. This youth, who was about sixteen, had entered the water just moments before with a wooden plank to hold out to Samuel, who apparently had been taken with stomach cramp. But the plank had floated away and now the rescuer himself was in distress.

John Hooley pulled off his shirt, kicked his shoes away and plunged down the bank into the carp pond. For years he had not swum anywhere but in a public pool. He had heavy work trousers on, the kind he wore as a circuit breaker assembler at Westinghouse Electric Corporation. Powerfully built, certain in any case that other rescuers would be bound to follow him fairly quickly, he thought he might wade out to the boys and at least hold them up.

But the mudbank plummeted sharply. Seven or eight feet out

Hooley was in muddy water over his head. He had to swim and in spite of the soggy drag of his trousers, he stroked out to the youths and put an arm around the one most in trouble, Samuel Stephenson.

"The boy was ice cold," he vividly recalls.

Lifting Samuel's face from the water, he turned him over, hooked him under the chin and started for shore. But instinctively the other boys grabbed him, too. The teen-ager caught his belt, young Bobby Tomer his shoulder. Suddenly Hooley was carrying the weight of all three. He had to strain to hold his face up. Sputtering and gagging, he struggled a few feet closer to shore and then sank, taking in more water and unable, at that point, to touch bottom.

He kicked upward and managed to just catch a breath of air before he sank under the boys again. He had only his right arm free and his legs felt like lead. He tried to shout as he surfaced but muddy water flowed into his mouth and for the third time he sank.

Blind in the coffee-colored water—carp love to slide along and roil the bottom—Hooley struggled, it seemed to him, for "quite awhile." There was one ineradicable moment when he knew what must be the imminent feeling of those about to drown: "Everything in my chest and head was like it was going to explode. I thought my heart was going to stop."

The boy Samuel, cold and inert, slid from his grasp; the other two released him; and touching for an instant on the mushy bottom, Hooley was able to heave up—up!—out into the air.

The teen-ager and Bobby Tomer both seemed to be unconscious now. They were floating beside him. He snatched each boy under an arm, the older weighing perhaps 160 pounds, the younger about 85. And still fifteen feet from land, John Hooley treaded water with his legs and let loose with his tongue at the men on the bank.

"What did you say, John?" a reporter later would ask him.

"Never mind," he said. "Sometimes you have to use strong language to wake people up."

One of his milder phrases was: "For God's sake, help me, somebody! I'm exhausted."

Hooley admits he's a man "easily worked up." Even several years later he could not speak of the incident without striding restlessly about the living room of his home and making sweeping, helpless gestures with his powerfully muscled arms and now and then slapping at the chest that had nearly quit on him.

People's inaction at the peril of others, either from indifference or "freezing," is a subject which invariably "works him up." He told of recently reading in the paper about a girl running from a rapist along a New Jersey highway. She had called in vain to passing cars to stop. Hooley thought that if only one motorist had done nothing braver than bring his car to a halt, the criminal would have been scared off. But no one did, and the girl was found later dead in a roadside ditch. "At least someone should have run to a phone," said Hooley. "People have to *make* it concern them!"

Two men did respond to his plea for help in the carp pond. They couldn't swim, they said, but they did come down the soft bank to chest depth in the water to reach out for the boys.

And so with his hands full and only his legs to propel him, Hooley had to wrestle both boys closer and finally was able to thrust them one at a time at the men on the bank. As he did so, however, his right leg sank to the calf in the soft clay bottom; and in wrenching himself free he pulled muscles in his knee and back. The incident left him with a slight limp and an infection from some mud clogged in his ears.

Having yelled for someone to give artificial respiration to the two boys, Hooley at once swam back, no matter his fatigue, to the point where he thought Samuel Stephenson had been lost.

He dived blindly in the muddy water and felt, at one point near the bottom, a body brush his leg.

Desperately, he submerged again. With his fingertips he had one fleeting touch of the lad's head but could not hold on. "His hair was too short. I lost him."

Again and again he dived but never could make another contact.

At last, unable to push himself any further, he stroked weakly to the sloping bank, where he hadn't the strength to drag more than his head and shoulders from the water.

A crowd had gathered. The other two boys had been revived with artificial respiration. "Thanks for saving my life," said the teen-ager, bending over his rescuer, but obviously in a hurry to get away from there.

For ten minutes Hooley lay on the bank, still half in the water, his chest heaving, his face streaked with mud. He was looking up at the blue late afternoon sky through tears of frustration and rage. The boy he could not save, for whom other men now were finally dragging through the pond in a human chain, that boy haunted him, and would in fact give him nightmares for many months: a cold body brushing his leg, a head of short hair impossible to grasp.

He remembers something else, too: a blurry stranger leaning over him as he gasped on the mudbank and admonishing, "You old fool, you nearly drowned yourself." □

"PEOPLE WALK AWAY from a 'bad scene,'" said Richard A. Mathieson Jr., who confessed that his twenty-seven years had brought him a certain measure of disillusionment. This was no cynic talking. Handsome and husky in the "whites" of a student of dental medicine, he had a mass of reddish brown hair and a tendency, when compelled to speak about himself, of blushing raspberry red.

He grew up, he said, thinking most people naturally good. But he had held many jobs during his student years—in factories and cafeterias, as a credit investigator, a state vocational counselor, even a Pinkerton guard in a New York department store—and had seen too much evidence the other way.

The way passersby, eyes rigidly ahead, could avoid people slumped in the street, even obvious victims of mugging and other violence: this troubled Dick Mathieson. The year he spent as a volunteer in a New Hampshire mental hospital he came to know men—some of whom had not set foot outside the institution for fifteen or twenty years—who were the objects of an entire community's averting of the eyes. What he had done was to buy poles and take patients fishing, or on walks through town, where store windows and the most commonplace artifacts of culture, like parking meters, gave them pleasure.

As the doctor of medical dentistry he would be some day, Mathieson was under no illusion that he would be able to save the world. "You wonder how much you can do," he said, "but at least you work with living people." That struck him as important: to work with people, not "things."

The morning of December 17, 1966, Mrs. Doris M. Eakin, thirty-eight, of Cortland, Ohio, was driving east on Route 358 at Greenville, Pennsylvania. With her in the front seat were her older children, Daniel, nine, and James, seven. In the back, Timothy, five, and Lisa Ann, three, were trying their best to behave.

The morning air, though windy, had warmed to 40 degrees, but there was a patch of melting ice in the road and Mrs. Eakin's car hit it at 35 miles per hour.

The auto skidded sideways, lurched into the opposing traffic lanes, then shot back across the road and through a cable guardrail down a six-foot sloping bank into the reservoir of the Greenville Water Authority. Five hundred feet long, 100 wide, the reservoir erupted in unaccustomed waves as the car's momentum sent it seventy feet across the water. It came to rest about thirty feet from the opposite bank and began sinking.

"Open the windows!" Doris Eakin cried to her children as icy water surged through the floorboards.

Daniel J. Fitzmartin and Dick Mathieson were en route back to a florist's shop in an empty truck after making a delivery. Both were college students earning some money during the Christmas recess. Dan, twenty, was driving; Dick, who was then twenty-two, glanced out his window on the passenger side. "Look at that," he said with a laugh as the truck crossed a bridge at the north end of the reservoir. "Some kids playing on a raft—in this weather!"

Then he saw a small form float to the surface from under the "raft" and realized it had come out of the window of an auto.

"Hey, there's trouble here," he said. "Stop!"

Fitzmartin turned into a side road along the east bank and before the truck quit rolling Mathieson was out the door and running between pine trees on the slope beside the water. "Can you swim?" he called but knew even before the screaming replies came back at him that it was a wasted question. Doris Eakin and her older boys, Daniel and James, were flailing in the water about five feet apart, alternately slipping under and bobbing up, desperately trying to cling to the car roof as it inexorably sank.

Mathieson ripped off his heavy jacket and ankle-length boots. In a sweat shirt, trousers and socks, he leaped down the bank and waded out across a five-foot "shelf" of the reservoir, where the water lay only two feet deep. At that point the bottom sloped sharply to a depth greater than ten feet where the car was sinking. Mathieson plunged off the shelf and began stroking toward the mother and two boys twenty-five feet away.

The water was barely above freezing, about 35 degrees, but

somehow, Mathieson says, he "didn't feel the cold." He was a strong swimmer, a veteran of many canoeing trips and, perhaps more important, had had rare experience with cold water. His college fraternity had offered freshmen the choice of waking up each morning to menial personal chores—or to an ice cold shower. Mathieson always chose the bath. He once stood it for an hour and a half and could hardly walk out when the shower stopped, but he never bent to the chores.

In a few strokes he reached Daniel Eakin, the 9-year-old, who at once seized his shoulders. But Mathieson deftly turned the boy, put a hand under his chin and sidestroked twenty-five feet back to the drop-off point. There he was able to shove Daniel into the shallows where Fitzmartin, who was only a weak swimmer, hauled him onto the bank.

Dick at once swam back for Jimmy Eakin and dragged him to the shallows in the same manner. By now Frank A. McClimons, fifty-eight, a bridge inspector, had come running; and though he could not swim, he helped Fitzmartin lift Jimmy onto the bank, while Dick Mathieson swam back out toward Mrs. Eakin.

Weighed down by a heavy winter coat in addition to her other clothing, the mother was exhausted and hysterical. What she knew and Mathieson couldn't know was that there were two more children in the car, now completely vanished.

When Mathieson tried to put a life-saving hold on her, she pushed him away, though she was gagging and choking. He took her right arm but both her arms immediately locked around his shoulders, and together they sank in frantic embrace. He thrust her from him and they surfaced. He had time for one breath and again went down under her weight as she tried to climb on him. "Timmy and Lisa," she gasped. "Timmy! Lisa!"

Mathieson couldn't understand. Did she mean the children already saved?

His head was cooler than those of the people on shore. To them it appeared as if the woman's struggles would drown both him and her. Mathieson was confident he could handle her. Swimming alongside but keeping his distance, he thrust out now and then with his hands. He pushed or pulled on her arms or any part of her coat he could touch and, though she continued to struggle, he worked her into the shallows.

But once there, sobbing violently, she would not let herself be pulled from the water.

It dawned on Mathieson now that more children were involved. He was getting tired but he swam back to where the car had gone down. And just then a child's hand appeared above the surface. It was Timmy Eakin. Unconscious, the boy had floated out of one of the open windows. Mathieson lifted the child's head from the water and with a hand cupped under his chin pulled him to the shallows, where the others promptly lifted him out and began artificial respiration—with success.

But once more, for the fifth time, Dick Mathieson swam out to the spot where the car had sunk. He dived under the surface. The cold water was dark, virtually opaque. He could see nothing, feel nothing. He was losing his bearings. The car had gone down here, hadn't it? Where was it? He strained to go deeper. Not a shadow, nothing; just himself in the midst of cold, black water.

He dived again, forcing himself to go down what he thought was about ten feet to where the bottom should have been; but he could find neither bottom nor car.

With all his back and forth rescuing, he had swum at least 250 feet and he was near the end of his strength. His breath was coming in harsh gasps, and it seemed to him that he had nothing left when he reached the shallows where Mrs. Eakin still sat in the water sobbing. With the other two men, Dick hauled her up on the bank and loaded her and the three boys, all now shivering violently, into the truck. Within two days all were released from the hospital. Mathieson himself was all right after an hour's soak in a hot tub.

A tow truck hauled the Eakin car out of the reservoir with hook and cable two hours after it had skidded in. The baby, Lisa Ann, was floating near the back window, arms stiffly outstretched.

Later Mrs. Eakin spoke in the warmest terms about the service Dick Mathieson had performed. But he remembers rising to applause at a public meeting where some honor or another was presented—and suddenly feeling that he could not look the woman in the eye.

He has often dreamed about the incident at the reservoir. There is no real satisfaction for him in being called a "hero." He recalls all too easily the frustration of searching in the black water for the little girl he could not reach, but whose picture he saw in the papers later, her hands reaching out.

"I think I'm always going to be asking myself," said Dick Mathieson, "if I could have done more."

———————

Based on the facts as told in the two stories related in The Nagging Doubt, *John Hooley and Richard A. Mathieson, Jr. were awarded bronze Carnegie Hero Award medals.*

A Walk on
the Crust of Hell

IMAGINE A GIGANTIC KITCHEN where the kettles are larger, far larger than the chefs; where the utensils, if not under strictest control, become monsters. The men who cook steel move among ladles big as houses. The big pots are lifted by crane and emptied with a clatter of tumbling ingredients into the kettles, which are electric furnaces twenty-five feet in diameter. This is the "melt shop" of Armco Steel Corporation at Butler, Pennsylvania, thirty miles north of Pittsburgh.

Carbon electrodes thick as tree trunks descend into the domed roof of each furnace. An electric arc rips and stabs through tons of cold steel scrap with a noise like a thousand urchins banging on pans. It is an inhuman racket, and it abates only to a deep, pulsing thunder as the scrap bleeds, melting down to a white hot soup, 300,000 pounds of it, pooled in the refractory floor of the furnace. Drapes of electric cables, thick as elephants' trunks along the furnace walls, shudder in the sonic pounding or with their own floods of energy. The entire furnace seems to jump in its bearings. From apertures in its dome, orange beams flare out beyond cables and craneways and glimmer to the cavernous reaches of the plant, lighting the web of girders at the roof 100 feet up.

An electric furnace "heat" takes about three hours. Limestone and other impurities rise to the top of the molten steel and at intervals have to be "slagged off." The whole furnace tilts forward, the slag flowing like foam over the lip of the front door and cascading with a sizzling, lumpy splatter into a large, square pit twenty-seven feet below. Then the furnace tilts back and the steel cooks some more, to 2,700 degrees . . . 2,800 . . . 2,900, far too dazzling to look at, save through a square of dense blue glass.

Since final temperature is critical, determining whether the batch is ready or not, the furnace's "first helper" has the duty of thrusting a pole through a peephole in the door. The pole is tipped with a thermocouple. Nothing can live in the steel bath, of course. But in the instant of dying, the thermocouple yields information. It signals along a wire the precise temperature of the melt, then disappears. This is how steelmen know that a batch has reached "heat" and—provided a small sample under test shows the proper metallurgical qualities—can be poured out into ladles.

In more than thirty years as a steel worker, Frank A. Simmer Jr., first helper on Furnace No. 4, had thousands of times plunged a thermocouple into a heat of steel. At age fifty-seven, the economical swing of his arms, the ease with which he stepped onto a platform only two feet square before the furnace to make his thrust, and then to stand in that fiercely hot spot not a moment too long but neither to hurry away: all this showed the sturdy grace of experience.

A few minutes before 4 A.M. on October 14, 1970, as Frank Simmer was withdrawing the smoking pole, the welds cracked open in the steel platform on which he was standing.

Arms raised, still holding the pole—therefore missing the one instant when he might have grabbed for something solid—Simmer twisted his face about and shot Joe Wiest a look of dreadful surprise. Then he plunged into the pit which had received, less than an hour before, a flood of slag at 2,000 degrees.

Joseph C. Wiest, third helper on the furnace, stood twelve feet away. He had spent seventeen of his thirty-five years at the steel plant working in Simmer's crew. They were pals. Like everyone, Wiest called the older man "Chubby"—perhaps just for the reason that he was not especially chubby. Nearly six feet and 168 pounds, father of three grown children, Simmer would smile and let the younger fellows josh, so long as they did the job.

Half a head shorter, Joe Wiest had been one of the smaller boys on his high school football team. Now with five young children of his own, he coached "midget football," and believed that coaching sharpened his reactions, especially to certain kinds of trouble. He hated to see a boy get hurt, and when one was down on the field after a play, Coach Wiest made it his business to get out there first to help.

And now Joe Wiest was leaping to the hole over the slag pit. He peered down through the rising fumes and saw Frank Simmer writhing on the bottom more than twenty feet below.

"Hold on, Chub," he cried, "I'm coming to get you!"

The closest stairs were 100 feet away and Wiest ran for them. "Chubby's in the pit!" he yelled to second helper Daniel A. Fleeger, fifty-three, the only other worker nearby, and Fleeger relayed the cry to the crew of the next furnace up the line.

Joe Wiest never heard the alarm which clanged through the vast plant within seconds. He was rushing down three flights of iron stairs, it seemed to him, "ten steps at a time." The need to act was like a huge bubble of panic growing in him; he had no idea how he could help, only that he somehow had to.

Under the raw lights of the basement he ran, past dusty stacks of stored materials and around the wall of the slag pit to its far end. At this level the pit was simply a large concrete bin about twenty-five feet square and open at one end. A bulldozer could drive in, smash up the partially cooled slag, and remove it for salvage; enough steel pieces were trapped in it to make this worthwhile.

From the furnace twenty-seven feet up, whose rounded bottom roofed the bin like an inverted dome, the last fiery shower of molten slag had streamed into the pit. It had rolled down a slope of older hardened slag and spread into a delta that stretched across the open end of the bin and, in fact, fanned five feet beyond onto the basement floor. This, of course, had had some time to cool.

But cool! A black crust had formed two inches thick, spiky and chunked as dirty frost. Even the crust was hot enough to boil water. It made a man's spit hiss. Beneath it, like embers of a charcoal fire, the slag glowed at 500 to 700 degrees, in places perhaps still molten. This was hell with a bit of shell on it.

Caught between two fires—the molten steel cradled in the furnace above and the mass of cooling slag on the floor—the air in the pit was heated to at least 150 degrees and filled with fumes that made the eyes water.

Frank Simmer had not, in falling, plunged directly into new slag; rather onto that slope of hardened, older material the bulldozers never quite cleaned out of the corners of the bin. But he had rolled down and the left side of his body and face had slapped against the newly formed crust of the slag. He immediately recoiled but he had many broken bones. In a roasting space of five feet on the slope between the hot mound of slag and a side wall, he could only flail helplessly as his sidekick appeared, his face lit by the glow at the open end of the bin. "Get me out, Joe," Simmer moaned, "help me."

Between them, however, lay the delta of slag at least fifteen feet across, its radiant heat blasting up at Wiest's face.

A bulldozer was parked several yards away. For an instant Wiest considered *driving* to Simmer. No—that would take too much time. In an agony to act, he suddenly stepped onto the mounded slag and began walking over it like a pedestrian hurrying across a busy street.

"I didn't think, you just don't think," he would later explain.

But he could feel: feel the weight of his work boots with soles an inch thick, and feel the clumpy slag under them. If he scampered across the crust at its narrowest point near the wall—and quickly, so that it wouldn't crack under him—there was a chance. If ever a man tried to will himself weightless, it was Joe Wiest in those seconds.

And he made it.

He ran, he stumbled up onto the slope of old slag. He couldn't do anything fast enough. With his gloved hands he batted at flames on Simmer's shirt while simultaneously trying to haul him up to his feet, all the while coughing encouragement to himself as well as the other man—"Don't worry, Chub"—needing the assurance of a voice, even his own, "we'll make it, we're gonna make it."

The heat was at the limit of endurance. He felt his face was frying. He tried not to inhale the air. With a power in his arms that, when he thought about it later, amazed him, he pulled Wiest up from sitting position, lifted him under the arms in an embrace like some giant baby, half over his own shoulder; and carrying the man who was six inches taller than himself and practically as heavy, he started back over the crust of slag.

Now the weight on his boots was doubled. Further, now he was blind to the clumped irregularity of the crust: the way he was carrying Simmer obscured his vision. He could only put his feet down, and hope, and lift his feet again as quickly as possible. If his boot broke through, if he sank to the knee in *that* . . .

At his second step he felt a sickening crumble—and quickly took a third step. He saw Dan Fleeger, the other furnace helper, waiting at the open end of the pit. Fleeger had been only a few yards behind him down the stairs and through the basement. He was saying, "C'mon, Joe."

Wiest was close now. Just a few more feet. A fourth, a fifth step. And then he fell.

He landed hard on his left hip, smack down on the slag crust with the full weight of Frank Simmer across him and Dan Fleeger's outstretched hand reaching for them.

"God had to be there," was the only way Wiest could explain it later. He does not know why the slag crust did not break, or how he could rise back up to his feet still carrying Simmer. It just didn't and he did. And he walked off the slag and laid the injured man down on the basement floor.

Other workmen came running now and doused Simmer's smoldering clothes with water. Soon there was an ambulance and Simmer was being lifted in on a stretcher, and that was when someone noticed the left side of Joe Wiest's trousers was burned away and he was near fainting.

En route to the hospital in the ambulance, Wiest heard Simmer repeatedly murmuring his thanks and then, deliriously, "someone take my shoe off . . . I think I broke my ankle." He had suffered second and third degree burns, fractures, internal injuries and shock. Two days later in the hospital he died.

Wiest's own second degree burns healed in a few days. Three weeks later he was back in the steel plant but not on No. 4 Furnace. Transferred to another department, he worked there for about eight months, but he had lost his taste for it. In June, 1971, he quit to start his own business as a paving contractor.

The steel firm gave him its "Armco Spirit" medallion. There were other recognitions by civic groups and in the press. But for him these had the leaden taste of the posthumous.

"If he had lived," said Joe Wiest, ". . . it would have been great."

Based on the facts as told in A Walk on the Crust of Hell, *Joseph C. Wiest was awarded the bronze Carnegie Hero Award medal.*

Tracking the Heroes

FAR AS I GO, MISTER," said the cab driver, and Herbert Eyman, peering down the lane into the swamp, had to see the man's point. A roadbed of crushed clam shells wound into the scrub. The path of sorts was elevated from the surrounding ooze but barely wide enough for a car. Branches of oak and pepper trees meshed overhead in a sort of canopy from which strands of furry moss hung down to the level of a man's face. Eyman was put in mind of a railroad tunnel, except that there was no light at the other end, only a deepening green gloom the farther the lane receded from the main road out of DeLand, Florida.

Not only the prospect of getting stuck had chased off the cab driver. Moonshiners lived in there. And they were known not rarely to greet uninvited guests with a cold squint at the other end of a gun barrel.

Herbert Eyman felt very much alone as he started into the swamp afoot. He was a pale man of quick, jumpy movements despite his robust build. In his late fifties, wearing a business suit into a swamp, he was definitely a city man, with smoothly brushed white hair, and spectacles atop a small, slightly hooked nose. A good many people knew and liked Herb Eyman but none in this neighborhood that he knew of. His purpose in life was to collect and report facts, not "hot" for the press but months or even years after the event, so that a group of gentlemen in Pittsburgh would have adequate data for deciding whether an act of heroism had occurred.

As a field investigator for the Carnegie Hero Fund Commission, Eyman's business in the swamp was to interview the mother of a child rescued from a fire. That this benign purpose might, in this day and place, get him shot or nipped by a moccasin or rattlesnake oppressed him. The crunch of his shoes on clam shells made the only sound under the mossy branches. With each advancing step the gloom around him seemed to intensify.

Professional duty over the years, a certain craftsmanlike pride, had occasionally goaded Herbert Eyman to acts of daring. He did not confuse these with heroism. A Carnegie agent was not only not expected, but practically forbidden, to try to re-enact deeds of courage. What might pass for bravery in another man, Eyman realized, was, in him, mere thoroughness.

Still, he had done some things . . .

Once he had gone to the top of a Texas grain elevator the only way to get there—by conveyor belt. There was no protective grating, only a belt a foot wide with blocks of wooden two-by-four bolted to it as steps. It looped out of a hole in the floor and quivered nakedly straight up 110 feet through a hole in the roof. Not till Eyman had leaped on, was rising giddily the equivalent of eleven yawning stories with nothing around him but hot rushing air, did the thought occur to him: what if the motor conks out? He would have been stranded like a bug on flypaper, and without the sticky stuff to hold him on. Yet a rescue had taken place on that roof after a dust explosion some months before, and Eyman never was satisfied with second-hand descriptions of the locales of courage.

"Generally I had to see the scene," he said. "It helped in

interviews with witnesses. You could tie questions to environmental features."

In 1950 a visit to a scene had helped him verify a tale of rescue that sounded like something Alaskan cronies might cook up for sport in the long arctic night. A fishing boat had sunk in a gale off Elfin Cove, but a wave had washed one survivor onto a ledge of rock which projected from the water 1,200 yards from shore and ten feet above the sea. Exposed to icy wind and spray—this was in November—Helvig Christensen, forty-five, huddled on a shelf a yard wide and even less, deep. His feet froze, consciousness ebbed and flickered, but somehow his cramped, fetal position conserved the spark of life through that day and night. And the next day and night! At last he was able to tumble like a block of ice into a boat which came out for him, though the storm had not fully spent itself.

Christensen lost both feet and two fingers but proved a cheerful fatalist in his interview months later with Eyman. The investigator was impressed, too, by the guileless accounts of other witnesses and of fisherman Thomas Allain and the two teen-age sisters who had gone out with him in his boat through the storm to rescue the marooned man. These people scanted many points that connivers would have dramatized. Still, Eyman made sure to hire his own boat. Nor was he satisfied until, piloted directly up to the rock 1,200 yards offshore, he was able to verify that ten feet up on its face there was indeed a ledge where a man might huddle for life.

A far more plausible story Eyman once exposed as fabrication. After a disastrous hotel fire in Atlanta, Georgia, an elderly tenant reported that a heroic bellhop had led her to the lobby down stairs choked with smoke. In this case the "scene" was no more. The hotel had been razed. But puzzled by the dowager's vagueness, Eyman reconstructed the scene from the architect's plans. He also tracked down the bellhop through several succeeding jobs. The fellow laughed. Him, a hero? He had never left the lobby, he said; had in fact seen the old lady simply step out of an elevator there. Why, then, had she constructed a whopper? Eyman's belief is that, finding herself "saved," she romantically assumed someone of mighty purpose had rescued her; or else, after an incident that gave rise to so many thrilling personal accounts, "the poor old girl just had to have one of her own."

It was not unusual for Eyman to have to run a hero to ground. Once it took him three years to make contact with a man who had hurled himself at a woman in front of a train at Elkton, Maryland. His force had pushed both him and the lady off the track and flush against a fence as the train, with just fourteen inches clearance, roared past. Witnesses reported the act but the good man was no typical storybook Galahad. He finally answered one of the notes Eyman had distributed in the shabby hotels and bars he frequented: an habitual drifter who had risen to one moment of glory.

A common failing of witnesses, Eyman learned long ago, is an inability to judge distance, directions, or speeds accurately. "Seventy-five miles an hour!" an honest man will estimate for the speed of a stream from which a struggling swimmer has been saved. Having scrutinized most of the fast waters of America, Eyman testifies that six or seven miles per hour probably is closer to the fact.

Such was the speed—he checked it—of the current sixty feet above Vernals Fall in Yosemite National Park in July, 1946, when Keen Freeman, who was twelve years old, leaned over to dip a canteen in the water and fell in. A 20-year-old sailor without hesitation vaulted a guard rail, leaped out in the stream and caught at the boy's shirt. Orville Loos had been discharged from the Navy at San Francisco just a few hours before; he hadn't wanted to go home to Akron, Ohio, without seeing the Yosemite. The water above the falls was just two and a half feet deep but it flowed at seven miles an hour—and seven looks like seventy from the bank. The current shoved Loos and the boy from one clawing handhold on the slippery bottom to another. If they shouted anything, no one could hear it in the roar of the falls. Twenty feet from the brink another man leaned far out from the guard rail and reached for Loos, but their hands never touched. Silhouetted clear of the flood for one instant against a painfully blue sky, sailor and boy, hands locked, plunged 317 feet to the rocks below.

Heroism—or reckless impulse? The final judgment on that is not the investigator's to make. In his own mind Eyman feels this way: "When a man loses his life to save someone else, how can you go beyond that?" Still, the cases he has admired most have occurred "when all the dangers are known beforehand—and still somebody goes!"

Sam E. Wohlford was Eyman's favorite. This ranch owner, fifty-seven years old, knew all about the sort of blizzard that pounded the Texas panhandle in February, 1948: one of those storms with which a north wind can torment a region for days, a mixing bowl of snow and howling darkness that can freeze a wandering man ten feet from his own front fence.

In the afternoon of the second day of such a storm, an Oklahoman named Reynolds staggered to Sam Wohlford's door. Reynolds's car had been buried in a drift three miles down the road all the previous night. His mother and three children, including a baby fifteen months old, were still trapped.

Rancher Wohlford got out his tractor and rigged a wood platform behind it for passengers. By cutting fence wires and driving across windswept areas in the open fields, he was able to avoid the heavily drifted roads and finally reached the car. It was buried hip deep in snow, but Wohlford and Reynolds were able to dig the family out. All but the baby were unconscious, however; and an older boy showed no sign of life.

Wohlford's house was too far to try to reach in the furious storm. The family would all be dead. So the rancher unloaded them at the first shelter he could find, a vacant bunkhouse. The nearest doctor was ten miles north, at the town of Stratford. No home in the area had a phone. The best Wohlford could do was to reach a neighbor's house a mile and a half away, and leave word there to stop any passing vehicle with a plea to send a doctor.

As he tried to get back to the Reynoldses, Wohlford's tractor stalled a half mile west of the highway. All he could do then was to stagger back, with numb hands and feet, to the neighbor's home. Hours passed, the temperature fell to zero and not a vehicle moved in the night.

At that point the neighbor's pregnant wife went into labor!

Once more into the storm went Sam Wohlford, toward a woman relative's house two miles away. For a half mile he could follow a fence, then a line of utility poles; though with icicles on his eyelashes and a whirling net of snow all around, a man could get lost between two poles! Every few steps the tired rancher had to sit down in the snow and squint up in the darkness toward the faint, glistening arcs of the utility lines to guide him. He reached the house, summoned the relative to the woman in labor—she was delivered of a girl—and, the next morning, brought an ambulance team from an army depot nineteen miles away. But for three of the marooned Reynoldses, Sam Wohlford's long night's struggle with the storm had been in vain. Only the father and the baby survived.

On another day in a better season the old rancher walked over every yard of the ground he had covered with Herbert Eyman. Such people have to be tactfully drawn out. Theirs is a quiet pride—and often mixed with a sense of guilt that they didn't accomplish more, or at any rate, that too much is being made of *this*. There certainly have been rescuers so modest that by withholding information they effectively parried any effort to honor them. But actual hostility is rare, said Eyman, and most apt to be shown by a "witness who stayed on dry land while somebody else went in the water."

When a witness would not help him at all, the investigator's soft twang, his gentle, almost pedantic punctilio, showed its cutting edge: "Then you are willing to take the responsibility for making it impossible to give recognition to someone else?" he would say. "In the absence of what you can tell me, we have nothing to go on." Putting it like that usually had a bracing effect, says Eyman—"You could hear them thinking: 'Well, so I *am* important.' "

Eyman may hold the world's record for having a job application on file. Judging the life of a Carnegie hero investigator to be "an educational way of living," he applied to the commission while he was still a senior in high school in western Pennsylvania. That was in 1922.

Twenty years later, in November, 1942, as telegraph editor of the Sharon (Pennsylvania) *Herald*, he received this message in the mail: "If you are still interested in a position with the commission, would you kindly call for an appointment."

What had happened was World War II. From a peak at one time of seventeen investigators, the staff had fallen to just one. Older men had retired, younger ones were being drafted for military service. But Herb Eyman never would be taken by the Army. "Apparently the commission remembered I had this deformity of the left hand," he said, with the same objectivity he would have noted that physical fact in any rescue victim or hero. His left hand had some utility, but from birth its fingers had not developed beyond tiny stubs.

And so in February, 1943, Eyman began a career which would for the next quarter-century keep him on the road eleven of twelve months of the year, and would take him to remote corners of every United States state and every Canadian province save Labrador. Evenings he spent pounding out his reports on a typewriter. In hinterland hotel rooms that lacked the amenity of a table, he typed many a page of official prose under a bare light bulb at a machine bouncing giddily on a mattress.

The glamor in such a life "wears off in a year," he says, but he never quite lost his reporter's eye for the flash of humor which unrolls past a bus window or across Main Streets strolled by a man who is always a stranger in town. "Frisky Worms" is a sign he once jotted down near a Georgia fishing village; a ramshackle house in Alabama tickled him with an offering of "Room and COOKED Board."

If there was one aspect of life on the road that irritated and challenged him, it was being stuck someplace with "no way to get there." On one of the earlier of his nine trips to Alaska, he faced six days in a tiny fishing village waiting for the next steamer out. But out of the fog dropped an old Navy patrol bomber which had been converted to cargo. The cargo was salmon. Even the co-pilot's seat had been sacrificed to this commerce. There was, accordingly, no co-pilot, just more space for fish. In spite of repeated baths and the best efforts of dry cleaners, Eyman and his clothes smelled of salmon for two weeks. He rode out of the village lying prone under the ceiling of the plane—on top of crates of iced fish.

At the other end of America he once investigated a rescue at Vinal Haven Island, off Maine. It was also off season: there was no public transportation. And the sea was rising in five-foot swells. But Eyman stood on a rain-swept wharf until the skipper of a seventeen-foot mailboat reluctantly took him aboard. The boat's wheelhouse was only big enough for one. The captain placed Eyman next to a small mast forward, and the man from Pittsburgh was astonished to find ropes being wound around his middle. Thus, with waves sloshing over the deck to his knees, his waist and once (he swears) to his neck, the hero investigator made his way to an assignment—lashed to a ship's mast.

Another investigator, not Eyman, once dramatically improved his waiting time. Finding no one at home when he knocked on the apartment door of a certain witness, he was invited to wait next door by a neighbor. She proved to be a comely widow, not without charm or sympathy for the lonely rigors of an investigator's life. Soon thereafter she had a new husband, and the commission was hiring a new field man.

The nemesis of Eyman's career was a witness who led him several miles up rough stony terrain to a mountain stream in Oregon where a drowning man had been rescued. The investigator was pushing sixty then and his guide, cruelly playful, insisted on showing him just how fast a fellow had to go to keep up in those parts. Just as stubbornly Eyman refused to say uncle. When he dragged himself into bed that night, his legs were numb. This was the first onset of a circulatory illness that later, sometimes, caused him to black out during interviews in witnesses' homes and, finally, forced him to retire from the road altogether in 1967.

But this twilight lay far in the future on that day when the Carnegie fund's most seasoned investigator walked into the Florida swamp, his shoes crunching on clam shells. He flicked garlands of dripping moss away from his face, and at one point when he looked back, the opening to the main highway was barely visible. "Hello," called Herbert Eyman to no one in particular. "Hello there."

No human throat gave answer.

But onto the road a quarter mile ahead leaped fifteen hounds in full cry. They assumed "a nasty, wedge-shaped silhouette in the gloom," Eyman recalls, and they were led by a particularly fearsome brute whose tail was stiffly elevated and his teeth bared.

Eyman hadn't a chance in the world to run. Neither did he, at that moment, remember the advice given him years before by a veteran postman: "Cover your face with your coat. A dog'll never attack a man whose eyes he can't see. He'll back away." In a long career of diplomacy with strange dogs, Eyman was pleased that he had never had to put this advice to the test. Yet now perhaps all his conquests were but prelude to this Waterloo of many fangs.

What he did was to employ his gift of address. He spoke to the lead dog. "Good dog," he called out, "good fellow," and expanded on the theme. He remarked on the animal's gentlemanly bearing, his noble mien, the vigor with which he was even now carrying out his sentinel duty. Eyman said things about that dog that would have embarrassed a candidate for President.

And the brute liked it. He stopped ten feet away, offered a quarter wag of his tail. His raised hackles receded. Eyman extended his good right hand. The dog permitted his head to be patted. He wagged his tail. It was a distinct, full wag.

In an instant his slavish minions surrounded the investigator, rivals for his pats and his flattering words.

The rest of Eyman's walk down the lane to a house in a small clearing, hailed and heralded by fifteen spirited dogs, was almost triumphal.

And when Herbert Eyman returned to the highway with the same frisky and loyal escort, the mossy green lane seemed not gloomy at all nor nearly so long, and his facts were in his pocket.

Based on the facts as told in Tracking the Heroes, *a silver Carnegie Hero Award medal was awarded to Sam E. Wohlford and bronze medals to Thomas F. Allain and Orville D. Loos, Orville Loos's posthumously.*

Tragedy on Tallmadge Parkway

THE TRAGEDY BEGAN INVISIBLY. Forty feet in the earth under Tallmadge Parkway, in Akron, Ohio, a storm sewer failed. It was a pipe of concrete barrels three feet in diameter, capable, in a heavy rain, of shooting water like an endless bullet down to the Little Cuyahoga River. But a six-foot section weakened and cracked open. Water burst into the surrounding earth-fill. Swirling, scouring, it flushed tons of soil, as well as most of the broken section of pipe, out through the sewer's lower end.

How long this erosion had been going on no one knows. A torrential storm in the early afternoon of July 21, 1964, dumped three and a half inches of rain on Akron in one hour; so the bulk of the damage might have occurred then, just before the accident. All that can be stated certainly is that by 3 P.M. on that streaming summer Tuesday, a piece of Tallmadge Parkway, formerly solid roadbed, had become bridge. Fourteen inches of asphalt covered a pit thirty feet deep.

Now the downpour was over. Traffic was moving again in Akron. Still the afternoon air clung to the middle 80's; it felt spongy enough to wring out. Mrs. Velma Shidler's car was a steam cabinet. In the rear seat her pert daughter Claudia, twelve, and a friend, Janet Lewis, thirteen, couldn't wait to get home. They had to keep their windows rolled up, because it was still drizzling. The glass was all misted.

Visibility ahead was clear enough. Mrs. Shidler noticed several trucks preceding her eastbound, their tires spitting up spray. Others were rumbling up the hill in the opposite lanes. Tallmadge Parkway at that moment and in that place was, in fact, taking a pounding from heavy traffic.

It is a pleasant suburban piece of road right there: wide and graceful to the eye as it descends a wooded hillside very much like a park, then curves out of sight down through the trees toward a bridge over the river in the valley. The roadside maples glistened, the tires sang on the wet paving, the girls chattered in the back seat, and Velma Shidler, carefully driving one of many vehicles on a busy road, had no reason for alarm when she saw—as a truck fifty feet in front passed over it—what looked like a pothole.

An ordinary pothole two feet wide in the paving.

She steered easily to the left, so that her wheels would miss it. Her left front tire did miss it. It had reached the other side—when her car suddenly crashed.

It surely crashed: that is, came violently to a stop. Mrs. Shidler was thrown against the steering wheel. She sensed the girls tumbling about behind her. But the car's impact was against nothing visible, only this shattering inability to go further . . . followed an instant after by a deadly plummeting weightlessness at the stomach, as in an elevator whose cables have snapped. There was no support under three wheels of the car.

It tilted backwards. Treetops and sky swooped across the windshield. The auto dropped back, straight down, into some sort of pit. Wrenched around, Mrs. Shidler stared with a terrified clarity in the direction of the fall.

The car landed hard on its rear end. The events that immediately followed happened so fast their precise sequence was unsortable. Inertia blew out the rear window of the car and young Claudia tumbled backwards down out of the rear seat toward the window space; her mother's hand darted after her—but missed.

Both girl and glass disappeared.

With a scream Mrs. Shidler caught the other child, Janet Lewis, around the waist. Though a tiny woman of forty-eight years, just five-feet-one and ninety-five pounds, and battered by the crash, the housewife somehow was able to haul the girl up into the front seat by main force. Janet was seriously hurt. Hospital examination later would show, along with many cuts and bruises, a fractured left arm and ruptured kidney.

Frantically the two tried to open the car doors. The one on Janet's side would not budge at all. Mrs. Shidler could move hers only a few inches. Her position was too cramped for any leverage. She felt her legs bowed over on top of her, and her whole weight resting on her neck. About all she and Janet could do to help themselves at this point was to scream.

John Wiebelt's truck had been rolling down Tallmadge Parkway at nearly 50 miles per hour, but Wiebelt never "tailgated." A safe hundred yards stretched between him and the car ahead. At first he thought he was seeing things: a crater coming open in the road directly under the car ahead, great chunks of paving sloughing off like so much wet icing with no cake under it, and then the car being swallowed into the pit. Wiebelt rammed his brakes. His tires skidded and squealed, but he wrestled his rig to a halt against the highway curb with the front wheels just three feet from the pit's edge. He jumped down from his cab and took one second to peer in at the damage.

The pit was a giant wastebasket. It was circular, roughly, tapering down from a top diameter of seventeen feet to about twelve feet on the floor, thirty feet below. The Shidler car stood in the bottom on its rear end but tilted slightly backwards. Its roof leaned against the base of the sloping side of the pit. The wheels still feebly turned, like the under parts of a helpless insect. Slabs of fallen paving also lay in the pit bottom, some flat, others poking from the dirt at angles. Here and there a clod broke loose and tumbled down the sloping walls. But there were no major slides.

And not a drop of water was visible in the floor of the pit, nor any sign that water could enter. The only sounds were feminine cries for help.

Wiebelt was a construction foreman, and he happened to have the means for a rescue on the back of his truck: an extension ladder, block and tackle, lengths of rope. He was thirty-five years old, handicapped years before by a polio attack that left him with one leg an inch shorter than the other. But his instinct was to get things organized to help.

He caught sight of a tractor-trailer laboring up the hill under a cargo of steel plates. A heavy load like that might collapse the highway more, widen the cave-in. With a shout Wiebelt ran limping into the westbound lanes, waving his arms, and flagged the heavy truck down. Other vehicles halted behind it. Then Wiebelt hustled around the pit and brought downhill traffic to a stop as well. Horns sounded, windows were rolled down. Motorists opened their car doors and asked each other what was going on. From these scurryings and worryings the driver of the steel truck preserved an olympian detachment. He never even got down from his cab. However, others permitted themselves to become concerned. And soon there was a ring of consultants around John Wiebelt at the edge of the pit.

It was not a wholly inexperienced group. Among the men flagged down were two from the municipal sewer department, dispatched through the city with many others on storm emergency calls. There also were a drainage ditch contractor and his young summer helper, and a fair number of other hands able, at least, to hoist a ladder or pull on a rope. The sewer man promptly ran down to the nearest home on a side street to report the cave-in and ask police and fire department assistance, along with heavy equipment to raise the car from the pit.

But the cries from within the crater were piteous—and urgent—and to some witnesses it appeared the wrecked car was settling, sinking perceptibly, into the soft bottom dirt. With a girl and woman crying, among other things, "Oh God, save us!" it was not a situation in which men of spirit could wait for "the proper authorities."

At Wiebelt's suggestion an 18-foot section of ladder was pulled off his truck and lowered into the pit on a rope tied to the truck bumper. In the excitement, the ladder's extension was somehow forgotten. Resting down the slope of the crater, the half-ladder awkwardly failed to reach the floor of the pit by a good twelve feet.

No matter. Young Jim Landis, the 16-year-old helper of the drain contractor, volunteered to descend. He was in the act of tying a safety rope around his belt when his employer, thinking of his own responsibilities, began worrying aloud that the boy really was too young for the job—when someone else put his hand on the rope and quietly said, "Tie it on me, I'll go down." They were the first words he had spoken.

Wiebelt and young Landis looked up into the calm, intelligent face of a boy of 19. He was athletic in build, had closely cropped blond hair and a finely chiseled but strong mouth and chin. There was no need or time for introductions, nor would the youth's name, Hugh Michael O'Neil, have meant anything special to the others.

Attired in work shoes, khaki trousers, and a plaid shirt, he was a typical college boy—in this case from Georgetown University— en route to a typical hometown summer job, which paid $45 a week, at the General Tire Company, one of Akron's largest industries. That his grandfather had founded the firm; that one of his uncles was now its president, and others, along with his father, important executives; and that he himself could, if he chose, look forward someday to considerable social and professional standing in the city: all this would have been irrelevant to the qualifications needed at the crater in Tallmadge Parkway.

Young O'Neil tied the rope around his waist and, with Wiebelt and a half-dozen others holding on to the loose end, he put his feet on the ladder and started into the pit. He hung from the lowest rung and dropped from it to the floor of the cavity. Then he tugged on the rope and called, "Give me some slack."

A brick occasionally broke loose from the crusty overhangs of paving and rolled down the slope, but none of these fell near O'Neil. The up-ended auto concerned him more. From the crater floor it loomed much taller than he, and at a crazy angle. He did not want to be underneath if the wall of the pit gave way and pushed the car over. So he made his approach warily from one side, placing his feet with care in the soft moist earth among the fallen chunks of paving.

Standing as tall as he could, he gripped the edge of Mrs. Shidler's car door in both hands and tugged it about one third of the way open. The space seemed sufficient to allow the exit of both victims.

Meanwhile, at street level, John Wiebelt was appealing for another man to enter the pit to lend assistance. A construction man on the scene agreed to go down but insisted on first running to his nearby car for his hardhat. In that small interval Patrolman Ronald D. Rotruck arrived in his police cruiser.

Getting the picture at a glance, Rotruck unbuckled his gun belt, had Wiebelt tie a rope around his waist, and descended into the pit. A strapping blond man, six feet two and 215 pounds, Ron Rotruck was married, the father of three girls, aged two, four and five. He had been a police officer five years. In the next fifteen minutes his work shift was scheduled to end. He would soon be off-duty. It is not unknown for policemen at such a moment to be idling back toward the station house and not looking for trouble.

Mike O'Neil on the bottom of the pit in fact needed assistance.

He was reaching with both arms up through the door opening and hauling gently on Janet Lewis. Mrs. Shidler, from her cramped position, was trying to lift the girl under the armpits and thrust her toward O'Neil. Several times the child cried out with pain. But gradually O'Neil extricated her without disturbing the balanced position of the car.

Then, holding Janet in his arms, Mike stepped carefully around the perimeter of the pit toward a twenty-four-foot ladder which meanwhile had been let down along the opposite slope of the crater. For the first time he now noticed Rotruck striding through the soft dirt. "There's a woman in there—maybe more," said O'Neil. The policeman nodded and continued on toward the car.

Reaching the ladder, O'Neil lifted Janet under the arms so that her feet reached the bottom rung. "I can't climb," she cried, appearing to be in severe pain.

Until this point Mike O'Neil had not needed the "life line" tied around his waist. Without hesitation he now removed it. He wound it around the girl and around several rungs of the ladder. He gave a signal, and the men at street level hauled upward till about ten feet of the ladder projected out of the pit. Then they lowered the projecting part to the horizontal and swung the end to which Janet Lewis was lashed in a wide arc from above the pit to the pavement at the east side of the hole.

Meanwhile, Officer Rotruck had reached the car. He helped Mrs. Shidler out to a standing position on the floor of the pit. The woman could walk but she was hysterical. "Claudia," she sobbed repeatedly, "Clauddie," naming the child she had last seen shooting out the car's rear window. At times she cried, "Floyd, poor Floyd," this being her husband's name.

Rotruck did not know what to make of it. Firmly he led Mrs. Shidler toward the long ladder, which had been reinserted into the pit after Janet Lewis's removal. Mike O'Neil helped Mrs. Shidler onto the ladder. She seemed strong enough to hang on by herself. Before she could be hauled up and away, Rotruck demanded, "Are there any more in there? Tell me!" The woman nodded. She held up one finger. Then the ladder lifted her away.

Rotruck at once slogged back to the auto. Its front seat was removable. He hauled the seat out and wedged it to brace open the door. Then he extended his body in to the waist. There was no one else in the car.

Withdrawing, Rotruck shouted up to the men on top: "I can't see anyone in there. Who am I looking for? A boy, a girl, a man?"

Someone yelled back that the Lewis girl had said Mrs. Shidler's daughter was still missing.

This was the last reasonably calm statement spoken at the scene.

With no warning, from some invisible source below, water suddenly bubbled up in the floor of the crater. Portions of the sandy slopes gave way and slid. The up-ended auto sank deeper and someone at street level noticed that the removed car seat was "disappearing into the water."

Ron Rotruck looked down in astonishment at his shoes. His feet were covered to the ankles. He tried to move them, exclaiming with no special sound of alarm but rather as a statement of a new and unusual fact, "I'm stuck."

The men on the street heaved up on the rope still attached to the officer's waist. But somehow it came loose, either untying at the knot or breaking, no one was sure how. And Ronald Rotruck was off the line—and sinking to his knees.

Again came a surge of water out of the pit floor, again some crumbling of the slopes, and this time when the water receded, dropping with a loud gurgle of suction, it dragged Ron Rotruck down to his hips!

"I can't get out!" he cried.

What Rotruck did not know, what no one at the surface could know, was that ten feet beneath the floor of the pit in a broken storm sewer which no one could see, tremendous pressures were being unleashed. According to the theory constructed some days later, the debris under the crater floor, including big slabs of paving and the broken crockery of the sewer pipe itself, must have acted as a temporary clog in the sewer's flow. This had allowed the interval of seeming safety during which Mrs. Shidler and Janet Lewis had been removed. But now a massive head of pent-up water evidently was smashing across the gap in the sewer, washing up into the crater and flushing out again as chunks of debris, crumbling, were swept into the lower end of the pipe.

The O'Neil youth heard Patrolman Rotruck's cries and was the only other person now in the pit with him. Mike saw the life line come away from the officer's waist and saw him sink to his hips as in quicksand. O'Neil, remember, had already surrendered his own life line, having used it to lash Janet Lewis to the rescue ladder. Nevertheless, the boy quickly and cautiously stepped around the perimeter of the pit bottom toward Rotruck and reached out his hands for the trapped man.

But at that moment another invasion of water welled up. The slope at O'Neil's back collapsed and thrust him forward. The slide imprisoned his legs in the bubbling mud. With relentless suction, the water's withdrawal hauled Rotruck down to his chest—and O'Neil to his chin!

The siren of an approaching fire department vehicle had been sawing the sultry air for at least a full minute now. Some 200 feet down the hill the ladder company came to a halt. Its captain feared to bring the heavy vehicle closer till he could survey conditions at the cave-in. As he came running up the hill, John Wiebelt ran down, imploring him to hurry.

Meanwhile, the commotion among the men around the rim of the pit was rising to panic. Some screamed at the firemen to hurry, others barked at each other as though by shouting they could bring some useful idea quickly to birth. The ladder by which Mrs. Shidler and Janet had been pulled from the pit was once more lowered. The men holding it by a rope swung it closer to Mike O'Neil's raised hands.

He reached up, obtained a grip on the bottom rung, and strained to pull himself out of the clutching mud. But the suction of retreating water was like a living force. Suddenly the men above felt the ladder "give." O'Neil lost his grasp. His shoulders and head sank into the muck.

For a moment his hands made convulsive clutching movements in the air. Then they, too, were drawn into the ooze.

A woman bystander screamed. The men moaned or swore or stood paralytically silent, hoping that what they were seeing could not be true, that the boy would naturally come up again like a swimmer in a pool.

The fire captain at this moment reached the crater's edge. With one glance he turned around and bellowed to his men: "Ladder and ropes!"

But Ronald Rotruck was sinking fast now. He was down to his chin. "Get me out of here!" he cried.

Two firemen were running up the hill with a ladder 35 feet long. "Move, move!" the furious John Wiebelt was storming at them. "You ought to have a pump, you ought to have oxygen!" he shouted at the fire captain. "Can't you guys move any faster!"

Into the pit dropped the ladder. "He's sinking!" someone cried. Rotruck's face went under. His hands clutched at the air as Mike O'Neil's had. "Get him, for God's sake, get him!" people were shouting.

Fireman C. J. Fox scampered down the ladder. He reached the bottom rung as Rotruck's hands disappeared. The fireman squatted. He fished with one hand under the surface. He touched something: Rotruck's arm, he was sure. But he lost it. It was too slippery. He thrust his hand as deep into the muck as he could. Nothing. Fox looked up at his captain on the edge of the crater and shook his head.

One of the civilian volunteers leaned over and breathed in another bystander's ear, "He's gone."

Two days later, the bodies of Rotruck and young Claudia Shidler were recovered by workmen digging within a special metal caisson lowered by crane to the pit bottom. Both were found wedged between chunks of broken concrete and the submerged sides of the car. A hiker along the pleasant banks of the Little Cuyahoga found young O'Neil the day after the accident. At first glance he looked asleep. But he was covered with mud and the body was quite cold. It was evident that he had been drawn into the sewer and swept its entire length down to the river, a mile and a half from the pit where two lives were saved and three lost.

Based on the facts as told in Tragedy on Tallmadge Parkway, *Hugh Michael O'Neil was awarded a silver Carnegie Hero Award medal and Police Officer Ronald D. Rotruck a bronze, both posthumously.*

Runaways on Wheels

HIGH, THIN, AND WHINING, like the song of a summer insect, the noise floated out of Vienna, Ohio, along the highway leading east. It could be heard at the Patrick Garage a quarter-mile from the center of town. On the warm clear air of early afternoon—it was 1:30 P.M., Tuesday, July 10, 1962—the noise intensified, and became something definitely mechanical, a metallic rasp, steel turning on stone.

Steve Patrick looked up annoyed, then astonished. An auto was bearing along the two-lane road at considerable speed, 40 miles an hour or more, but with its right front fender sagging down, *really* down. In fact, there was no tire on the wheel. The fool was driving like that on his rim! Weaving, too. If he wasn't careful, he'd hit those boys . . . "Hey!" shouted Patrick.

In front of the garage, a few feet off the highway shoulder, Jim Mack, fourteen, was pedaling a bicycle at just enough feet per hour to keep it up on balance. A few yards ahead of him, Billy Merrifield, also fourteen, was pushing a homemade go-cart occupied by its builder-driver, Peter Shanaberg, sixteen. This vehicle did not depend on esthetic beauty for the satisfaction it gave Pete. It was five feet long and three wide, a contraption of metal pipes and wooden panels built close to the road—it was less than two feet tall—but actually capable of self-propulsion, a

136

true automobile. A small gasoline engine behind the driver's seat drove it, when it drove it. Right now Billy Merrifield was pushing it.

But *right* now that loud metallic sound getting closer on the road had become very loud indeed, alarmingly, threateningly loud. Pete Shanaberg turned in his driver's seat just in time to see a lopsided automobile looming behind him. It hurled Jim Mack aside on his bike. It knocked Billy Merrifield away. And it crashed into the little car Pete was sitting in.

He felt no pain at first. Just the wide open slap of an irresistible force, followed instantly by a great dizzying sensation of being scooped up, lifted, carried along at breathless speed. It was over the threshold of this sensation that pain came rolling in on him. His whole left side felt bitten. He cried out but the auto's clatter drowned out his voice and he continued crazily moving, the gravel of the highway shoulder streaking to a blur, just inches under his ankle. The fleeing beast had him in its teeth.

The noise of the passing car summoned into the sunlight, blinking, John Patrick from inside the garage. He saw the boy struck from his bike, saw the second lad batted from behind the little go-cart, and saw the cart itself, hooked somehow under the auto bumper and with a boy still aboard, getting dragged on down the highway by the hit-run madman at undiminished speed.

John Patrick looked at his father Steve, who was standing out front, nearer the road, flabbergasted. Both had the identical thought. That driver had to be drunk! Or crazy. For sure he'd kill the boy trapped in the go-cart if he weren't flagged down right away! Not a word needed to be said. Father and son simply dashed for the younger man's five-year-old sedan parked alongside the garage. John Patrick rammed the vehicle out onto the hot road, tires screaming, while his father held on in the passenger seat beside him.

Steve Patrick, at forty-eight, was an assistant foreman in a steel mill as well as co-owner of the garage with his mechanic son. He also had once served three years as town constable, and had often flagged down speeders and reckless drivers. So the challenge of holding one car hood to hood with another in a test of wills, the two of them blasting down the highway with the whole countryside ripping past and death no more than a hairline turn away . . . well, he had lived through a few of those. And now, older, his reflexes a bit slacker, he knew he could rely on the driving skill and judgment of his son John, twenty-one. The lad turned on his headlights to catch the attention of any motorist who might be coming the other way—it was just a two-lane road, after all—and leaned into his car horn for long blasts of warning.

This noise did nothing to slow the crazy man ahead, however. He had a start of 200 to 300 yards on the Patricks and he never let up speed. Even if he had been aware of it, the go-cart was out of his line of sight, below the horizon of his right front fender.

Somehow the cart was caught up between bumper and fender, sweeping along with only its right rear wheel spinning on the highway paving. Pete Shanaberg's left leg also was wedged under the fender. The boy was bleeding heavily. He tried to lift himself up higher than the car's fender, so that he could at least be seen by the driver.

Far back, John Patrick pounded his horn and pressed his accelerator to the floor. He sped to 60, giving chase for half a mile and steadily narrowing the gap. With profound gratitude he noted that far up the road the westbound lane was empty. And now he smoothly drew out to the left, into the opposing traffic lane, and abreast of the fleeing car. He eased up, to exactly match and hold its speed, and his father shouted at the other driver through their open windows:

"Pull off the road! You'll kill that boy on your fender!"

There was no reaction.

Steve Patrick might as well have been yelling at a statue. The other man's hands gripped his steering wheel, his speed did not slacken; his eyes, staring, never left the road before him.

"Hey, you!" Patrick shouted.

Nothing.

"Get closer to this guy," Steve said.

His son, with one eye on the road ahead—still nothing coming, thank God!—leaned two tons of automobile a little to the right, and a little more. Ten inches now separated the speeding cars. They were practically door to door. Steve Patrick reached out his window into the other car and slapped the other driver on the shoulder.

Still no reaction.

Patrick hit the man again. He didn't even blink.

By this time young Shanaberg had managed to raise himself up and twist the upper part of his body so that he could see back over the hood. He held onto a projecting piece of metal trim on the front of the car and shouted back at the driver, "Stop, please stop! I'm hurt!"

But the crippled car rolled on. Its wheelrim ground on the hot asphalt pavement; its rasp counterpointed by the warning blasts of the Patricks' car horn. For half a mile now the vehicles had run side by side in what threatened to be a suicidal embrace, the one doomed and the other powerless to abandon it, till some car or truck inevitably would come hurtling toward them from the other direction. Now, in fact, there was a curve ahead. The road was turning left, and Steve Patrick realized at last that the driver an arm's length from him was locked into some incomprehensible stupor which, on the curve, could kill them all. Desperately he reached for the man's steering wheel . . .

About an hour before the bizarre chase, Kenneth Kelly had begun feeling drowsy at the wheel of his car. Kelly was a 28-year-old married man who suffered from diabetes. Away from home the night before, he had missed his usual insulin injection and had slept poorly. Now, in mid-day heat, he was paying for it. The torpor caused by excess sugar coursing through his blood was catching up with him, though he had the windows open and the breezes blowing at his face. Home was only a few miles away now. He would be able to reach that medicine shelf soon. There was no cause for panic. He had the presence of mind to stop his car, get out at a store and buy a snack for quick energy. Then he resumed driving east on Route 82. The gray belt of roadway sped beneath him between the green Ohio fields that rolled out and out, and up to a dusty blue sky, hot and far away. His foot was on the gas, his hands tight on the steering wheel . . .

The conscious part of his mind snapped shut. The condition is called "acute insulin trance." His eyes were open. He drove. To curves and certain other highway situations he evidently could make coarse reflex adjustments. But a shock as concrete as the loss of a front tire did not faze him; he continued to drive on the rim. Police never did learn how he had lost the tire. The groove his wheel rim had laid in the road could be traced back three miles west of the Patrick Garage, where it disappeared.

As the two cars approached the curve, Steve Patrick lunged for Kelly's steering wheel. He could not get a firm grip but he pawed the wheel just enough to get the sick man's car directed safely into the curve.

Then he heard a groan from his son. Seven hundred feet ahead, speeding westbound in the lane occupied by the Patricks, a station wagon appeared. John sounded his horn desperately, long blasts and short. Up ahead the station wagon still came on, but suddenly it seemed to hesitate, to waver. It squeezed farther to its own right side of the road—the Patricks' left—then went off the road, slashing through gravel on the shoulder, forced out there by the two cars abreast, and John Patrick, with an apologetic glance, caught one look at a motorist's face contorted with fear and outrage.

But there was no time for explanations now. As Kelly's car came out of the curve, the go-cart somehow became detached from the bumper and fender. Set free at a tangent, Pete Shanaberg's little vehicle spun off the highway on the right. It raced across the shoulder, sagged down into a roadside ditch with soft walls, and came upright to rest.

Seeing this, Steve Patrick immediately ordered his son: "Ditch him!"

John slowed his car to let Kelly's move ahead a few feet in order to improve the target against which he would nudge. When the other car door was opposite his own front bumper, John nosed it over to the right and made a brushing contact. Then he bore more forcibly in at the side of Kelly's car, presently shoving it off onto the right shoulder amid tremendous spits of gravel and into the side of the ditch—to a full, jarring stop!

The Patricks were not unhappy to stop as well. They gave one glance at Kelly in his front seat—unscratched, not at all annoyed, he still stared ahead in his unaccountable coma—and then they ran back 200 yards to where Peter Shanaberg had gone into the ditch on his go-cart. Neighbors already were gathered about the bloody boy.

After a week in the hospital and five more under medical treatment at home, Peter recovered. His friends who had been struck in front of the garage luckily proved to have only minor injuries.

The entranced Kelly was taken by highway patrolmen to a hospital where, at last, an injection of insulin brought him around and his wild ride could be medically explained.

However, the Patricks still had one more danger to overcome before they could leave the accident scene. The station wagon driver they had forced off the road was not of the sort to continue on his way murmuring blessings to himself. The man parked and got out of his car. He came stamping back along the road to—just as he expected!—a scene of wreckage, cars in ditches, people gathered around a bleeding boy. His fists were clenched, his eyes blazing, and no one, least of all the Patricks, could blame him for the sulfurous tones in which he let fly at unrepeatable "fools who'd drag-race on a public highway without a bit of concern for other people's lives . . ."

It took more than a few carefully chosen words to calm the good man down. □

ON TOP OF THE DIVIDE! The groan went out of Don McClain's engine as though a long pain was finally allayed in its organs of internal combustion. From "5" the speedometer needle at last shook itself over toward "10," then "15." The tractor-trailer seemed to lean ahead into the road. A sweet quickening flowed up through the seats, and the driver's face cracked into a grin. "Glad that climb's over," he said to his helper, Sidney Wallace.

Donald I. McClain, aged thirty, father of four with a fifth on the way, owned his truck as well as drove it. Its loads were his loads (in a more intimate way, certainly, than they could ever be the bank's loads, though $7,000 was still owing on the truck). Right now McClain was pulling fifteen tons over the Continental Divide.

There was nothing abnormal about his cargo. Still, a fanciful observer having emerged, say, from the dense pines along the Trans Canada Highway into the sunlight of noon on that Wednesday, August 12, 1959, might for a half-second have thought some huge beast was crouched behind, trying to get in at Don McClain. Actually, it was a piece of road building machinery. Forty feet long and chained down on the flatbed trailer, the machine's slender body reared up on giant tires and carried, at the end of two elbowed arms, a wide heavy spiked roller for tamping roadbeds. McClain had a contract to haul it 300 miles from Wetaskiwin, Alberta, to a highway construction project at Golden, British Columbia. Now his destination lay just forty miles west "and all downhill," for he had reached the summit of Kicking Horse Pass.

The pass lies in that spine of the Rockies which divides the streams destined for the Pacific from those for the Atlantic Ocean. It is a passage a mile high between snowy peaks a mile higher. Two of Canada's provinces and two of its national parks, Banff and Yoho, flow up on opposite timbered slopes to the rim of the pass.

McClain had driven this way before. For him the summit meant the start of seven and a half miles of easier, yet still careful, descent. Like a hunter with an eager hound on the leash, he let his rig enjoy a bit of slack, out to 20 miles per hour, and then he geared for that speed and started down with great intermittent snuffles of the air brakes. The first three-quarters of a mile the descent seemed normal enough.

Then McClain realized he had no brakes.

His first reaction was disbelief. Pumping the pedal, he was answered with shooshes of released air. Air but no brakes. The trouble had to be in the braking drums themselves. (Later examination, in fact, revealed them cracked. The braking fluid had leaked out.) Cursing the fickleness of machinery, McClain hit the pedal again and again, trying to coax a final ounce of decelerating action from it. But any real hope, he now knew, depended on his being able to reduce gear. The engine's compression, leaning back through a sufficiently low gear ratio in the transmission, might neutralize gravity enough, just enough!

But how the truck leaped downhill in the intervals of gear shifting! The lever shook in his hand. Gear teeth gnashed on each other. The lowest position to which he could shift was the third.

The whine of his engine rose higher. Luckily he had the westbound, downhill, lane to himself, but a few scattered autos were visible below, coming up the pass. He began pressing on his horn. In the seat beside him, Sid Wallace saw the gleam of sweat on McClain's brow and realized his own was clammy.

McClain wrestled the rig through a long concave turn gouged from the mountain slope on the left, but this was only delaying the inevitable. The speed was already much too fast; the truck was bucking and wobbling, and it could only stop with a smash. The mountain wall slid past on the left, solid stone to crumple vehicle, cargo and men; on the right, which was worse, stretched nothing but beautiful scenery. There was no guard rail on the highway shoulder, and it was a long, long way down. The noise of McClain's horn, bouncing off the mountain wall, sounded a tiny wail for help over the splendid reaches of Yoho National Park.

The speedometer needle crossed "25."

McClain glanced at Wallace. "Jump while there's a chance," he said.

"What about you?"

"Soon as I get it past there."

He nodded down the road toward the one spot along the western slope of Kicking Horse Pass where, though he might be throwing away his last chance to jump and live, he could not turn loose fifteen tons of driverless truck. The place—a tourist vista turn-out—was a mile down the road, and he would try to stick with it that far. "Jump!" he said.

Wallace opened his door. He quailed at the blur of road beneath, but then, crying out a strained "Good luck!" he stepped out and down. His right foot hit the road at 30 miles per hour. His left ran to catch up and couldn't. He shot forward onto his hands and knees, rolled and was up again, rolled and came up, to his own numb astonishment, all right, his clothes flapping in the hot, oily slipstream of McClain's truck which boomed past with the chained monster on its back, flying down toward the tourists and their cars.

The paved parking area of Spiral Tunnel Viewpoint bulged out above the precipice on the right side of the highway going down. Nine hundred feet long and sixty wide, the viewpoint provided motorists with the safest spot for pulling off the road and gazing into Kicking Horse Canyon. Far below, the Canadian Pacific tracks wound through tight curves and curved tunnels under massive overhangs of rock, the "spiral tunnels." The view was particularly dramatic when a train was snaking through: a train was going through now, both fore and aft visible outside the ends of a short tunnel. Could that sound, people wondered, be the train's whistle? A dozen cars were parked at the Viewpoint and thirty persons were standing out near the edge. As the "whistle" grew louder, a man pointed up the highway and exclaimed, "Look, it's that truck!"

McClain was sounding his horn continuously. His increasing speed—near 50 now—caused his trailer to fishtail. Two cars which happened to be climbing the hill in the opposite lane cowered over to the rough rock wall to get past. To the watchers on the Viewpoint it was obvious that the truck driver was struggling. It wasn't until later that they understood his struggle was only to guide his missile of a truck safely past *them*.

A hundred feet beyond the far end of the Viewpoint, there was one place where the rock wall on the other side of the highway was split. An old gravel road, some thirty feet wide, descended this cut to a dead end in the forest below.

Don McClain apparently knew of this highway offshoot. As he reached the lower end of the Viewpoint, he was observed opening his door and then standing out on the narrow metal step outside his cab. He still had his right hand gripped on the steering wheel. The nearest oncoming traffic was half a mile down the hill. Then

McClain whipped his wheel around to the left. His truck roared across the empty opposing lane toward the gravel offshoot. Its left front fender glanced off a projection on the corner of the rock wall. The impact jabbed the rig outward, but it at once teetered back. McClain leaped from his step.

His truck, starting to topple, managed to get completely off the highway into the gravel road. Then it immediately ran head-on into another projecting rock and completely buckled.

The tourists on the Viewpoint heard a tremendous crash. They ran down the highway, across it and into the gravel road. The offshoot road was clogged with the twisted wreckage of both the truck and the huge machine which had ridden its back. In rolling over, the heavy roadbuilder, with its mighty weight, had lifted the front wheels of the truck-trailer clear off the ground.

And under the roadbuilder, arms and legs splayed against the mountain, lay owner-driver Donald McClain with a crushed skull.

Based on the facts as told in the two stories related in Runaways on Wheels, *bronze Carnegie Hero Award medals were awarded to John G. Patrick, his father Steve Patrick, and posthumously to Donald I. McClain.*

In Deep and
Narrow Places

Jesus Manuel Corral lay on the ground attempting to breathe calmly while men tied ropes around his ankles. One asked him in Spanish, "Are you ready?" Corral nodded. He seemed determined enough but his face, under a mass of sweaty black hair, looked yellowish with the pallor that fear spreads on a dark skin. A wiry five feet five, 125 pounds, and seeming even smaller within the knot of Texas farmers, Manuel Corral looked more like a frightened boy than a man of forty-two years.

"Who is this feller?" a man on one of the ropes asked, nudging his neighbor.

"Mexican. He works on the place."

"This ain't part of his job, I wouldn't imagine."

The other clicked his tongue. "I wouldn't want it. Look at that!"

Allan Hill was lifting the little Mexican upside down. Hill was chief of the Dell City, Texas, volunteer fire department and a mountain of a man. For a moment in the crisp morning air he seemed to be trying to shake a dollar from Manuel Corral's pockets, holding him aloft like that by the ankles.

Then he lowered him head first into the earth.

Slender as the Mexican was, it seemed impossible that he could fit into the hole. It was just fifteen-and-a-half inches in diameter, the top of an abandoned irrigation well. Corral's shirt rubbed rust from the metal casing inside. His shoulders twisted in, snug as a bolt in a nut. But they did go in; and then his back, his hips, cotton trousers, till all that showed above the tawny soil of west Texas were his feet in frayed tennis shoes. Then Allan Hill let go of his ankles. The ropes, tightening, took up his weight: each rope fifty feet long, knotted around an ankle and grasped by ten men stretched out on the field like tug-of-war teams.

And Manuel Corral disappeared into the dark.

The blood which quickly flowed to his head seemed to pool in his cheeks and to want to gush from his eyes and ears. He had known this would not be easy, he was not a fool. But already his head burned and roared. To be so painful so soon! And what a darkness!—as though his head were sinking in layer after layer of wet black wool, except that it smelled of rusty pipe. He mastered an urge to scream to be pulled out. Yes, he must think of the child crying somewhere down below him, and of the child's mother hysterically begging him to help: he, Manuel Corral, who earned $35 a week, being the only man on the place small enough to fit down the well.

And what if even he were not small enough?

Ai, if he got stuck in the dark, upside down, suffocating and vomiting, the blood flooding his brain and no way to squirm free—*Dios,* Merciful God, let that not happen!

Up above, a farmer was shouting down at him in Spanish to brace his spirits. How was it going, Manuel? Did he see anything, *amigo?* "I can see nothing," Corral called back in his native tongue, the words heavy, seeming to turn like stones through his sinuses. "But I am going down all right."

He reached ahead with his fingers, down, down, touching

nothing but the harsh metal casing. Below, he heard the little boy's cries—but how far? "Cold," the child kept whimpering. "The water's cold, Mommy!"

At the age of three, Randy McKinley also was three feet tall, thirty-five pounds in weight, and considerably less than fifteen-and-a-half inches in diameter. On this morning two days before Christmas in 1959, his family was visiting his grandparents on a farm near Dell City. While his mother talked with other women in the house, Randy and an older brother and sister and some cousins went out to play. The sun over the Guadalupe Mountains in the east had drawn up the morning haze and was sweeping the valley with clear, warming light. In the fields scattered workers bowed to their labor of picking cotton.

About a quarter of a mile away the youngsters wandered down a dirt road past a workers' bunkhouse with laundry blowing on a line in the yard, and across the road to a neighboring farm. A few yards inside the fence an oil drum turned over on a mound marked an irrigation well no longer in use. The older children began playing and only thought after a time: where was Randy? They noticed the oil drum toppled from the wellhead; came closer, heard muffled screams and the distant, faint splashing of water.

Now it was forty-five minutes later. Astonishingly, the tot had held on all this time, or else he was wedged at some point in the well. His continuing cries goaded the men on top to hurry. Yet what could be done? There was no time to drill a parallel shaft; the boy might be fifty feet down. His mother, who had come tearing down the dirt road in an auto with other women, was pushing the edge of hysteria. She moaned from the open door of a car parked in the weeds by the fence.

More autos kept arriving. There were now thirty men at the wellhead. They came in response to the fire alarm in town or to neighbors screeching to a stop on the roads, spreading the word. A doctor also was there, and farmhands from the nearer fields, including Manuel Corral. Some of the neighbors made eager motions to enter the well on a rope, but it was obvious they could not fit. Only the little Mexican was small enough, and willing.

Yet as they put the rope around his waist, the leading men realized the futility of sending him in feet-first. The pipe was too tight. He would not be able to bend over to grasp the child. Nor could a lad of three be expected to have the strength to hold on to a man's feet long enough to be pulled out. On the other hand, to put him in head-first . . .

Corral had refused. He was not an uneducated man nor one easily moved against his will. In Mexico he had worked as a tax collector, had taught school, and then had tried his hand at farming, but could not scratch a sufficient living from his native soil to keep a wife and four children. And so, for six years he had worked as a migratory farmhand on the "other side," in Texas. And now he wished to help the trapped child. But head-first! The danger of becoming trapped like that!

It had been necessary for the friendly farmer, the one who knew Spanish, to explain to Manuel Corral with patience and clarity why it had to be head-first or not at all, why this was the only practical way: hanging by the ankles, the hands freely reaching down to seize and to hold . . .

Down, down, Corral felt before him in the darkness. He was descending so slowly—and unevenly! Now all his weight hung by the right ankle, now by the left. Could they not lower the ropes together, he cried out; they were twisting him!

Ray Collier, the Spanish-speaking farmer, relayed Corral's plea to the men on the ropes. And from his own position, peering into the well, Collier grasped the ropes, one in each hard hand, and made sure to feed them evenly into the darkness.

Corral had descended about twenty feet when the ropes suddenly went slack. "What is wrong?" Collier shouted. It was a narrowness in the metal casing, the irregular welded joint between two sections of pipe. Corral was wedged there. It was the perfect opportunity to say, "No farther," and to demand to be drawn out. But instead he called up that he believed he could . . . yes, by squirming and wriggling . . . he could get past. And he did (but tried not to think about coming back *up*).

Now he descended more steadily. He was past thirty feet; past forty, the men holding the ropes moving in step by step more tightly around the wellhead. At forty-four feet the ropes again slackened. This time Corral had reached the bottom end of the metal casing. The rim was warped and narrowed with knuckles of rust. But he squirmed through.

And now, below the casing which had conveyed the well through layers of gravel, clay and shale, he found himself in a circle of solid rock, but wider, perhaps two feet in diameter. The walls were of limestone. His body was hanging more loosely than before, so that a trickle of light from above now flowed around him and reflected wanly from a surface of water below.

"Can you see the boy?" came Ray Collier's voice hollowly from far above.

"Not yet," grunted Corral. "Too dark. But I hear him."

The ropes to his ankles had almost run out of footage. Someone came running with another coil, cut it in half, and the two halves were spliced to the lines rubbing taut over the rim of the well.

The descent resumed.

Corral's eyes were playing tricks. The dim reflection in the pool below rose—it seemed to rise, or was it receding?—beneath his outstretched hands. How close was he now? His head was buzzing like a hive of wasps. He had a horror of passing out. If he did that, the men above, receiving no signal from him, would simply lower his face into water. He would drown. He must not pass out! His fingers touched cold water and he screamed: "Stop!"

"Hold it!" shouted Collier on top. The men on the ropes froze. "Do you see the boy?" Collier yelled down the well.

Silence.

And then, from the bottom, an exclamation in Spanish: *"Lo tengo!"*

"He's got 'im!" Collier whooped, and the men on the ropes sent up a cheer, and out of her car Randy McKinley's mother rose with a sob of joy.

But it was still a long way up, too far to begin any celebrating.

Corral by now had been hanging for ten minutes. He was light-headed. His feet were cold; they felt like blocks of ice above the agonizing pincers of the ropes around his ankles. Sweeping the water with his hands, he had caught the boy about the waist and lifted him, immediately feeling two tight little arms circling his neck.

The child apparently had fallen like a shot, in fact with such exquisite verticality that he had not even taken a brush burn down the rusty casing. Landing sixty-eight feet below, at water level (which could have been worse: the well's total depth was 300 feet) he had gone under, then bobbed to the surface at a point where the walls funneled somewhat beneath him, giving purchase for his hands and feet.

Corral peeled the boy's hands from his neck. In such an embrace the two never would be able to squeeze back up through the casing. He took the child's left wrist in his right hand, the right in his left, and held him suspended below. The boy offered no resistance. He had already stopped crying.

"Up!" Corral now shouted. "Up!"

He was terrified to think of blacking out now—*ai,* not now!—to lose his hold on the child's wrists and hear him screaming away down again into the blackness.

On top, the men began marching the ropes out from the wellhead. Ray Collier, fearing that too rapid an ascent might injure Corral or jar loose his hold upon the boy, grasped both ropes tightly in his hands to restrain and control their speed. They burned across his palms.

Corral cried out when he was drawn, like a cork, feet-first up into the neck of the metal casing. It was so much tighter. But he pleaded only for more speed: *"Pronto, pronto!"* His back and shoulders and a patch of hair at the back of his head scraped on metal. Friction was burning away the shirt at his shoulders. The constriction at the pipe joint weld seemed to strip off an inch of his flesh but he did not care now. Anything was better than passing out, or losing hold of the tiny wrists in his hands.

The demons in his skull were buzzing so loudly . . . hammering, shrieking. If only he could hold a little longer, bear the pain for a few more feet of ascent . . .

Suddenly hands were gripping his legs. There was light. On the ends of his fists as they emerged from the blackness he saw a small, dripping child.

Red-faced Texans were surrounding him, massaging his legs. It appeared he was weeping. He had been upside down in the well for fifteen minutes. His ankles, when they cut away the ropes, were discolored black. And Ray Collier had to *pry*, gently, Corral's fingers from the child's wrists. The Mexican could not seem to let go of his own will.

That night the people of Dell City spontaneously collected a purse of $108 for him. Later came other gifts and awards, including honorary Texas citizenship from the governor. More tangibly there was a pledge of regular employment, so that Corral could move his family from Mexico to the United States under a permanent visa. A day after the rescue he was fully recovered; six months after, he had a job in the Dell City public schools at $50 a week and was planning to buy a home. □

ROBERT BAUER KNEW MORE than the average householder about sewage systems.

He personally had installed the one which served his home in
Sarver, Pennsylvania. Consisting of a sewer line 200 feet long and
two septic tanks, it was a sophisticated achievement in do-it-
yourself. Especially since each septic tank, though buried under
four feet of earth, could be entered for cleaning through a tile
pipe that extended up like a chimney to the ground level.

The pipe was only sixteen inches in diameter. But Bob Bauer
could climb through it.

And on December 29, 1967, a few minutes after noon, he did.

Bauer had called a sanitation crew to unclog the sewer line
leading to his septic tanks. First one tank was drained, except for
a pool of sewage about three inches deep on the floor. The
sanitation people then advised letting the tank "air out" a few
hours. After that it would be safer to enter it and flush out the
clogged line.

Bauer thought differently. Without so much as a rope attached
to his belt, he lowered himself down the 16-inch pipe into his
septic tank. It was a confining space, just five feet in diameter,
four feet high. A full grown man in there was about as cramped
as a mouse in a tin can.

Bauer had to bend over from the waist as he worked.

He attacked the clogged line with a crowbar. He dug in,
gouged, chipped and scraped—for about ninety seconds.

Then the crowbar dropped out of his hands.

His knees became rubbery. He sat down in the three inches of
sewage on the tank floor, leaned back against the wall, and
passed out.

"Mr. Bauer, you okay?" someone on top shouted. "You all right down there?"

Their client not answering, the people in the sanitation crew ran across the snow in the backyard to his house to telephone for a rescue squad.

Just one crewman stayed behind, peering down into the tank. James A. Christopher saw Bauer's legs jerking and heard him gasping, and Christopher could not bear that. He was twenty-two, had been a septic tank cleaner for three years and knew the dangers of noxious gases, but now he unzipped his jacket and dropped it in the snow. And without waiting for the others to return, or getting any ropes from the truck, or giving any thought to how he would get *out* again—he lowered himself down the pipe into the tank.

He knew he didn't have much time. He tried his best to hold his breath. Bauer weighed 145 pounds and despite being unconscious, he was flailing his arms about. Christopher, who was ten pounds lighter, somehow wrestled the man to his feet, moved him upright into the exit pipe and struggled to boost him up toward fresh air.

But Bauer's own bulk acted as a kind of cork in the pipe, blocking the supply of air. It seemed to Christopher that what he was breathing was no longer air but something wet and pulpy like sopping rags. A kind of darkness was wavering toward him. He felt a stab of fear for his own life and then his strength and his will oozing from him. This man he was holding, this soft shapeless mass . . . meaningless. He dropped Bauer to a sitting position, and then, pawing upward at the tile pipe, Christopher realized he had no hope of getting out. He had been in the tank less than two minutes. He sank to his knees. A blanket seemed to float down over him. He fell across Bauer's outstretched legs, and laid his face down—in the pool of sewage.

Some two minutes after they had left the tank opening, other members of the sanitation crew hurried back. They saw Christopher's jacket in the snow. Crewman John N. Galbreath looked into the tank. He saw both Bauer and Christopher motionless. The latter, his face in the sewage, was making gurgling sounds.

"He'll drown," said Galbreath. "I've got to get his face out of that."

And that was all Galbreath meant to do. It was obvious by now that, whatever the tank atmosphere consisted of, it did not allow men to remain conscious. Galbreath planned to waste no time. He stripped off his jacket and shirt to ease his passage down the pipe. He was a bigger man than either Bauer or Christopher —five feet ten and 170 pounds. He was twenty-four years old and a printer by trade; but he had formerly worked for the lady who ran the sanitation service, and this day he was helping just as a favor, because she was short-handed.

First he had the other crewmen tie a rope around his wrists. If he fell unconscious, he wanted to make sure he could be dragged out again. Arms raised, he was lowered into the tank. He held his breath, knelt down and, with his wrists still tied, pulled Christopher's head out of the sewage and leaned him back to a sitting position against the wall. Then Galbreath lifted his arms into the pipe, stood up, and was pulled out.

He had performed the one emergency act absolutely required, and for a moment or two he was satisfied.

But as yet no rescue squad siren could be heard on the cold, clear air. Galbreath stamped about in the snow impatiently. How long could they wait!

"Tie that on me!" he exploded at last, holding out his wrists again.

This time, when lowered into the tank, he held the end of a garden hose between his teeth for breathing. But when he tried to inhale through it he found it was clogged with ice. The hose was removed, and the ice was blasted out of it by a pump on the sanitation truck.

Now, kneeling in the floor of the septic tank and breathing through the hose, Galbreath wrapped another rope around Bauer's wrists and wrestled the householder up into the exit pipe. Two people hauled from above, Galbreath pushed from below, and the unconscious man was removed after having spent a quarter of an hour inside his ingenious tank.

The rope was taken off Bauer's wrists, returned to Galbreath, and bound around Christopher's wrists. He was hauled out by the same method as Bauer.

And now Galbreath was feeling weak. The rope around his own wrists proved to be needed, after all. He was almost helpless when finally pulled out.

Later that night John Galbreath would be a sick man from delayed reaction. But lying on the snow now in the fresh cold air, he looked over and saw color return to the faces of two unconscious men, saw their chests moving and their eyelids trembling, while across the snowy Pennsylvania hills floated the belated siren of a rescue squad. □

BEFORE DAWN of a starry summer morning in 1960, the supply ship *Borie* steamed out of one of the mouths of the Mississippi River and rode sluggishly into the mild swell of the Gulf of Mexico. She was a small workhorse of a vessel, 135 feet long, and at the start of her delivery run to oil drilling platforms offshore, awkwardly laden. Behind her bridge, which stood well forward, pyramids of drill pipe towered on her deck. She was top-heavy.

Four miles out on the Gulf a swell no higher than most tickled her belly at precisely the moment of balance. Tons of drill pipe shifted. There was a shriek of clonking metal, and *Borie* violently rolled. Over the side went her cargo, plunging the deck in water as it slid. The keel rose into the air and snapped over like the lid of a box. She was left wallowing upside down in nine fathoms.

The heavy black wash stirred by her capsizing rolled out, flattened, and died. It was 4:30 A.M., August 14, 1960—a Sunday: though scattered lights twinkled ashore, there would be little shipping coming the way of the *Borie*.

Four men had been aboard her. Alton Fogg, the mate, and deckhand M. R. Bates were hurled clear as the ship turned over. They swam back and were able to clamber onto the keel. Presently an inert body floated alongside. Bates and Fogg hauled Captain M. L. Deakle aboard their shallow metal island: he was dead. The two men covered his face with his jacket and sat beside the body on the gently rocking keel and waited for the pale ghost of day to rise in the east. The only sound was that of the water lapping softly against the hull.

But then another sound came to their ears from within the ship—a faint, hollow metallic tapping. They thought at first it might be loose gear clanging about in the drowned passageways, but this sound was too rhythmic, too purposeful. *Bang-bang, bang-bang,* it went. The mate removed his shoe and hammered it on the keel, and at once the signal quivering from inside the ship responded with eight or ten quick taps—and they knew that somewhere down in there Jim Darby was alive.

Marine engineer James E. Darby, forty, had been on watch alone in the engine room when the ship turned over. Every light aboard had gone out as instantly as if the *Borie* had been a torch snuffed in water. Darby found himself tripping among a tangle of pipes. Water was shooting up through them. But he knew the network of pipes was at the engine room *ceiling*. Desperately backing away from the incoming flood, he found himself bumping through a space about six and a half feet high and three and a half feet wide that he sensed was the passageway—upside down—leading forward to the crew's lounge in the bridge superstructure. He slogged forward on the passageway ceiling only to find that water was pouring in up ahead as well.

So he was trapped. All he could do was stand his ground, wait for the passageway to fill totally and choke off his final breath on earth in a sinking ship. It would not take long.

The water rose over his knees, then his hips. It smelled of diesel fuel. Rotten luck, he thought, to have it happen like this, in stinking pitch darkness with no way even to see if there might have been a chance at a way out. The water rose past his waist . . . to his ribs . . .

And stopped there.

It had been gushing in; suddenly it was as calm as a pond. In fact, the surface of the Gulf had merely found its level within the ship.

The point is that the *Borie* was not, at that moment, sinking. She was lying upside down in the water; and as she lay, sea level happened to cut four and a half feet deep through Darby's passageway. Locked under the vault of the ship's bottom, a layer of air two feet deep was trapped with him. It was as though he had got his head up inside a submerged balloon. Under pressure, the trapped air surged and swelled with every rise and fall of the ship, squeezing at Darby's ears. His eyes smarted from diesel fuel in the water and from instinctive straining to see, though utter blackness surrounded him. He felt with his hands along the walls under water. There should be something there . . . yes, a loose metal fitting. He tugged at it and tore it from the wall. He began rapping it against the metal of the passageway floor over his head.

The answering taps from outside he heard with a deep thrill of joy. He had no idea how long it would take rescuers to come after him, but he would force himself to stay calm. And he would keep tapping. As long as he tapped, he was saying, "Here I am. You must do something."

It was not until daylight, two hours after the accident, that *Borie* and her forlorn crew were sighted from another supply ship cruising by. Captain Leon A. Williams of the *Halliburton 212* sent a lifeboat to bring off the marooned. The news that a man was alive inside the hull—was, in fact, still tapping out frantic signals—was radioed at once to the Coast Guard and to the firm which owned the *Borie*.

But it was a Sunday morning, replete, in Louisiana as elsewhere, with the difficulties of snapping the weekend state of mind to attention. Phone calls wakened men groggy with sleep in their beds. There were reports unclearly repeated, inevitable confusions and delays while good men fumbled for a revived sense of concern and awareness.

The helicopter bringing out a deep-sea diver could not risk landing on the rocking upturned belly of the *Borie*, as the pilot somehow had been led to expect he could. Nor could he land on Captain Williams's loaded deck, nor on the *Tioga*, an exact sister ship of the *Borie*, which had made way out of the harbor in reply to the call for help. Kenneth W. Daniels, the diver, had to be flown back to a cove of quiet water and transferred to a boat. When finally deposited on the *Borie*'s keel, along with his tender and two sets of diving gear, Daniels still was at a loss how to proceed. A handsome, sturdy man of twenty-five, he had had just two years of diving experience and all of that on pipeline work. He had been misinformed that the problem at hand was "to recover a body from a small overturned boat." To recover a living man locked inside a blind maze of decks, stairs, doors, and passages, and he having no true familiarity with ship construction—where could he even begin?

"Well, I guess I'll go with you," said Captain Leon Williams.

If there was one thing the skipper of the *Halliburton* knew, it was ships. Born a few miles from the Mississippi mouth, where earning a living from its traffic is second nature, Williams had left school in fifth grade and had worked on ships ever since. He was thirty-five now, a powerful five feet eleven and 210 pounds, and, rare for a man who worked on the water, he liked playing in it, too. He had often been skin diving, wearing self-contained breathing apparatus. In fact, scuba gear was exactly what the job of searching for Jim Darby called for. There was certain to be a maze of pipes, wiring and floating debris to thread through in the darkness below, just the sort of mess to foul a diver's air line.

But two sets of face masks and air lines to a surface compressor were what Daniels had been told to bring to the scene, not scuba equipment. That was the final flowering of the weekend state of mind.

But it was 8:30 A.M. now. Jim Darby had been trapped for four hours and this was recognized as fully sufficient. The Gulf sun beat down on *Borie*'s keel as on a solar roasting pan. The stern definitely was slipping deeper. About half the keel still sloped out of the water, the forward half, making a tiny island seventy feet long and thirty wide. While Ken Daniels's father-in-law, J. R. Elliott, tended the air compressor, Daniels and Williams in their masks, work clothes and shoes, trailing lines, walked down the *Borie*'s belly into the Gulf of Mexico.

The air lines to their masks were 150 feet long. Daniels also had fixed to his belt one end of a guide rope reeled out by his tender—the type of rope professional divers habitually use to find their way back.

The two men sank along the port side of the overturned ship. She seemed grotesquely bulky in this posture, still and swollen, like a dead whale, belly-up. The divers swam two fathoms down along her black side and then perceived the metal railing that circled three feet above—now, of course, below—her deck. They swam under the railing, pulling their lines carefully after them. The bubbles from their masks rose against the deck above, hesitated there, then scooted horizontally to the edge and up like fleeing sea creatures.

In the massive shadow of the wreck visibility shrank to only six feet. Williams led Daniels toward the center of the deck where a murky, triangular structure loomed. The skipper recognized it as the engine room companionway, which contained stairs heading down (now *up*) below the deck. He swam a few feet into the structure, and darkness closed on him like an eyelid. Wait a minute, he thought: whether or not Darby had been working in the engine room when *Borie* capsized, he must now be far up forward in the sloping ship to be above water. To try to reach him through the engine room would be going the long way, the tangled way, with the air lines most likely not reaching. Williams tapped his finger on the visor of Daniels's mask and shook the finger. This signal said: "Out. No good."

So they returned to the surface and the ship's keel and slipped off their masks to confer.

A thousand feet across the water, bobbing gently in the sun's glare, stood the *Tioga*, sister ship and identical twin of *Borie*. Leon Williams gazed at the other vessel and turned her over in his mind's eye. His index finger traced a path over her. Now where would a fellow climb from the engine room to get his head out of water, and how would you reach him from somewhere near the bow . . . ?

A door was plainly visible leading into *Tioga*'s galley in the superstructure one deck above the main deck. Turned over, that would be one deck below.

Williams and Daniels donned their masks again and this time went directly over the side, aiming for *Borie*'s galley door. Deep in the green water they found the door eerily propped ajar. A screen door inside had to be forced open. Then the two carefully drew plenty of air hose inside.

It was foully dark, save for a dense green smudge at the doorway. Williams and Daniels swam slowly into the gloom. They kept close to each other. It was necessary to keep brushing away canned goods and utensils floating in the inky water.

Williams was searching for a stairway down (now *up*) to the crewmen's lounge. He reckoned that that room would give onto some sort of passage leading back toward the engine room. But no stairway could be found. The two men groped blindly through a darkness clogged with floating solids like a cold black vegetable soup.

The galley was eighteen feet long and eight feet wide. At its far end Williams's hands came in contact with another door. He wrestled it open, and Daniels followed him out into another inky space which Williams judged to be a corridor between the galley and the crew's sleeping quarters. Mattresses, furniture, and personal gear floated in the space. Doggedly the two men pushed through, searching for the stairway. But it was no use, they were getting nowhere. Once more Williams tapped a finger on Daniels's visor, and hand over hand the two followed the guide rope out and withdrew.

They moved over to *Borie*'s starboard, swam down along the superstructure and, finding another doorway, entered it. A great sopping mass of puffy, yielding substance pressed against Williams's chest and face. Thrusting it away with disgust, he recognized it as a floating mattress and realized that he and Daniels had simply got into the other end of the same corridor between galley and sleeping quarters. Again, retreat.

"There's got to be a way to cut out this guesswork," said Williams when he and Daniels had climbed up onto the *Borie*'s keel and removed their masks.

Across the water, 1,000 feet away, lay *Tioga*, the identical twin of the ship that was mystifying them. Williams slapped his forehead, immediately called for the little motor tender that served his own ship, and buzzed across the water with Daniels to the *Tioga*.

They climbed aboard, marched immediately to the galley and found the stairway to the crew lounge on the deck below. Aboard

Borie, upside down, they must have swum right *under* that stairway. Now they fixed its position in their minds. Then they descended to *Tioga*'s crew lounge.

"There, y'see?" Williams shouted jubilantly. He pointed around an L-shaped bulkhead to another stairway. This one led down below the main deck, into a passage heading back toward the engine room.

Turn her upside down, that passage would be the *highest* point a trapped man in a capsized ship could get to. It was where Jim Darby *had to be!*

Williams noticed something else, too. The crew lounge had another door leading directly out to the after-deck. Entering by that door would be a good deal easier, less risky than pushing through the canned goods and swimming up the inverted stairs from the galley.

Williams and Daniels went over it again to make sure. In fact, they walked the route three times: in the door, turn right around the L-shaped bulkhead, turn right again—no, turn left, *left* both times, the *Borie* was upside down, remember . . .

"Think we've got it?" said Williams.

Daniels nodded.

"Let's hope he's still bangin' on the furniture, then."

As their tender drew alongside the *Borie*, Williams called out: "He still knockin'?"

The men standing on the keel yelled back that Darby was, indeed, still knockin'.

Quickly donning their masks, Williams and Daniels walked down the slope on *Borie*'s port side. They slid into the water about thirty feet back of her bow, allowing plenty of room to get aft of her superstructure. They swam down along the ship's black flank and under the guard rail.

The main deck was above them now, shadowing visibility down to just about two feet. They swam forward and the water darkened even more as they approached the superstructure. There it was: a solid metal wall descending before them, with the deck a metal ceiling above. Peering ahead, feeling with his hands, Williams found the door that must lead into the lounge. Luckily it was open. How foresighted of *Borie*'s crew to leave their doors unlocked! There was a screen door inside, though. This had to be forced open against its spring and tied back with an odd scrap of rope from Williams's belt.

Entering a realm of zero visibility did not disturb the plucky seaman now; it was like walking into a familiar room in the dark. There should be an L-shaped bulkhead on his left . . . yes, he ran his hand along it. Daniels, directly behind, hauling his guide rope, followed Williams's dark green back as it melted into blackness.

They proceeded seven feet along the bulkhead to its corner, followed the expected left turn another five feet to the end of the L, and turned again. Williams felt for the inverted stairway that he was sure must be before him, the one leading to the passage under the after deck toward the engine room.

His hands touched the edges of steps in the blackness, and he swam slowly up under them, feeling them above with the backs of his fingers like the ribs of Jonah's whale. Daniels's hand was holding onto Williams's feet.

Now at last they were going up in the only direction there could be any air; and feeling out above him in the syrupy blackness, Leon Williams's fingers closed upon the jeans and the muscular thighs of James E. Darby.

The trapped man recoiled. He kicked out in terror at the unexpected touch. But then the faces of Williams and Daniels were beside his in the darkness, invisible but talking to him and telling him that he was rescued.

With their masks off the divers could barely tolerate the locked air in Darby's passage. Its very blackness seemed a burning, ringing thing on their skins and in their throats. The stench of diesel fumes was nauseating. Even worse were the pressure pulsations as the vehicle rocked, squeezing the balloon of air. The jaws of a vise seemed to open and close on the men's ears.

Nor could Darby be immediately removed. To get him down the inverted stairway, around the bulkhead in the lounge, out the door, under the deck and up to air, he obviously needed a mask. And so he would have to wait a few moments longer.

Daniels tied the end of his guide rope securely to a pipe alongside Darby and put the trapped man's hand on the rope. "I just have to follow that back to you," the diver said. "It won't take me a minute."

Darby just said, "Hurry."

He heard them say good luck; then heard some splashing, and sensed them swimming down and away from him in the darkness. He kept his hand on the guide rope tied to the pipe. It quivered as his rescuers found their way out by it. Then it was still. Darby hoped, he prayed, that this interval meant the divers had got out of the ship, that Williams was now removing his mask, handing it to Daniels . . .

Now the rope was quivering again! It vibrated with the grip of a man's hand climbing back along it through the darkness toward him. Jim Darby, who had endured so much, suddenly found it a struggle to hold back tears.

There was a splash beside him. Ken Daniels's voice in the dark: "Here's your mask. You still okay?"

Darby cleared his throat. "Right," he said.

With the mask he was able to descend into the water and follow the diver out with no more difficulty.

He had been trapped in there for five hours. His eyes, his ears and skin all were severely irritated, but he healed in a week.

His rescuers reverted to normal living at once.

Ken Daniels returned home for what was left of Sunday.

Leon Williams mounted the bridge of his ship and put her out to duty on the Gulf. He also, of course, for comfort and the dignity of his command, changed into dry clothes.

Based on the facts as told in the three stories related in In Deep and Narrow Places, *J. Manuel Corral, James A. Christopher, John N. Galbreath, Kenneth W. Daniels and Leon A. Williams, Sr., were awarded the bronze Carnegie Hero Award medal.*

Life by a Fingerhold

FOR FOUR MINUTES, the space of 300 heartbeats, no one could think of a way to help Jim Miller, though fellow workmen were close enough to touch his hands and pull at his denim shirt. His eyes, turned up to them, squeezed tears, and his mates frantically but futilely scurried for some answer to his dilemma.

He was hanging straight down by his fingers from a steel beam over a drop of forty-five feet.

He did not precisely have a grip; that is, his fingers could not close on anything. Their first and second joints were only splayed out on the flange of the beam. As the seconds went by, he felt his fingertips slipping, yielding here a sixteenth of an inch, there a few more epidermal cells of contact with steel.

Below him lay the bottom of a ship's hold, that of the *S.S. Delos Pioneer*, an obsolescent merchant vessel whose poor maintenance was threatening to take his life. Not that James W. Miller, longshoreman, was thinking of grievances against shipowners now. He was totally concerned with pain. It seemed the worst he had ever known. An unbearable tension stretched from the skin of his fingers through his arms, shoulders and neck, and pulled from ear to ear. Neither a young man nor a light one, Miller, who was forty-eight, would not have dreamed his arms could support his six-foot, 210-pound frame for so long. But hold they had to. The only relief from his agony would have been to die. In the sweet instant of muscular release, the sky would shoot away from him, a receding rectangle of light, and the bottom of the hold would come up to smash his bones.

"Do something," he gasped. "I can't . . . hold much longer."

About twenty years before James Miller's ordeal, the *Delos Pioneer* had started life reasonably trim, as a wartime "liberty ship." Now under Greek registry, she could still eke out a cargo here and there in the ports of the world, but where repairs were concerned her owners appeared to have sworn vows of poverty.

Everywhere she showed the stigmata of neglect. On her hatches, for example. These great mouths in the deck were twenty-five feet long by twenty wide. They were not, as a landsman might suppose, closed by a single "hatch cover." Instead, fifty wooden "cover panels" rested on a series of parallel beams that stretched across the hatch at five-foot intervals. The cover panels, being five feet long, spanned from beam to beam. Theoretically.

In fact, had the beams not been battered and warped by years of hard knocks, the covers not riddled with dry rot, this arrangement might have made a smart fit. But most of the panels were worn and chafed. Their ends lay loosely between the beams. Others had been forced in tightly where the beams were warped, creating a springy tension.

And so, onto this house of cards, of obsolescence, weathering, and neglect, one mild fall morning in the Port of Houston, Texas, stepped a crew of longshoremen to open the hatch.

It was 7 A.M., October 29, 1964.

The easier cover panels had already been removed—some toppling into the hold, which should have been a warning— when Jim Miller tried to loosen a particularly tight cover with a long crowbar. He stood on a panel several feet away which seemed secure enough. But no sooner did he free the tight cover than the supporting beam sprang with released tension.

Four other panels jarred loose and plunged into the chasm of the hold—including the one Miller was standing on. He fell across the supporting beam, glancing hard on the inside of his thigh, tearing muscle. The crowbar flew from his hand.

As he toppled, he instinctively grabbed. The beam, from its upper to its lower flange, was two feet high, the vertical part being crisscrossed by metal struts in a series of open triangles. Miller's left hand caught the lower flange. For an instant, as he rolled over, he had a pinch of the upper flange in his right fingers, but he lost that hold as soon as he had it. He made a second, desperate stab at the lower flange—and caught it.

He was left swinging by his fingertips from the midpoint of the beam, ten feet away from either side of the hatch. Everyone on the bustling deck of the ship seemed to freeze—no one breathed for the second or two it took Miller to stop swinging. Then he just hung there.

A shocked murmur arose—not loud, as though the slightest breath might blow him to eternity. It seemed at any second he must fall.

His mates immediately tried to get him. Three of them mounted the beam, straddling it, two on one side and one on the other, and went inching out toward him on their haunches. They reached down, tried to grab his wrists. But this was awkward. Not daring to move directly over him for fear of jarring him loose—the beam vibrated like a harp string—they could not, from where they sat, reach low enough to get a grip on Miller and still keep from toppling over themselves. He was so near—but out of reach.

"Rope! Get a rope!" someone yelled.

What could be done with a rope nobody had a very clear idea;

but obtaining one seemed the thing to do. And so, the end of a hawser was swung out to one of the men straddling the beam. A hawser is two inches thick; it is the muscular line used for mooring a ship to a wharf. When it was dangled down in front of Miller, he naturally refused to release his fingerholds in order to try to grab such an unwieldy, fat snake. The hawser had to be tossed aside, and the men straddling the beam resumed their vague pawing for a grip on Miller's wrists and shirt.

Robert Lewis, foreman of the crew, had swung into action on another front. He had led a gang down a manhole ladder to the sub-deck fifteen feet below. On that level the hatch was spanned by a similar network of steel beams, and similar cover panels were stacked in the wings. Lewis's thought was to "lay a floor" beneath Miller.

But the first nine panels his gang tried to put in place were too worn at the ends. They all fell clattering to the bottom of the hold another thirty feet below. A tenth panel broke in half even as two men were carrying it.

Foreman Lewis was badly shaken. He dashed back up the manhole ladder with his men and, at a loss for what to do next, he called out for help to another crew working at a hatch farther forward.

This brought other men running, among them Raymond W. Allen.

Allen, thirty-five, had been a longshoreman for nine years. Five feet eleven, 160 pounds, he ran along the deck in work shoes and jeans, stripped to the waist, his tanned physique just beginning to sweat from the first few whacks at the job that morning. As he approached, he recognized the hanging man as Miller, with whom he had sometimes worked.

"Hold on, Jim, I'm coming!" he yelled, and seemed at that moment, by reflex, to form an instant plan.

He stepped onto the lower flange of the beam to which Miller was clinging, then moved out on it, working himself smoothly around the men straddling it—till he stood directly above and facing Miller, with his feet opposite the hanging man's fingers.

Crouching, Allen inserted his bare arms between the triangular struts of the beam's vertical brace. He knotted his fingers together so that his arms formed a locked circle through the bracing. Then he dropped his feet from the bottom flange, swung his legs forward to a scissors grip around Miller's waist, crossed his ankles, and squeezed.

Immediately, with a huge relief that was almost pleasure, Miller felt some of the burden on his arms flow to the other man. Allen was fifty pounds the lighter man. But with his arms locked through the beam, his legs around Miller, he was like a steel link in a chain. He would hold—for a while. Miller kept his fingerhold on the beam, of course, and was able, in fact, to slightly improve it; he did not dare trust all his weight to Ray Allen.

The metal struts were digging painfully across Allen's bare arms, but he kept speaking reassurance to Miller, urging him to hold on "just a little bit longer"; the other men would be sure to think of something.

This was optimistic. Most of those on deck seemed as paralyzed as the suddenly idle winches and cranes. Before there had been one man hanging. Now there were two. But how to get them off!

The commotion kept attracting more men. From the hatch farthest forward came stevedores G. Howard Bruner, fifty-nine, and his son John, twenty-one. The father's first thought was to hustle down the manhole and lay a floor under Miller and Allen on the sub-deck. He did not know the foreman's gang already had tried that.

Not surprisingly, the Bruners, too, tried to place several hatch covers under the hanging men, only to lose them into the hold, too short.

Then they found one panel too long!

It was only one, but John Bruner squatted down and braced it from one beam to another against his thigh. And out onto this uncertain bridge five feet long and just two feet wide, his father walked directly under the hanging men.

By standing on tip-toe, Howard Bruner could just touch the soles of Jim Miller's shoes. But he could not make sufficient contact to bear any of Miller's weight. Still, Bruner held his precarious stance, arms upraised. He felt that if Miller let go, he, Bruner, should make one supreme effort to catch the falling man before both of them toppled over into the hold thirty feet below.

By now Miller was so near exhaustion, he was urging his rescuer to release him and save himself. "Let me go, Ray," he said. "No use both of us falling."

But Allen was adamant. He told Miller to rest more of his weight on his, Allen's, legs. "I can take some more," he said.

Allen had by this time been helping to support Miller for four minutes and the pain across his arms was intense—but he never viewed the release of Miller as a feasible alternative. He had an absolutely clear vision of what would happen: Miller, in falling, would convulsively grab at his legs and wrench him too from the beam. The only thing to do was to hold.

At last, someone with a clearer head than most arrived with a sturdy rope about an inch in diameter.

Several men took holds on one end of this rope from a position alongside the hatch. A longshoreman named Freeman Bell went straddling out onto the beam with the other end of the rope. He dangled it down between Allen and Miller.

"Can you loop it around him?"

"I'll try," said Allen.

He had to break his locked fingers and instantly grasp the metal bracing with his right hand and hug it to him. Now his left hand was free, though nearly numb.

With his full weight—and most of Miller's—supported by his

right arm, Allen took the end of the rope in his left hand. "Give me some slack," he said, breathing heavily. He slipped the end of the rope beneath Miller's right armpit and flicked it across the lower man's back until he could catch it between his own thigh and Miller's back. Then he pulled the rope up under Miller's left armpit and handed it upward to longshoreman J. D. Reeves, who also had come out on the beam.

Reeves made a slip-knot and cautiously drew the rope tight around Miller's chest.

A dozen men now held the other end of the rope from the deck. "Let go, let go," they called to Miller. He released his fingerhold, hanging for a moment inside the still scissored legs of Ray Allen. "Let 'im go," the men yelled. The scissors opened.

Miller swung down fully suspended by the rope. Its loop tightened around his chest, stopping his breathing. But he held his arms rigidly down to hold the rope in place, and in a second or two they had him hauled up on deck. His first breath, after they loosened the rope from his sweaty shirt, was a sob.

Ray Allen tried to swing his now free legs up onto the beam and climb out, but he could not do it. He was too weak. He had supported Miller for more than five minutes and there was no response left in his muscles. "Help me," he called.

Below, still standing on the one rickety cover panel, stubborn Howard Bruner tried to reach up to Allen's feet.

But it took two longshoremen to come out on the beam and haul him up by the belt. Now he was slung over the beam on his stomach. Still he could not help himself, and a man had to physically place one of his legs over the beam so that he could straddle it.

And then a little feeling slowly came back into his arms. With the aid of others, he was able to inch along on his haunches till he reached the solid deck.

Miller required treatment at a hospital for shock and his thigh injury; he was several weeks out of work.

Allen felt strong enough after an hour to continue on the day's job. But for three days he carried deep welts on his arms, where he had locked them across the metal bracing: the service stripes, in this case, of a man who wouldn't let go.

Based on the facts as told in Life by a Fingerhold, *Raymond W. Allen and G. Howard Bruner won Carnegie Hero Award bronze medals.*

"Shark!"

James Jack Bolger had no sooner splashed into the ocean in his wet suit, fins, and scuba gear when a word he detested rang out over the water.

"Shark!"

Someone on the *Salmon Queen* had spotted a fin and if the rest of the shark was proportioned accordingly, it must be a monster. The dirty gray triangle slicing the surface looked three feet long.

It was not to mingle with sharks that Jack Bolger went scuba diving on weekends. An auto mechanic of forty, with a heavy face that tended to fall into solemn lines in repose, Bolger felt that it added nothing to the savor of his recreation that at any moment, from any direction and without warning or logic, a mouth might close upon him and remove a section of his abdomen or leg. His legs had taken enough beating already. They had been frozen in World War II and even now pained him in extreme heat or cold. But at this precise moment, in water of 56 degrees, his legs were quite fit enough to propel him back to the boat, up a ladder, and straight out prone onto the deck—as if the shark's jaws were snapping across the very gunwales. He did not mind how graceless an image of the sportsman he presented. He removed with some haste, in fact, his hood, mask, air tanks, fins, and weighted belt. He just was not about to go back in.

But six other men were still in the water.

Until that moment, the day and the place had seemed fine for it: a cool, not cold, winter Saturday, January 11, 1964, off the Farallones, a group of barren islands twelve miles out in the Pacific from San Francisco. The Farallones had no human habitation but were a marvelous playground for fish. A vivid color chart of species darted among the crannied walls and rock chimneys dropping sixty-five feet to the ocean floor. There was no beach, no crowd; only the misty line of California on the eastern horizon, and here, standing off from the rocks, the sport fishing boat *Salmon Queen* bearing twenty-two members and guests of the Southern Pacific Scuba Club.

Tom Shea and Bruce Bolger, Jack's brother, were swimming near the bottom, investigating caves, pits, and whatever life forms swam into the blurry globe of their visibility, which extended out about twenty-five feet. The shark never broke into it.

Bruce and Jim Davis, brothers, did spot the beast. Their instinctive reaction was to become stone. Holding as still as possible on the bottom, they saw the shark swim over and pass them, unseeing.

Jack J. Rochette first saw the shark from the closest imaginable position—within its jaws.

A handsome six-footer, Rochette was twenty-one, weighed 180 pounds and was in the top of condition as a water sports enthusiast. He read meters for a utility company for a living, but surfing, deep sea fishing, and scuba diving were his ideas of how to live on a weekend. At this moment—it was 11:30 A.M.—he had a fish on his spear. He had just shot a sea bass. Its body trailed threads of blood in the surrounding green. Rising with this trophy, Rochette, who was attired in hood and fins, black rubberized suit and air tanks, came to within four feet of the surface when he was struck.

He thought he had collided with his buddy, Gary Neu, or

some other diver. There was no pain, not right away; only astonishing, irresistible force.

"This tremendous power," as he would describe it later, "started to take me down in its mouth."

Staring through his face mask, he saw both his thighs, from his hips to several inches below the knees, locked in the jaws of a Great White Shark.

There are experts who believe that when a Great White attacks a man, it is essentially a mistake: the shark believes the man to be a seal. The man seldom lives to forgive the error. Some Great Whites reach thirty feet in length; the one attacking Rochette happened to be about twenty-two feet long and a barreling four feet in diameter. The species has the mouth of a chain saw and the appetite of a moving van. With thirteen huge teeth along each of four sections of its jaws, the Great White gorges on the ocean's larger viands, a walrus or a seal. It seizes the victim in its trap of teeth and, with violent twists of its head, saws it to meat.

For one instant as it bore Rochette under water, the shark broke the surface. It showed most of its body and flipped up a spray of water that looked, to one witness 100 yards away on the boat, "as if a depth charge had gone off."

But immediately, the shark seemed to sense its "mistake."

It released Rochette and backed away. Its teeth, as it pulled off, shredded both legs of his diving suit down to the ankles. Then the shark circled four or five feet below him, as Rochette bobbed to the surface—in a pool of red.

Nobody on the boat missed seeing the blood. It was very visible. That there should be so much of it—so vivid and spreading a stain on the frothy green water—horrified the watchers. They were sure the diver's leg, or both legs, had been torn away. Only Rochette's air tanks were visible above the surface. These churned around in tight circles. The swimmer had not lifted his head.

Captain Herbert Schramm on the ship's bridge pointed a rifle out toward the water, but how could he fire? The shark was out of sight. A bullet could as easily strike Rochette, or perhaps some other submerged diver.

In fact, Rochette still had both his legs, but they were lacerated to the bone. They hung quite uselessly in the water and bled. The swimmer had not raised his head for the simple reason that nothing topside was so hypnotically compelling as the huge fish he was staring at through his mask.

The beast was now circling slowly downward and away from him; puzzled, perhaps, but still menacing, still considering. Four feet, six feet, nine feet deep the shark's downward spirals carried it. Rochette, stroking with his right hand, clutching his spear-gun in his left, kept turning in his own frantic circles on the surface, to keep the shark in view. He was conscious that the sea was growing bloodier around him, but he could not tear his gaze from his massive, circling assailant.

For the men on the *Salmon Queen,* all this posed a growing dilemma. More than a dozen grown males lined the ship's railing. At least seven of them, a later count disclosed, were excellent swimmers. And a woman aboard was screaming for someone to go to Rochette's aid. "Help him, somebody, please!"

But the men were locked in a kind of mutual, straining hesitation. It seemed no more possible for them to act than for single links to spring by their own volition out of an iron chain. "I, like the rest on board, found at the time of crisis that my feet were firmly planted to that deck," one would afterward admit. "Even if I had been wearing a wetsuit, I doubt that anything could have induced me to go to Rochette's rescue."

Suddenly the tension broke. Jack Bolger dived over the gunwale into the ocean. With long slaps of his arms he stroked toward Rochette 100 yards away, churning in his circle of blood.

Of the men available for the task, Bolger might have been judged among the least likely to hazard it. First, he was acutely fearful of sharks. His panicky return from the water just a few moments earlier had proved that. Physically the government, at least, regarded him as "30 per cent disabled"—and pensioned him accordingly—for the war damage to his legs. He was not a powerful swimmer. A quarter mile was the farthest he had ever swum, unburdened and in calm water. Now he was weighed down by his heavy wetsuit. It was more a hindrance than a help. He had thrown aside the air tanks, mask, and fins which could have aided his breathing, vision, and speed.

But the irony that it was he who had broken the chain of inaction along the ship's railing did not now occur to Jack Bolger. His mind was absorbed in one thought: that unless *someone did something*, Rochette would drown or bleed to death, or be torn by repeated slashes of the shark.

Yet as he flailed ungracefully through the choppy water, his arms growing heavy and tired and feeling his age, Bolger received a boost from his own terror. He felt that if he once stopped moving, something massive, fast, and ferocious would dart for him from beneath the opaque surface with mouth wide and tearing.

This sensation was so sharp that he hated to stop moving even as he reached Rochette.

He kicked his feet, treaded water, and put out his right hand to lift Rochette's head. He had not actually known till then that the younger diver was still alive. Recognizing Bolger, Rochette shook his hand off and dunked his own face back in the water.

The shark was still below.

But now, curious at the arrival of another seal-that-was-not-a-seal, the Great White swam up closer. Rochette jabbed at it with his spear-gun. He made a lucky stab. The point struck between the shark's eyes. The beast recoiled. No seal had ever done that to it! With a whip of its tail, the shark shot out of sight.

Bolger, seeing none of this action, took hold of the straps of Rochette's air-tank harness. He meant to haul him back to the boat like that. But it was hard going. His wetsuit was weighing on him like armor now, and Bolger realized he was a very tired auto mechanic.

He noticed that Rochette—who still had his face in the water, on lookout for the shark—could stroke with one hand while holding his spear-gun in the other. All right, then, let him stroke. Releasing Rochette, Bolger simply began shoving him toward the boat—in the intervals between his own labored swimming strokes.

The *Salmon Queen* might have made these efforts easier. It might have come toward *them*. But the skipper feared that spinning propellers might injure other divers unseen in the water. So Jack Bolger had to struggle on, trying to make progress himself and pushing at Rochette between his strokes.

He got them to within forty feet of the boat and could go no farther.

"Rope," he gasped, near exhaustion. "Throw rope!"

Someone on board did. Bolger caught the line in his right hand. He gripped Rochette's tank harness in his left. Then he held on as the two of them were hauled through the water to boatside.

It was still a struggle to get the maimed diver aboard. In his full gear Rochette weighed close to 300 pounds. Bolger had to push him from below, while others lifted from above, and he was hauled in.

And only then was Jack Bolger able to climb up out of the ocean he so sincerely desired to leave. Till the last instant the ocean, for him, meant teeth and terror. Once on deck, dead tired, panting for breath, despite the relief and the admiring back-slapping, he slipped into the emotional backwash of the ordeal. He started shaking. Someone put a blanket around him. If he weren't on guard, he might have started bawling.

But in a few minutes he was breathing normally and had his composure back. Another man on board, studying Bolger's stolid, heavy-jawed face, thought to himself, "There's a fellow nothing bothers."

Jack Rochette's recovery took longer; many weeks. Flown by Coast Guard helicopter to San Francisco, he needed blood transfusions and surgery. Both legs had been deeply torn. In the left leg a nerve which controlled his foot had been severed. The surgeons managed to repair it.

After the operation they also were able to give Rochette a souvenir guaranteeing him forever against anybody's casual suspicion that he had only got hurt by a jagged hunk of underwater metal. They had cleanly extracted it from his left leg.

It was a large, sharp white tooth.

———

Based on the facts as told in "Shark!", a silver Carnegie Hero Award medal was awarded to James J. Bolger.

Disaster at Point 16

DENNIS LONG WAS READING A BOOK when the four girls invited him for a walk. It didn't take much time for him to decide which mode of recreation deserved his preference. He and the girls stepped down from the porch at Rock Harbor Lodge at 7:30 P.M. Somehow at the time it seemed important for them to reach Scoville Point two miles away before the last sunlight of that Wednesday, August 6, 1969, fled through the pines, across the lake, and over the horizon forever. Soon the five of them, in sheer exuberance, were running.

Dennis was twenty, the girls the same age or near it. All were college students on vacation jobs in Isle Royale National Park, Michigan; and being bright, articulate, self-conscious, very much a "group," they enjoyed a shared sense of the splendors of nature attending on the twentieth summer of their youth.

Isle Royale can easily invite such feelings. It is a noble place, a wilderness of forests and rocky shores thrusting from Lake Superior like a muscular, hairy forearm. The island is forty miles long and, in places, eight wide; but it is a safe bet that boat oars log more mileage there than auto tires. Accessible only by ferry and only in summer, Royale is a fortress for the camper, the fisherman, the seeker of quiet; and the lake is its moat. Such blessings of local government as the island requires are extended

183

from Keweenaw County, Michigan, out of sight over the pale blue water to the south. Canada is closer but just a smudge on the northern horizon. In short, Isle Royale is away from it all. Out of the woods which surround its glistening interior ponds, under the moon, wolves come down to drink.

The summer of 1969 was Dennis Long's third on the island. He was between his sophomore and junior years at Northern Michigan University and had written his parents that he was beginning seriously to consider a career in biology or forestry. True, his summer chores stood in rather humble relation to these goals: that day he had mowed grass with the grounds crew at the lodge.

The girls were Amy Cort, Margaret Johnson, Patricia Stimac, and Carolyn Torma. The routine domesticity of their tasks at the lodge sloughed away from them as they ran: four spirited females making frisky, coltish patterns in the long slants of sunlight as they vied for the lead with each other and with the boy. Their arms swung, their hair flowed in the breeze, and the act of running seemed to feed their freedom on itself and spark a euphoria of purest innocence.

Their route lay along a marked nature trail between woods at the left, the rugged shore at the right, on the peninsula running to Scoville Point, a rocky finger stretching northeastward from the island "arm."

Breathless, exhilarated, the young people had run about a mile and a half when they noticed—not unhappily, for it was a stirring event to witness—that a gale was coming up. Nature's moods on the Great Lakes are quicksilver. A moment ago had been brilliant slants of sunshine; now black clouds herded low across the sky. Gusts of wind fluttered the youths' sweaters and jeans. The blue faded from the lake like the light of a smiling eye. As if burners had come on under the surface, the water began boiling and leaping. It surged into a small cove beside the trail, and it rolled and eddied and foamed among a half-dozen boulders which lay scattered just off the shore.

Dennis Long suddenly declared, "I've got to get into that water!"

The girls stared at him. He was a tall, athletic boy with serious eyes set close together and a firm mouth; but now, with the wind lifting his thick brown hair into a shape of flame, he had the look of a man sniffing the storm as if it were a feast to be devoured. The girls voiced conventional protests but, in fact, they too felt the urge not merely to be spectators. One youth's fire ignites others, and as Dennis stripped off his jacket, removed his watch and billfold, and got set to wade into the growing surf alone—he wasn't going to let the girls dissuade him—Patricia and Carolyn impulsively decided to join him.

The danger seemed not unreasonable. All the youths had swum in the cove before, in calmer weather. They called it "Beach Sixteen," situated as it was at "Point Number 16" on the nature trail. In fact, there was no true beach but in contrast to the island's usual precipitous meeting with the lake, this point was favored with a rocky shelf which extended about twenty-five feet out from shore. Onto this shelf the lake lapped at wading depths. Large boulders also were scattered on it. The cove was about fifty yards wide; walls of steep rock bounded it at both sides. These jutted out past the wading shelf to where the water depth plummeted to 100 feet or more. Leaping six to eight feet high, waves dashed among the boulders on the shelf "beach" as if through so many gapped teeth: it looked like the very mouth of the storm.

Dennis and Patricia Stimac strode out hand in hand into the line of breakers. The other girl, Carolyn, hesitated. She strolled another fifty feet on up the beach closer to the rock barrier at its upper end, then entered the water there alone.

Such sport was not for the other girls, Amy Cort and Margaret

Johnson. They climbed out on the rocky point to its end, where they could look straight down, about twenty-five feet, at the waves smashing into the sheer rock wall.

For some eight minutes the boy and the two girls played out on the shelf in water to their waists and let the waves tumble over them. Patricia and Dennis were within arm's reach of each other, Carolyn a bit farther away. The water was cold: in Lake Superior it always is for swimming; but at 50 degrees and foaming, the dashes of surf felt like brisk avalanches of ice. The two girls had their sweaters and jeans on; the boy was bare-chested. All three whooped and gasped in the sting of the battle.

Suddenly the fun ended. An especially strong wave flipped Patricia against a sharp edge of one of the boulders under the foam. Her leg was gashed. It started bleeding. Dennis at once took the girl's arm and began wading toward shore with her. They were within fifteen feet of the bank and Patricia was saying, "I can get out alone now," when they heard over the wind and the hissing waves a scream for help.

A large wave had batted Carolyn Torma off her feet and before she could regain her footing, with a terrifying swiftness, as though she were sliding down the rim of a bowl, the retreat of the swell swept her out over the shelf into deep water; and sped her in a matter of seconds on beyond the tip of the rocky point at the end of the cove.

Hearing her cry, Dennis immediately plunged back into the breakers and swam toward the girl with long, powerful strokes. He was a skillful swimmer and could go about two miles, though not in water this rough. He had sprinted about 100 feet when he caught up to the girl some ten yards off the high point of rock. He was calm, she was thoroughly shaken. The wind had been knocked out of her, and the undertow had held her down long enough that she was coughing and sputtering from taking in water.

Worse, she was unable to move her legs.

Though a strapping, energetic girl, who had often swum in competition, Carolyn Torma had been troubled since infancy by a pinched spinal nerve. At times this caused a temporary but vexing loss of mobility in her lower limbs. Her legs hung helplessly straight down in the water.

She was trapped in the trough, unable to stroke over the first huge swell beyond the breaker line, when Dennis Long's hands came in under her left arm for support. He treaded water and held her up as a wave rolled over them.

"I can't . . . raise my legs," she gasped.

The boy understood at once; they had talked about her spinal difficulty one time.

"I can tow you in," said Dennis.

He reached down behind the girl's thighs and lifted her to a nearly horizontal position. Then with his left arm across her shoulders, his elbow under her chin, he began stroking toward shore. Unfortunately the girl was still gagging on water she had swallowed. The boy's arm across her throat choked her and she fought to break free, drawing both of them under. As they surfaced, gasping for air, another large wave rolled over, and this delayed both of them from catching their breath.

Head out of water at last, Dennis sucked in a deep, groaning quaff of air. "I'm . . . I'm winded," he panted.

"I couldn't help it," Carolyn said, ". . . choking."

For a moment they tried to rest in the turbulent water. "We'll try again," said Dennis.

This time, having once more raised the girl to the horizontal, he cupped his left hand under her chin and began stroking toward shore. But the incessant rolling of the waves made it impossible to hold the girl's face above water. Once more, gagging and struggling, she fought free.

Both were thoroughly winded now. And it seemed to take so long for the waves to pass over their heads! The boy's mouth was close to the girl's ear as he continued to tread water and support her. "I'm tired," she heard him say. They rested as well as they could for close to a minute, during which a dazzling jagged line streaked down the sky and heavy rain started to fall. As it stabbed into the water, billions of silver drops seemed to pop an inch above the surface in tiny blossoms of splash, instantaneously vanishing; but if this was beautiful to watch, there was no one now to be exhilarated by it, not those struggling in the water, nor those above on the rocky point fearfully watching them.

Dennis managed to recover a trace of his strength. He thought of a plan. If the two of them could only cut through the swell before them, staying close to the surface and above the undertow, the waves breaking on the other side would push them on toward shore.

"I'm going to give you a shove," he told the girl. "Then stroke with everything you've got!"

He took a breath and sank down beside her. He seized her two feet in his hands, pulled the feet together. And then as suddenly and forcibly as he could, he thrust her legs to the surface. She, fully horizontal, climbed at the water with flailing arms. She hauled herself up over the swell to its breaking side, and the dash of surf hurled her in along the flank of the rocky point.

She was coughing and choking, but she was able to cling and move hand over hand along the steep rock wall into the shallows. Patricia Stimac stretched a hand to her, and she crawled out, able at last to rest. Certain that Dennis would be close behind her, she sobbed in tired elation, her heart booming.

But Dennis did not immediately follow her.

The life-saving shove he had given the girl from underwater had depleted his strength too much for him to launch himself over the swell. Surfacing, he continued to tread water while he evidently was awaiting the return of more strength or a favorable opening in the waves.

Meanwhile, however, the current was moving him steadily

farther off the point of the cove. From atop the rock Amy Cort threw two slender driftwood logs toward him. But they landed five yards away and—irony of ironies!—they floated closer to the rock while he drifted farther away, treading water, uttering no cry.

And now the rain was lashing the lake's surface in great driving sheets. The clouds were descending like a black lid over the cove. The darkness and mist intensified. "Dennis!" Amy Cort shouted. She had a glimpse of him still treading water out in the lashing gloom. "Dennis!" The clouds and the lake met.

Two weeks later a hiker on Scoville Point Trail found the boy's body rocking gently at the edge of the calm blue water.

———

Based on the facts as told in Disaster at Point 16, *Dennis A. Long was posthumously awarded a bronze Carnegie Hero Award medal.*

The Heroic Act

AT THE CORE OF THE HEROIC ACT is mystery. A rescuer, personally safe, pitches his life into danger on the chance of saving someone else's, a stranger's—why?

This question holds fascination and disquiet for the modern mind. Not alone because each of us in the secrecy of his heart wonders how he would react to the terror and challenge of a cry for help; but also because locked in the enigma of what makes a hero could be one of the keys to a better world. A society in which anyone in distress could rely on the selfless assistance of others, even to the others' last breath, would seem to be a long way in the direction of utopia.

The science of social psychology employs a broad, rather tame designation for acts of heroism. They are classified as a form of "helping behavior." So, by the way, are acts of charitable giving. But the hero obviously is an extreme form of "helper." The donation he is prepared to make is his life.

How is it that he is able to commit so much more than the mass of mankind?

Clues begin to emerge when the question is put, as society these days increasingly puts it, negatively: What is it, we ask, which is *missing* or which has *failed* in most people that they seem (to us) to look on anesthetically—awake, possibly annoyed, but without agony—at the destruction done to others?

Let one of us tumble innocently into peril, especially in a large city, and there is strong popular notion that no one's hand would be raised to help us. No one would dare to "get involved." It's every man for himself.

This species of pessimism found classic justification in a crime which occurred on March 13, 1964, in a middle-class neighborhood of Queens, New York. While returning home from work at 3 A.M., a young woman named Catherine Genovese, whom her friends called Kitty, was stabbed to death outside the apartment where she lived.

By actual count, thirty-eight persons in neighboring buildings saw or heard what was happening from their windows. But they made no effort to save the woman. None even called police. It was not that the victim's plight was ambiguous—"Oh my God, he stabbed me," she clearly cried, "please help me!" Or that there lacked time to take action: the attacker drove away and returned twice to renew his ultimately fatal assault as his victim crawled bleeding toward her door.

Why then had the thirty-eight witnesses watched and done nothing?

To police and reporters later most of them gave explanations of numbing incredibility. They "didn't know" why they hadn't notified police. Or it looked like a "lover's quarrel" in which they had no business meddling. Or they were "afraid," fearful even to get involved in a phone call to a precinct house. And one witness actually said, "I was tired. I went back to bed."

The failure of anyone to lift a hand for Kitty Genovese was a sting to the nation's consciousness and its conscience. The explanation most commonly put forward by experts was "apathy." The shocks of metropolitan living had left people unable to *feel* anymore; they were past caring about each other; leave them alone. A. M. Rosenthal, the *New York Times* editor who directed coverage of the Genovese case, concluded there exists a "terrible reality in the human condition—that only under certain situations and only in response to certain reflexes or certain beliefs will a man step out of his shell toward his brother."

For science, the Genovese outrage had one positive effect. It stirred a new wave of inquiry into the mechanism of bystander reaction to emergencies. Could it be that individual personality had atrophied to the point where it could no longer respond to another's distress? Or was there rather some psychological germ in the situation, in the "behavioral setting," which inhibited even humane, much less heroic, action?

A series of laboratory experiments in the late 1960's threw fascinating light on how people behave in emergencies. It is against this light that the mystery of heroic behavior perhaps stands out in a kind of relief.

The most famous experiment, reported in professional journals by John M. Darley and Bibb Latane, involved seventy-two university students. They were placed in a series of intercommunicating but private offices, ostensibly for interviews with a stranger over an intercom. They were instructed not to leave their individual rooms during the session. Some students thought they were alone in the suite with the unseen stranger. Other subjects knew that adjoining offices also were occupied, singly, by as many as six other persons. Suddenly from the intercom came a realistic cry for help. The stranger was suffering, evidently, an "epileptic seizure."

What happened next casts grave doubt on the old notion that "there is safety in numbers."

Eighty-five per cent of the students who believed they were alone—the only person with a chance to aid the "stricken" individual—came out of their rooms in less than a minute (actually fifty-two seconds) to offer help.

But when students were in groups of three, thus knowing the cry had been heard by at least two others, just 62 per cent moved to help, and in a 90-second period.

And if the group was as large as six, it took 166 seconds—with the poor "victim" babbling over the intercom the whole time—to draw help reactions from just 31 per cent of the subjects.

"The more bystanders to an emergency," wrote Darley and Latane, summarizing their results, "the less likely or more slowly any one bystander will intervene to provide aid."

Additional experiments tended to confirm the phenomenon. Heavy smoke was shot into a room through a ventilator. When one person was in the room, he reported the smoke quickly 75 per cent of the time. When three were in the room, even after the smoke grew thick and irritating just 38 per cent reported it. In another test, people heard a woman scream in an adjoining room; she had fallen off a chair and twisted her ankle, she clearly cried. Seventy per cent of subjects alone in the next room opened the door to offer aid. Of those in groups only 40 per cent made the helping gesture.

What is it, then, which hinders persons in groups from taking actions that come readily to them as individuals? Primarily, the researchers concluded, the "diffusion of responsibility."

"If only one bystander is present at an emergency, he carries all the responsibility for dealing with it. He will feel all of the guilt for not acting. If others are present, the onus of responsibility is diffused."

In other words, whatever guilt feelings may arise from not helping are diluted by the knowledge that other bystanders acted just as weakly or wrongly. In short, it takes a load off a person. "Each individual's feelings of personal responsibility for helping are weaker."

But something else happens in a crowd to discourage "volunteers," too: something that Darley and Latane called "pluralistic ignorance." Each bystander is picking up cues on how to react from other bystanders. Given the American ideal of trying to keep poised, "cool" under stress, a witness may see only calm, unconcerned faces around him.

"If everyone else in a group of onlookers seems to regard an event as non-serious and the proper course of action as non-intervention, this consensus may strongly affect the perceptions of any single individual." Thus, the crowd "can suggest by its passive behavior that an event is not to be reacted to as an emergency, and it can make any individual uncomfortably aware of what a fool he will look for behaving as if it is."

It is significant that the people who did not *help*, in the experimental "emergencies" cited, were not on that account *unconcerned*. In fact, the researchers found most non-helping subjects sitting there with sweating palms and trembling hands, when the office doors finally were opened. "Is he being taken care of?" they would ask. "He's all right, isn't he?"

These persons seemed to the psychologists *still undecided.* They had not decided not to help. They were locked between two unpleasant alternatives: rushing out of their offices, against previous instruction, to help—or letting the victim continue to suffer.

Even the thirty-eight real witnesses to the very real murder of Kitty Genovese appear less monstrous in the light of "diffusion of responsibility." Darley and Latane suggest that these witnesses "did not merely look at the scene once and then ignore it. Instead they continued to stare out of their windows at what was going on. Caught, fascinated, distressed, unwilling to act but unable to turn away, their behavior was neither helpful nor heroic; but it was not indifferent or apathetic either."

But however enlightening laboratory studies may be with their statistics, percentages, and probabilities, something in the heroic rescuer slips out of this test tube precisely by performing the improbable. And because his act involves actual risk of life, the rescuer's impulse may well be impossible fully to simulate.

"Heroism is an individual phenomenon," said psychologist Ervin Staub, of the University of Massachusetts, in an interview. "The only thing you can do is draw conjectures from when it occurs."

Staub notes, for example, that in spite of the laboratory evidence supporting the diffusion of responsibility theory, in real-life emergencies some one person does frequently emerge from a group to assume responsibility. The hero seems able to crack out of the general clutch of inaction.

Dr. Martin Greenberg, of the University of Pittsburgh, says this phenomenon has been likened to that of a "particle in a force field" being able to surmount the force.

Heroes, of course, are always being asked directly how or why they were able to do it. The typical answer tends to be brief, honest—and unenlightening. "Somebody had to do something." "I couldn't just stand there and let him die." "It seemed like the right thing to do."

Such answers beg the question. Other onlookers must have felt the same way: why didn't *they* act? According to some psychologists, a norm like "the right thing to do" is exactly the sort of reference point people do *not* check in the heat of the moment, but do fall back on as a convenient explanation for their acts after the fact.

Elusive though the specific trigger may be for an act of rescue, Professor Staub for one believes that certain personality traits and tendencies might come into clear focus, if sufficiently large groups of heroes—and "control" groups of non-heroes—could be interviewed in depth.

A few years ago, Dr. Perry London, of the University of Southern California, questioned twenty-seven immigrants to the United States who, in Europe during World War II, had helped to rescue Jewish victims of Nazism. The group was, of course, too small to draw important statistical conclusions. But Dr. London's impression was that these rescuers generally evinced (1) a spirit of adventurousness; (2) intense identification with one or both parents as a model of moral conduct, and (3) a sense of being "socially marginal," of not quite belonging in their own society and class.

The first two of these traits, Ervin Staub believes, would be visible in the make-up of most rescuers. "My guess is that a fair percentage would be action-oriented, in some sense of the adventurous. People like this might find few opportunities for adventure in their everyday lives, and so would exercise it in a rescue opportunity. Also," adds Staub, "I would expect to find a moral orientation handed down by the parents, a concern for others' lives."

The latter point was strongly in evidence among groups of civil rights activists interviewed some years ago by Swarthmore College's David Rosenhan. In contrast to those who merely gave financial support or went along on a single "freedom ride," what Rosenhan called the "fully committed" workers, who labored for a year or more often at severe personal risk, were "very much influenced by identification and learning from the past. . . . They were taught not only to believe but to do."

It is, however, also a fact that some heroic rescuers have been criminals and that some Carnegie Hero medals have been delivered to prisons.

Whatever the moral freight carried by the hero, he probably has the faculty of being able to make a decision quickly, according to psychologist William Meegan of the Eastern Pennsylvania Psychiatric Institute. "I have suspected that the kind of person who comes quickly to the aid of another may have a particular kind of cognitive or decision-making capacity."

Others have suggested that a hero rescuer may be blessed with unusual empathy: a gift of being able "to experience vicariously the relief felt by the person whose need has been met."

A "risk-taking" trait is one that Dr. Joel Goldstein of Carnegie-Mellon University would expect to see. In the main, however, he feels that heroism "is largely pulled forth by the characteristics of the situation. . . . Almost anyone is a potential hero if the circumstances are appropriate." That a fair number of heroic deeds are performed by "socially marginal" persons—immigrants, members of minority groups, the very poor—does not surprise Goldstein. A rescue, he says, can be "a way to gain acceptance, an opportunity for proving your loyalty."

The fact that a rescuer is able to perceive the distressed person's need and then decide, in effect, "I'm the only one who can give help," is a significant one to the University of Pittsburgh's Martin Greenberg. He says it implies a "high self-esteem" on the part of the hero. True, it can also imply the miscalculation of the foolhardy.

Greenberg believes that however quickly it zips through the rescuer's mind, some reasoning process does occur, a weighing of the "costs" of helping against the costs of failing to help. Such costs, he says, in attempting a rescue "could range from your own death, to getting blood on your coat, to missing a train." And the cost of not helping? "A nagging sense of guilt for violating what you thought was your duty."

But the decision also is complicated by ambiguity in the roles of the good citizen. "A man feels himself to be father and provider for his children," says Greenberg. "For him to try to play the role of rescuer may threaten his family role, to which most people would give priority."

The question of role-playing impinges on another aspect of heroism: the general impression, not readily provable with statistics, that more acts of rescue occur in small towns and rural settings than in large cities. In cities there are specialists paid to deal with certain problems. "If you see someone getting beaten up in the street," says Greenberg, "you might react that it's not your job to intervene; why not call an expert?—the policeman."

On the other hand, rural areas tend to be undermanned, and social pressure focuses on each individual to respond in situations requiring help. Hence, a "volunteer" fire department in the absence of the city's professionals.

It seems logical, too, that the sheer opportunity to perform a rescue occurs more often among fields, streams, mountains, open highways, lakes, and seashores than in urban environments where the opening sound of trouble is often followed quickly by the policeman's whistle or the fire engine siren.

And yet the psychological wounds left by degrading social conditions in cities cannot be discounted. Says Ervin Staub: "People in cities may be simply overwhelmed by the needs of others. If you stopped to help everyone in need, you might never get home. In some emergencies passersby immediately turn their heads and never look back. They are trying to protect themselves from even psychological involvement in the distress of others."

A fascinating correlation has been found experimentally between personal good fortune and willingness to help others. Change has been "planted" in a public telephone booth coin return. The person who finds the change is extremely likely, upon coming out of the phone booth, to help a "victim" who has just dropped an armload of books. Is it possible there would be less "apathy" in large cities if people had more happy experiences in their daily lives?

The psychological springs of heroism receive marvelous physiological assistance in the actual performance of the deed. The "strength of ten" that some rescuers report feeling—able to climb mountains, swim miles, carry a heavy victim—is no doubt an exaggeration. But under stress the strength of "maybe two—or two and a half" is believable indeed, according to Dr. Francis B. Colavita of the University of Pittsburgh.

He explains that under the challenge of life-or-death situations the autonomic nervous system switches fully on. This is the "primitive" nervous system, which controls the involuntary processes of the body and in which man is not dissimilar from many "lower" animals.

Stimulated by stress or danger, massive amounts of adrenalin pour directly into the blood. Chemical changes occur which cause the blood, for example, to clot more quickly (in case of a wound). Blood distribution is also radically altered, the supply to unimportant (at least for the moment) digestive organs being cut to a trickle, while the muscles are virtually gorged with oxygen-rich blood. The mouth dries, the pulse pounds, the arms and legs tremble and shake with the sudden access of power—or, in some cases, "freeze," becoming so tensed that they can't function at all. This magnified strength is only temporary but sometimes sufficient to enable a woman to lift one corner of an auto off a fallen child. An accompanying decreased sensitivity to pain lets one understand how a rescuer might swim for some time in water that would turn the casual summer bather blue with cold.

The sheer physical ability to perform great feats under stress goes back to the dawn of the human race and before: the power of "fight or flight" to assure animal survival. It explains why an insignificant beast like the rat, whose whole instinct is to scurry away from danger, becomes, when cornered, a ferociously effective fighter. The rescuer performing beyond his powers is in tune with mighty primeval forces.

That the Carnegie Hero Fund has made awards to over 6,000 heroes since 1904, and regularly finds them out at the rate of about 100 a year, surely is some proof that the Kitty Genovese murder does not tell the whole story of man's current concern with his fellow man.

A century ago, in *The Descent of Man*, naturalist Charles Darwin wrote: "As man is a social animal, it is almost certain that he would . . . from an inherited tendency be willing to defend, in concert with others, his fellow men, and be ready to aid them in any way which did not too greatly interfere with his own welfare or his own strong desires."

Many people today would regard belief in an "inherited tendency" to do good as too optimistic. Yet the findings and conjectures of modern social scientists cited here are not so very far removed from an intuition expressed by another 19th century optimist. "Heroism feels and never reasons, and therefore is always right," exulted Ralph Waldo Emerson. Don't look for reason or logic in heroic acts, he said; they are by nature intuitive, impulsive, "an obedience to a secret impulse of the individual's character."

Having observed the phenomenon in 2,300 documented cases across three decades, the late Thomas S. Arbuthnot, long a president of the Carnegie Hero Fund, had this to say in a 1935 book commemorating the centenary of the founding philanthropist's birth:

"The Carnegie Commission has found it impossible to answer the question, 'Of what are heroes made?'

"An individual stands apart in one heroic, sometimes sublime act of self-forgetting, then melts back into the common composition of humanity. The commission is forced to the conclusion that it is not the individual altogether but the inspired moment that accounts for the deed. . . . Perhaps all of us are eligible for acts of heroism if the spark comes at the right time to set aglow the impulse. Heroism is not made; some tragedy finds it out. Like gold, it is uncovered."

These majestic phrases do not make heroism the less a mystery. But the grand old rhetorician and the modern man of science would seem agreed that the mystery might blaze into light within any of us. And this is a thought worth placing beside the other irrefutably solemn one that any of us might also have stood watcher at the window when Kitty Genovese cried, "Oh my God, please help me!"

A Lion by the Ears

BRIAN KILBREATH was six years old and three feet seven. What tried to eat him was a year old and—from its nose to the tip of its tail—four feet three. It was also starving. A full grown cougar in good flesh weighs about ninety pounds; this one weighed twenty-four. Only driving hunger could have accounted for its having ventured into the outskirts of Hinton, Alberta; for a cougar nearly always makes it a point to avoid the locales of human habitation. But this one, on Friday, March 16, 1962, lay up in a pine tree in the tall grass fifty yards beyond the end of Simpson Street, when Brian Kilbreath with two friends came out to play.

Still and silently the beast crouched, with that iron control instinct exerts even over the gnawing torments of the belly, till the prey came closer . . . just within leaping . . .

A tawny flash burst from the green branches; there was a snuffling sound, a vision of the longest, whitest teeth Brian had ever seen—and he was down on his back, screaming, claws scratching his chest and belly through his jacket, the cougar growling and biting at his throat. Its breath on his neck felt like warm sprays of water.

Brian's friends ran off through the tall grass shrieking. They ran nearly 200 yards before they saw anyone they could tell what was happening. One of the first houses at that end of town was the McEvoys'. To Mrs. Elsie McEvoy, standing on her back porch in a blouse, slacks, and slippers, the boys cried out:

"A cougar's eating Brian!"

Particularly horrifying this choice of words, for Mrs. McEvoy herself had an 11-year-old son named Brian. "Oh, God!" she cried and leaped down the steps and across her yard with unaccustomed energy toward the clearing of tall grass. The fact was Mrs. McEvoy was in frail health for a lion fighter. Though just twenty-eight, married to a turbine operator and mother of two children, she tended to tire easily and was sometimes prostrated by attacks of "nerves."

Upon reaching the clearing 125 yards from her porch, she was out of breath. But such relief! She saw her son Brian with other children, unhurt; thus knew that the boy in danger was not hers. Screams and growls carried from the brush.

"Get the kids in the house!" Mrs. McEvoy shouted to her son. "Phone the police!" And then she charged head-on into the waist-high grass, in the direction of the screams.

A broken tree branch, five feet long and about two inches thick, lay in her path. She picked it up and ran blindly on. Abruptly she came upon the deadly struggle at the foot of the pine tree: the boy flat on his back, bloody, writhing in the grass; the cat, its ribs showing, on the child's chest—gnawing.

The woman screamed, "Get out! Out!"

The beast's back was to her. Except for growling louder, it ignored her.

She stopped just short of the animal, lifted her tree branch in both hands, and brought it down full force on the cougar's skull. Astonishingly it paid no attention. She might have hammered on stone. Again and again she swung the club. At her fifth or sixth blow the beast turned its head to growl at her, but immediately resumed trying to chew at the boy's neck.

Mrs. McEvoy returned to the attack. She struck at the brute

again—only this time a piece of the dry branch broke off and flew into the grass. And as she continued to pummel the cougar, the branch broke down even more until it was a blunt wand no more than fifteen inches long in her hands. Her arms seemed to have no strength, or there lacked enough weight in the club; or else the cat embodied some indestructible passion that no effort of hers could deter.

Suddenly Mrs. McEvoy recalled having heard somewhere that animals—cats especially—were painfully sensitive at the nose. She gripped the stick in her right hand and reached forward with her left, grabbing the cougar by the scruff of the neck.

She jerked its head upward and gave it a solid whack flat on the nose.

The beast staggered. It suddenly drooped like a bag of bones in her hand. She shoved at its head, and the animal fell over on its side.

Zoological curiosity did not now detain the lady.

She lifted the boy by his torn and bloody clothing, clasped him to her breast, and turned and ran.

Once she stumbled. It happened only a few yards away, and in terror she looked back for one instant, catching a glimpse of the cougar with its front legs planted, quivering: it was trying to rise to its feet.

Mrs. McEvoy gave a scream and fairly leaped onward through the tall grass, which whipped at her legs. It seemed to her that at any moment she might hear the whispery rush of the beast behind her, slicing through the grass, inexorable, indestructible.

She was sobbing wildly, near fainting from exhaustion, as she burst out of the brush with Brian in her arms. By then, the boy's mother and other neighbors were standing by the dirt road. They took the child from her at once, and Mrs. McEvoy, at last, could give way to the relief of an attack of nerves. She felt much better afterwards.

Weak from loss of blood, Brian required 146 stitches in the

face, neck, chest, abdomen, hand, and leg but recovered after several weeks in the hospital.

The cougar was shot where Mrs. McEvoy had left it. But later examination revealed that the cat's skull had, in fact, been mortally fractured in several places. The power of a frail tree branch in the hands of a frail housewife cannot be underestimated when a child's life is at stake. □

IT NEVER HAD OCCURRED to the Reverend James E. Simpson how cunningly designed the antlers of a buck deer are for inflicting damage on an opponent in battle. While the upper and outer tines surround the foe in a fence of hard, sharp bone, the snorting buck stabs its shorter inner tines into whatever soft surfaces may be exposed to them. The Reverend Mr. Simpson had not been aware of this mode of attack until, one Monday morning, November 23, 1959, he found himself within the antlers of a furious white-tail deer.

Mr. Simpson, a Presbyterian minister of thirty-six, was driving past the Volunteer Park Zoo, in Pasco, Washington, when he observed through the wire fence of the deer pen—a full grown buck attacking a man.

Park caretaker Levi Yates had been about to feed the animal when it charged him. There was no warning. Yates turned around in the split second necessary for making a grab at the antlers, but the buck's charge drove him back against a shed wall. As he tried to wrestle, one tine of the antlers punctured his lower abdomen, another pierced deeply in his right knee, and he went down, crying out in pain and for help, as the buck pinned him inside the spread of its hammering horns.

Mr. Simpson was en route home after delivering his daughter

to school. Immediately upon seeing Yates's plight, he slammed on his brakes and, leaping from his car, ran to the deer pen's wire fence. It was seven feet high. "How can I get in?" he shouted.

Somehow the struggling Yates was able to indicate that a gate around the corner was unlocked, though closed. The minister ran toward it. He had had time to notice blood smears in the trampled soil around Yates; and he remembered a newspaper account of an enraged buck at the zoo—this one, very likely—having killed its mate just a few weeks earlier by driving an antler into her belly and ripping the poor beast open.

As Mr. Simpson came running through the gate, Yates cried to him, "Hit him! Hit him with something!"

But there was nothing suitable for a club except a salt block, which the deer in more docile moments used as a lick. It lay on the floor of the pen. It was four inches square, about eight inches long, and weighed barely more than a pound. Mr. Simpson seized it in both hands and hammered it down hard on the animal's skull, just behind the antler beams.

The blow failed to stun the buck, but it did get his attention.

In fact, the beast sharply raised its head, backed off from the fallen Yates, and charged head-down toward this new candidate for its rage.

The minister caught the antlers in his hand. But the tines ripped through his jacket and poked painfully at his abdomen as he gave ground backward. Pawing and snorting, the buck violently shook its head, trying to jerk its horns free of the man's grip. And though he held on, Mr. Simpson was pushed back hard against the wire fence.

The buck spread its legs. It nodded its head in, in, and in again at the minister, who now at last comprehended the deadly use to which those smaller, forward-pointing horns could be put.

Desperately Mr. Simpson strove to wrestle the deer off balance—but only lost his own. Down he fell on his back, still holding onto the antlers as the deer dragged him like a rag doll a dozen feet across the turf. The horns ripped the upper part of his trousers to shreds.

Meanwhile, Yates, though wounded and bleeding, had managed to drag himself up to a standing position by the wall of the feeding shed. And another rescuer was charging into the pen.

Joseph J. Kauer, forty-five, a pipe fitter, also had been driving by, had seen what was going on, and had come running through the gate to help.

As the buck belabored the fallen clergyman, Kauer grasped the beast's antlers and tried to force it to lift its head. He could not. But then Yates hobbled over. He gripped the antlers on the other side of the buck's head and also tried to lift. Together the two men forced the head a few inches upward. Suddenly, to throw off their holds, the buck jerked its head up. The alert Mr. Simpson rolled out from under, sprang to his feet, and again seized both antlers near their base at the deer's skull.

There was a moment of balance. The opposing strengths of the animal and of the three men neutralized, quivering.

What to do now? Kauer had a suggestion: that all three should twist the head in an agreed direction and try to bulldog the buck off his feet.

"Okay," he said, "heave!" But it was like trying to pull a tree out by its roots. The buck shifted his hooves—and stayed up.

All three men were breathing heavily now. "Let's see," said Kauer, "if we can . . . get him over . . . closer to the gate." His thought was to work the animal over to a point where all three men could let go at once, jump out, and leave the deer dumbfounded inside.

And so with much strain and effort they hauled the resisting animal a few inches at a time until they were about ten feet from the gate. All were extremely tired now and practically out of breath. They were not going to get any closer.

"Okay," said Kauer, "when I say 'Now!' let go."

"Wait," Mr. Simpson said. "This is stuck." A torn sleeve of his jacket was fouled on one of the deer's horns. He removed the snagged part.

"Okay?" said Kauer—"Now!"

The three dropped their holds and rushed the gate. The deer charged right behind. It got its antlers around the minister's waist just as he left the gate. Following him out—which was not the plan—it pushed him back, back, and down against the trunk of an elm tree outside the deer pen.

The deer seemed just about ready to pierce Mr. Simpson with a half-dozen points of its horns when, in the very climax of its fury—it suddenly, incredibly, paused.

It backed away.

The Reverend Mr. Simpson held his breath as the buck lowered its head again, brought its antlers down once more, but this time gently, and began to graze peaceably in the shade of the elm tree. □

"THE LION IS LOOSE!"

The woman's scream rang with the impact of gunshots through the lobby of the Houston, Texas, animal shelter. Jerrol P. Lowe sprang up from his desk. He did not have to ask which lion.

As manager of the Houston Society for the Prevention of Cruelty to Animals, Lowe three weeks previously had accepted for shelter a 200-pound African lioness named Lisa. The beast had been raised in a private home until, growing too large and unmanageable for a pet, she had been offered to the zoo in Beaumont, Texas. But until she could be transported, an unused kennel at the Houston SPCA shelter had been strengthened to hold her. And now she was out!

At 3 o'clock in the warm afternoon of Tuesday, August 15, 1967, Rebecca Green, who was four and a half years old, had come to the shelter with her mother to take home a puppy. While her mother talked to an attendant, Rebecca wandered off unnoticed. She went back to a cage she had passed before, where prowled a beast more fascinating than any puppy: a real lion which walked about on great, furry pads and flicked the puff of hair at the end of its tail around the bars of its cage like a duster.

Rebecca spoke to the lion. She wanted it to look her way with its big yellow cat's face, its eyes like pale green marbles, its whiskers sticking out straight from its flat, neat nose. But the lion insisted on looking away. It sulked at the far end of its cage. Rebecca rattled the lion's gate.

The metallic clangor had startling effect. The cat sprang with a roar from the back of its cage squarely into the gate. The child recoiled, screaming. There was a rattle of bone and muscle crashing into metal. The hasp which held the gate shut bent outward, and, though a loop of rope secured the gate at another point, the opening was forced wide enough to allow the lion to wriggle through.

Rebecca ran, but with a few bounds the cat was on her. It tumbled her on the lawn just ten yards from the office door of the shelter. And holding the child down with one of its great paws, the lioness began biting at Rebecca's shoulder.

Thirty persons were inside the nearby lobby. At the electrifying cry—"The lion is loose!"—a thrill of panic shot through the room. There were screams, starts of fear, impulsive rushes; mothers seized their children.

Manager Lowe ran from his desk to the door. He saw the child down in the grass with the big cat on top, pawing and biting at her.

There was no time to summon the "right person," no time even to remind himself that he, Jerrol P. Lowe, administrator, had no responsibility for direct care and handling of animals and certainly no competence at subduing wild beasts. The worst he had ever dealt with was a vicious cat or dog. Lowe, who was forty-nine and had a long, serious face and thinning hair, was not a veterinarian or zoologist, but a retired Army major. Toward the lion and the child writhing in deadly struggle on the lawn he felt, however, the immense personal draw of a moral obligation.

"Get me a crowbar, somebody!" he shouted. It was the instinctive first thought of man versus animal: to have something heavy in hand, a weapon, a club. But he immediately dashed out the door bare-handed anyway.

The people in the lobby saw him sprint hard across the grass, reach forward with both hands toward the beast's head, and lift it up—somehow—at the same time butting his hip against the lion's side and actually jostling the animal off the fallen child.

The lion jerked its head loose from Lowe's grip and caught his right arm in a full bite.

One fang entered the upper side of the forearm and broke through flesh on the lower side. Another tooth penetrated two inches. But the lion at once relaxed its bite, and Lowe pulled his arm free. The child, Rebecca, meanwhile profited by the distraction. She sprang up and scampered along a walkway to her mother, who carried her screaming into the lobby.

Jerry Lowe's arm was bleeding. But he could not just walk away from a lion on the loose. Coolly he backed step-by-step toward the lobby door. He put his hand out behind him, and James Jackson, an animal attendant, passed over to him a rubber squeegee at the end of a six-foot pole. Used for scraping water off the floors of kennels after cleaning, it was not quite the heavy crowbar that Lowe had called for.

Yet the shelter manager made good use of it. He held the

squeegee out toward the lion and twirled its rubber blade before the beast's face. Puzzled, the animal backed off. Lowe's thought was to work the cat back toward her cage. Meanwhile, another attendant with a crowbar—a real one—would be trying to stretch the gate wide enough to re-admit the beast.

But this plan, so reasonable to the human mind, failed to secure the cooperation of Lisa the lioness. She loped off across the shelter grounds, and Lowe gave chase, his squeegee held out ahead like a lance, his arm flowing blood.

Back and forth the pursuit wended across lawns, through shrubbery, under trees, and along the empty walkways beside the shelter buildings. At one point an employee brought heavy twine and tied it in a knot around the shelter manager's arm as a tourniquet. Lowe made one close approach to the lioness with soothing words and a gently twirling squeegee; she crouched suddenly as though to spring—and then leaped past him. At another time the beast appeared poised to leap right over the shelter's outer fence; and Lowe realized that the present danger was as nothing compared with the nightmare of allowing the lion loose in the community.

By now two police officers had arrived with rifles. "She's got to be shot," they said. "There's no other way."

And in view of the impossibility of trapping the animal, and the constant danger of her escape, Lowe reluctantly had to agree.

The women in the lobby heard a shot and screamed. The first shot was followed by two more. Then there was silence. Soon uniformed men came to the door and announced, "It's all right to leave now. Everything's under control."

The little girl, Rebecca, had not been gravely maimed. After hospitalization for cuts and scratches, she completely recovered.

Lion-chaser Lowe's wounds were dressed by a physician and he was under treatment for a month, but came through, though scarred, without physical impairment.

But how, police were curious to know—how had Lowe got hold of the lion with such force that he could pull its mouth away from the fallen child? How *would* a man grab a lion's head anyway?

Jerrol P. Lowe did not know if his was the textbook answer. He only knew that it had worked.

"By the ears," he said.

Based on the facts as told in the three stories recounted in A Lion by the Ears, *Elsie H. McEvoy was awarded a silver Carnegie Hero Award medal and Joseph J. Kauer, Reverend James E. Simpson and Jerrol P. Lowe won bronze medals.*

Storm, Ice,
Wind and Tide

MRS. OTTAWA BENSON had no reason to expect a visitor the night of February 25, 1963. In the best of weather her doorstep was little frequented by society. Her husband kept the lighthouse on the southwest promontory of Grand Manan Island in the Bay of Fundy. And this particular winter's eve, the eye of South West Head turned its great glance through blearing masses of cloud.

From Maine to Nova Scotia the bay was lashed by storm. Sixty-mile winds stampeded through the night, howling like all creation in torment. The temperature was below freezing and going down, the stars and moon invisible above the black veils, the darkness all but absolute. At the base of the 200-foot cliff over which the lighthouse raised its gauzy beacon, a violent surf dashed flowers of dimly reflected light, at once doused. A foot of snow had already blown down. In fishing villages huddled around coves along the island's craggy fifteen miles, people who were so blessed felt grateful for thick stone walls, snug windows, and logs snapping on the hearth.

Thus Mrs. Benson was quite startled, at a quarter past midnight, by a loud pounding on her door. She opened it and, amid a gust of blown snow, a man lunged in and dropped on her floor. "My brother . . . my brother . . ." he was babbling. William Jones was nearly delirious with what he had been through. Warmed by a drink, hugging himself before the fire, at times sobbing, he told a broken, frantic story. Even as Benson was summoning other island men by telephone to help, he could scarcely believe it.

Jones, forty-two, and his brother, Floyd, thirty-seven, were laborers in the town of Lubec at the eastern tip of Maine. That morning—meaning sixteen hours earlier—they had gone out fishing in the Bay of Fundy in a light 15-foot motorboat. Their carburetor froze. This they discovered too late, while trying to restart the motor with a squall coming up.

Wind and current beat them away from shore as they tried desperately to paddle. In the choppy water their oars were useless matchsticks. For hours their little boat tossed helplessly in the channel twelve miles wide between the mainland and Grand Manan. Darkness fell, and freezing cold, and high, rocking seas. All the brothers could do was bail and shiver—and pray. Accustomed as both were, lifelong, to the water, they became wretchedly seasick. At last, Fundy seemed to grow bored with them. A strong flood tide was bearing them toward Grand Manan. By the logic of that terrible day it seemed certain to dash them on reefs at the foot of South West Head. But instead a wave lifted them in, dropping them on a miraculously tiny patch of beach at the foot of the cliff with no more smack than a newspaper on a front porch.

That was the first miracle.

The second was that William Jones somehow climbed the cliff.

Had he had the benefit of prior advice, the islanders would have told him the cliff was unscalable. Its walls were of volcanic stone: jagged, crumbling, and, on this night, spotted with ice and snow. Extremely steep where it was not perpendicular, the climb called for 200 feet of blind exploration up into the unknown for handholds—if they would hold!—in nearly total darkness, under blasting winds, by a man as weak and chilled as a sick cat from fighting the sea all day.

Before William's successful ascent, both brothers had tried to climb, knowing that the tide soon would cover their tiny beach. But after getting up just a few feet, both had tumbled back. The last William Jones saw of his brother, Floyd lay on the beach virtually helpless and far too thinly clad against the punishments of the night. He had on a light wool jacket, a cotton shirt and trousers, shoes, rubbers, and rubber gloves.

It took William Jones three hours to reach the top of the precipice.

Then he stumbled three-quarters of a mile through the snow toward the one light turning in the stormy sky.

Jones had no true hope that his brother still lived. Neither did the fifteen men of Grand Manan, who, summoned by telephone, drove and slogged through the snowy night to follow Jones's tracks to the edge of the cliff. Huddled on the stormy height in caps and boots, wool jackets and mittens, they peered down toward a sea far more audible than it was visible. Beneath the shrieks of wind they could hear the surf's explosions as it smashed the foot of the cliff. Could any man be alive down there?

It was possible for the islanders to get, at least, a bit closer to the answer. Ropes were tied around the trunks of trees on the summit, and six men lowered themselves to a broad ledge thirty feet below. They hallooed into what seemed an immense black pit, its bottom swept by sheets of foam scarcely less tarry than the night itself. There was no answer but the wind.

Any chance of recovering a body much less rescuing a living man seemed nil. But two islanders quietly stepped forward and asked to have ropes tied around their chests, so that they could essay a further descent. They were Vernon P. Bagley, forty-six, the island game warden, who lived at Seal Cove, a village five miles from South West Head; and Sidney A. Guptill, thirty-four, the assistant lighthouse keeper.

While others put their backs into the ropes, Bagley and Guptill went over the side and began inching down the cliff. They had descended no more than six feet, however, when their boots set off slides of rock and dirt; and the two had to scramble back on the ledge.

It was as every Grand Mananite had suspected, in spite of the marvelous climb of William Jones. The cliff's steepness and crumbly structure, not to mention the wind, cold, and darkness, made it simply impossible to descend by foot. In the morning, if the storm died, perhaps then; but now, sheer madness.

Even game warden Bagley agreed, and he was not an easy man to turn off course. A wiry man with a shrewdly lined face, Bagley stood five feet seven and 160 pounds and was tough as a walnut. He had lived and tramped all his life on Grand Manan; there weren't many pieces of its rock on which he did not have some informed opinion. He had seen tons of cliff plunge away at what seemed the merest touch, and he knew of major slides set off by a single rifle shot.

If he were sure the man was alive down there, well, then it might be different. Or if the fellow were his, Vern Bagley's, own brother, what then? "Sure I would!" he exclaimed audibly, arguing with himself aloud. And he continued to search the rim of the ledge, almost unconsciously looking for a safer route down the cliff he had decided not to descend.

The wind all this time had been deafening. And then for a moment it died. To the men on the ledge there arose a faint but unmistakable human cry. "Help!" It escaped and flew through a hole in the wind, before the howling curtain of sound crashed down again. It proved Floyd Jones was alive!

And it decided Vernon Bagley. "I've got to try again," he declared to the others.

He tied the rope once more around his chest over his wool

hunting jacket, and he started down the cliff at a point on its south face where the rock seemed sturdier to him. The other men on the ledge drew back on the rope and kept it taut, except when he signaled for slack. Feeling cautiously for footholds and handholds, he was utterly out of sight and earshot of the men above when he had descended just fifteen feet. The night was that dark, the wind that loud. Bagley's only way to signal was with tugs on the line; what these meant the men above could only guess.

Still proceeding southward as he descended, Bagley crossed a gash in the cliffside which was about three feet deep and four feet wide. It formed a kind of gully. He decided to follow its south rim downward; any rockslide would be likely to collect in the gully's bed rather than along its rim, and thus would roll past him, he hoped.

And so, placing his feet and hands with utmost care, he inched downward, but he also lost all sense of contact with the men above. True, his rope was by turns taut or slack, but not through volition, only because it kept getting snagged and unsnagged. If he fell, the rope would—might—serve him as a life line. But any real chance he had of safety, or of helping Jones, depended on an intimate sense of the icy stone that lay under his hands and boots, along his legs and outstretched arms, the stone whose edges poked through his jacket and against his weathered cheek. Never to trust his weight to a piece of stone that might "give"—that was Vern Bagley's true life line.

For a quarter of an hour the men on the ledge, stamping their feet with the cold, paid out rope inch by inch into the roaring abyss. They judged that about 100 feet of rope had gone over the side, but beyond this they had no idea how Bagley was faring.

In fact, he had moved about twenty to thirty feet south of the ledge in descending 100 feet, and he decided to stop there and try to get another fix on his man. "Where are you?" he shouted.

"Where are you?" He tried to pitch his voice into spaces in the wind.

It worked. "Over here!" a voice came back, from somewhere down and to the left, northward along the cliff face.

So Bagley recrossed the gully, gingerly, knowing well that all it would take was one stone rolling down the channel onto his head to mark a period to this and all future exploits of the game warden of Grand Manan. As he crept downward and to the north toward where he thought Floyd Jones's cry came from, his path now formed a rough figure "7" with the first leg of his descent. Fifty feet below the angle of the "7" and about ten to fifteen feet north, he came to a small earthen mound. The surf boomed in just twenty feet below him in slides of blackish foam. Spray wet his face. He stretched out at length on the mound and crawled on top, embracing it. Floyd Jones could not be much closer to the water.

Bagley took a flashlight from his belt. He played its sickly beam—the batteries were nearly dead—across the cliff face immediately before him.

In the niche between the face of the cliff and the slope of the mound Bagley lay on, he saw Floyd Jones.

In desperation after his brother had climbed away, and with the tide evicting him absolutely from the beach, the mainlander had worked himself up about twenty feet off the sand. He was crouched on a ledge about three feet square, barely large enough to hold him, in a kneeling position, with his face toward the cliff, slumped over. But he was conscious enough to tell Bagley, after the game warden had scrambled down onto the ledge, a piece of most discouraging news.

"I can't move," he said. "My legs are froze."

It was the nature of Vernon Bagley that in this ominous report he somehow found a positive to accentuate. Floyd Jones's arms were *not* frozen. Bagley stood over Jones to lift him, circling him around the midsection, and he felt the injured man's arms tighten: he still had strength in them.

The game warden took a spare pair of mittens from his jacket pockets and pulled them over Jones's hands. "If you want to get out of here," he yelled in the other man's ear, to make himself heard above the wind, "you're going to have to use every bit of your strength and help me as much as you can."

Jones nodded agreement. Bagley ordered him to grip with both hands, grip as hard as he could, on the rope circling Bagley's chest, where it came around his back. Now the game warden stood up, facing the cliff. Floyd Jones took hold of the rope behind him, and the weight was like a noose tightening on the older man's heart and lungs.

In this posture, with another man's weight equal to his own dragging at his back, Vernon Bagley began what was surely one of the epic personal struggles a volunteer ever has undertaken for a stranger on a stormy winter night.

Literally towing Jones behind him, he climbed back over the earthen mound and inched southward up the leg of the "7" down which, a few minutes before, he had crept. Jones simply could do nothing to help except hold onto the rope; and that was effort a-plenty. Both men groaned and gasped with the brutal struggle of it. Every few feet Bagley had to stop to rest.

His fellow islanders far above in the storm could neither see nor hear what was going on below. Their only clue: the rope kept getting slack. "He's comin' back," they shouted to each other. "He must be comin' back with 'im!" So with each few inches yielded from over the edge, they hauled the rope taut; and, by pulling, they started giving Bagley some small aid upward.

The game warden had risen only a few yards when he felt a stab of horror. Peering up along the quivering rope, he saw that it had got snagged on a projection of rock which even now stood ten feet higher and about five feet forward of him. It obviously had got hung up on his descent!

This meant that for the past quarter of an hour—encompassing his last few steps down, his retrieval of Floyd Jones, and the beginning of his ascent—his life had hung over the boiling, black surf by no more than the scrape of a rope on an angle of rock. At any moment it could have, could still, slip off!—and the yards of slack which *that* would suddenly turn loose would catch the men above flatfooted and send Bagley and Jones tumbling.

But there was no quick help for it. All the game warden could do now was keep climbing, with exquisite care, and pray that the projecting rock would not let slip the life line. Inch by inch he drew himself closer to the snag of rock. He pulled it within arm's length and finally, with a groan of relief, past his face. The rope twanged free; the slack was drawn up by those above.

Now Bagley came to the gully which had served him so well on the downward route. No mystery about the *way* up—if he and his passenger had the strength to follow it. He crawled and scraped on his belly, with Jones hanging on behind, into and out of the gully and wormed up onto its southward lip. By this point he had ascended approximately fifty feet.

It was his passenger who could go no further. "I can't . . . hold on anymore," Jones gasped.

Bagley stopped and hauled Jones around in front of him, pinning him to the slope. The younger man said he had no more strength to cling to the rope around Bagley's back. He was desperately fearful of losing hold and falling into the sea.

And then Jones made a request, pleaded actually, that Bagley remove the rope from around his own chest—and tie it around his, Jones's!

The game warden stared at him for a moment. Then, without a word, he selflessly slipped out of the rope and knotted it around Floyd Jones's waist. If Bagley lost his step now, he was on his own.

What he proceeded to put in effect, however, was a reversal of their previous positions. Bagley crept around Jones, who now faced the cliff, and seized the rope at Jones's back. In this position Jones was practically sitting in the older man's lap. And now, with exhausting awkwardness, Bagley nudged Jones upward from below, while the men above steadily hauled in the inches of slack.

And that was how the progress was measured, in inches sorely won, under the buffeting of the ceaseless wind and with the snow pelting Bagley in the face. He was, in effect, alone much of the time, for at several intervals during the climb Jones blacked out, resting in his life line; then he would come back to himself with a start like a man awaking, but still locked in the same nightmare. Inch by straining inch up the rim of the gully, then across it again, for fifty more feet Bagley lifted and shoved his helpless charge. The rope that was around Jones no longer gave Bagley the lifting sensation, such as it was, that he had enjoyed before. He came to a point where his trembling arms and legs simply could perform no more. He tried to raise Jones, and the man would not budge.

There was no more strength left in Vernon Bagley.

"I got to leave you a couple minutes," he shouted in Jones's ear. "Hey, you hear?" Jones seemed to emerge briefly from the most profound and sickly sleep. "You hear? Got to go up . . . rest . . . be back for you in a couple minutes." Jones nodded and dropped back into lethargy. "No," said Bagley, shaking him. "You got to hold on. Hold!" He put Jones's mittened hands on the rock slope, and the injured man wearily nodded. In fact, of course, with the rope around him he could not fall.

Bagley reached up and seized the rope a foot or two above Jones and began climbing on it hand over hand. It was still a good fifty feet up to the ledge, but his own weight felt almost light compared to the burden he had been raising with so much struggle. Far below him the surf boomed; little stones skittered

from under his boots; he skinned his knees, elbows and, once, his nose; and his arm muscles began to feel like spring wire twisted too far, but with the last ounce of his energy he put a hand up over the rim and was pulled onto the ledge by the others.

Ninety minutes had passed since the game warden had gone over into the storm and cold and blackness.

He tried to explain that he only wanted to rest before going back down for Jones, but the others, especially Sidney Guptill, would not hear of it. Not only had Bagley run past the point of dangerous fatigue but, from what he had reported, time was critical. Exposure might snuff out Floyd Jones's life at any moment.

Guptill volunteered to follow Bagley's rope down to the helpless man. In another half hour, the hardy lighthouseman, with others hauling from above, at last got Floyd Jones onto the summit.

To the summit, not necessarily to safety.

Jones's legs were so badly frozen, the doctors thought at first they surely would have to be amputated. Yet Jones responded to treatment so well that in only three days, his legs still intact, he could be discharged from the hospital.

Vern Bagley's legs were sore *that* long!

Mentally, the game warden's ordeal lasted longer. He had nightmares for three months, awakening to the cry of wind around his house and the feel of sliding stones under his hands and feet, and a tightness, like that of a weighted rope, around his chest.   □

In the clear, warm, breezy noon of July 20, 1959, the Clark family's plight was annoying but hardly alarming. Their 26-foot sloop *Sea Dog* was hung up on a submerged sandspit in the Atlantic Ocean outside St. Andrews Sound in southern Georgia. The nearest land, an uninhabited island called Little Cumberland, raised its low, brushy profile a mile and three quarters to the east.

Skipper Harold R. Clark, who was forty and a lawyer from Jacksonville, Florida, wisely hauled down his nylon sails as soon as his craft sliced bottom. He didn't want her structure strained by the wind. A good swimmer, certainly not troubled at the shallow bottom he saw over the side of *Sea Dog*, Clark jumped in the water and tried to pull the ship free with his anchor line while his wife Vivian and son Harold Jr. rocked the vessel from side to side. It would not budge.

As the minutes went by and the tide continued to recede—it still had an hour to go to "low"—*Sea Dog* yawed slightly higher and drier. But the air was fresh, the sky clear, the ordeal one of enforced idleness rather than hard effort. So Clark philosophically decided the family might just as well wait for high tide to float them off. Besides his wife and son there also was a daughter, Christine, who was five. Harold Jr. was four.

Sea Dog happened to be well appointed for this sort of inconvenience. It had a roomy cabin. There was comfort and no apparent danger.

About 1:30 P.M. the charter fishing boat *Zoemar* approached. She was taking a party of eight sportsmen out to sea from Jekyll Island a few miles to the north. With a powerful diesel engine and deck winch, *Zoemar*'s captain, M. L. Winner, figured she could spare a minute or two to haul the beached sloop off the sandbar. Piloting his craft into water five feet deep about fifty yards from *Sea Dog,* Winner sent his young mate splashing overboard to wade with the end of a hawser—a husky rope, two inches in diameter—over to the sailing sloop.

Clark jumped down to help the youth tie the hawser to *Sea Dog*'s bow. Then Winner started the deck winch; the hawser came out of the water dripping, tightening, and *Sea Dog* began scraping across the sandspit, but with such a creaking and cracking that after twenty-five feet of tortured progress, Clark cried out to *Zoemar* to please desist rendering aid. He feared his craft would split open with the strain. "We can wait for the tide," he called.

Captain Winner was put in a quandary. He did not like leaving a small craft in any sort of trouble; on the other hand his own ship was chartered for deep-sea fishing, and his patrons deserved a certain consideration, too. At this point his young mate took the good skipper off the hook by offering to stay behind and help Clark refloat his *Sea Dog* after the change in tide. Winner agreed, and *Zoemar* rumbled away on the blue water and over the horizon toward the fishing grounds.

"I'm Harold Clark," said the lawyer, holding out his hand to the new man in his crew.

"Don McGregor, sir. Pleased to meet you."

Donald E. McGregor, of Brunswick, Georgia, was fifteen and already over six feet tall, but with not an extra ounce on his sapling frame. Stripped to the waist, his jeans rolled to his knees, Donald was dripping wet. He had small ears that stuck straight out from his crew-cut head, but his face was serious and strong, and he had that air of tanned, sinewy competence which comes to seacoast boys who, from their earliest days, emulating older brothers, spend most of their time on or in the water. The sixth of seven children, Don earned $12 a day on his summer vacation from school by assisting on fishing cruises. It was a daily wage that, now he thought of it, he probably had just volunteered himself out of.

The first thing the boy and the lawyer tried to do was to rock the *Sea Dog* from side to side by lines tied to the mast. Back and forth she crunched and creaked, but did not come loose. At about 2 P.M., when the tide began to change, Clark and Donald entered the water again, took the anchor line from the bow and tried to haul the sloop free—again without success.

Meanwhile, the wind had veered from west to northwest. It was blowing fresher and a bit colder. The sea started to kick up. Waves a foot high slapped into the sloop broadside and rocked her, but she still stuck fast. Lawyer Clark pulled life preservers out of a cabin locker and tied them on his children, his wife, Don McGregor, and himself.

The wind tightened to 12 miles per hour. Now came breakers, piling up and thundering over the shoal to an average height of three and a half feet, though some were bigger. A strong tidal current westward and northward nudged the ship toward land, but futilely; it was as though she had put down a root in the sandspit, determined not to be moved but only pummeled by the sea.

A wave fully six feet high jarred the *Sea Dog* so hard that little Christine, who was trussed up in two life jackets, bobbed off the deck like a cork. Her father and Donald were already in the water, jumping in the surf, looking for an opportunity to pull the ship free; both of them charged through the foaming water after the child and hauled her back to the deck.

But the seas were surging regularly across the cockpit and into the cabin now. At 3:15 P.M.—the punishment had been going on for a good hour—a breaking wave tore a five-inch hole near the ship's bow at the water line. Clark climbed aboard and set up a gasoline-powered bilge pump, but it could not keep up with the flow of water dashed in by the waves. The true situation could not be denied any longer.

Sea Dog was breaking up.

"We're going to have to get off," Clark informed his wife.

It was not a shining marital moment. The day had begun with the unfortunate idea of sailing instead of driving to a religious conference only twenty miles or so up the coast from their home. And now they had spent hours stranded on a sandspit, missing the meeting, missing even the chance to get off safely onto *Zoemar*; only to see their boat being beaten to shreds beneath them, and to be forced now to climb out with two little children onto a sandbar swept by tides.

Apart from the danger of drowning, there was another peril the Clarks were not aware of. Don McGregor kept that from them, not wanting to intensify their fears.

Sharks.

Many a fin had been sighted in these waters, and Don himself the month before had caught a five-foot shark in the vicinity. He passionately desired to see none of such game on the present outing.

Before abandoning ship Harold Clark removed from the cockpit two life preservers of the seat cushion type and another in the form of a small raft, three feet long, eighteen inches wide.

Clark placed his son lying prone on the air raft. He sat his daughter on one of the seat cushions, and placed the other under his wife's arm. And then Mr. and Mrs. Clark, wading on either side of the children, pushed the "rafts" slowly out into water chest deep, with Don McGregor in their wake, until they drew about 100 feet away from the disintegrating *Sea Dog*.

The sandbar under foot had a name: Pelican Spit. It was more than two miles long, and extended in the general direction of land; but its depth varied so much, that the little group could not expect to wade much farther. They paused. The push of the tidal current streaming past their bodies made standing difficult, but Harold Clark thought it wisest not to stray far from where *Sea Dog* had been sighted. "A boat has to come by soon," he said.

Don McGregor would not bet on it. *Zoemar* was the last vessel they had seen. That had been two hours ago. Soon the incoming tide would lift their feet off Pelican Spit willy-nilly. The youth pointed to the low smear of Little Cumberland Island, a mile and three quarters to the west. "We've got to swim to that island," he said firmly. He argued that the way the tide was running now, it would push them toward land. Later, when it turned, it would be sweeping them outward, toward the sea. The boy's other good reason for making for land—sharks—he still kept to himself.

Harold Clark's decision was not easy. Tricky though the footing was on Pelican Spit, it was a place to stand. On the other hand, land was nearly two miles off; his wife was a poor swimmer, his children could hardly dog-paddle. True, they had life preservers, and Don McGregor, from the look of him, would be a sturdy right arm . . .

Nonetheless, the lawyer decided to accede to the leadership of the 15-year-old boy.

The rubber raft on which Clark's son was riding had a pullrope attached to it at the front, in the shape of a "U" about three feet long. Don McGregor swam up inside this loop and took the rope around his waist. The Clark parents tied the belts of their life preservers to the belts of their children's.

And now with Don McGregor swimming, towing the raft behind him by the rope around his waist, and the Clarks holding onto their children and kicking their feet behind, the tiny human convoy set out northwestwardly from Pelican Spit, splashing and struggling between waves three feet high.

Clark began to tire after a few minutes. He proposed that they stop swimming; simply float on the tidal current till a boat would hove into sight. Don McGregor was not only tired, the rope around his waist was beginning to chafe painfully. But he urged strongly that they all keep swimming. Their best hope was to reach the island before the next change in tide. Otherwise there would be no way to avoid getting dragged out to sea.

And so they swam.

There were long minutes when they appeared to make absolutely no progress. The salt water seemed like a syrupy green treadmill, endlessly stealing back whatever yardage they managed with leaden arms and legs to achieve. They did not resent the occasional wave that washed over their heads, welcoming, rather, the impulse it provided toward land. At times, too, the stream of the tide along their chafed limbs told them that though their way was slow the oceanic forces were somehow on their side.

An hour of their toil had passed . . . more than an hour. Far behind them now, invisible, probably scattered and sunken, lay the wreckage of *Sea Dog*. It was about 5 P.M. They had swum or been pushed by the tide perhaps a mile and a half. With each stroke he took, the rope around Don McGregor's waist smarted unbearably. His skin was welted and inflamed by the salt water. He had an idea. He removed his arms from his life preserver and slipped it down around his waist. Then he placed the rope of the life raft around this thick "belt" and thus got some cushion against the pain. He was able to resume swimming. The Clarks by now were kicking only sporadically. If the raft had any power left at all it was named McGregor.

Six o'clock came. The island, lying so low in the water, didn't look much closer. But in fact, less than a quarter of a mile now separated the struggling swimmers from the north tip of Little Cumberland. The tide was a train from which they now had to debark, however: it no longer bore them toward the island but beyond it, still northwestardly, on into St. Andrews Sound.

They *must* move southwestwardly, cross-current to the tide, or be swept past the nearest point of land! And so Don McGregor turned the group southward and, despite the aching fatigue in his arms, stroked with a renewed determination. "Kick hard! Kick with all you've got!" he exhorted the Clarks. They tried. All three tried, punching and splashing at the choppy water. They were gasping for breath, hearts pounding and red in the face. They couldn't be balked now, they just couldn't! Another stroke . . . another kick . . . one more effort . . .

But 250 feet was the closest they could approach.

"You go," Clark, panting, told the boy. "Swim in . . . Get help . . . We'll float . . . be okay."

The boy hated to leave the family so close to shore. What if the tidal current carried them out? And yet this might be the only chance now to help them.

He slipped the rope of the life raft over his head and stroked alone for shore.

Even now his progress was maddeningly slow. The undercurrent surged strongly and the breaking waves seemed to comb across rather than toward the Cumberland beach. The exposed parts of Don's body collected disgusting blobs of jellyfish, which he tried to brush away. Still he swam on and, at last, with a sob he felt sand under his feet.

He waded onto the beach at just about 7 P.M.

He had been pulling the Clarks for most of three hours.

Though near exhaustion, he thought that if there was to be any chance at all of saving the family, he must run for help without a moment's loss. So he ran southwest on the beach toward the quiet, warm waters west of the unpopulated island, hoping to find shrimp fishermen there.

Heavily tangled with brush to the very water's edge, save for a section or two of sand beach, the island was not designed for navigation by foot. Mostly Donald had to wade along the land's edge, sometimes crashing barefoot through swampy thickets.

By 9 P.M. he had tramped only a mile and a quarter south along the west shore, but 300 yards out in the water toward the mainland he spotted a shrimp fishing boat. Don waded toward the boat till he was chest deep; then he cupped his hands to his mouth and shouted to the fishermen to notify the Coast Guard about the shipwrecked family off the north tip of the island.

Don dragged himself back to land. Night was falling fast. He had done all he could. Wearily he slogged back northward along the rim of the island under the stars toward the beach where he had first come out of the water hours before.

It was 11 P.M. when he stumbled onto the beach again—and to his joy found the Clarks there. With a favorable shift in the tide, they had been able to climb up onto the beach an hour after he had.

Swarms of mosquitoes, gnats, and sand-flies proceeded to feast upon the survivors of *Sea Dog*, but there came also the vision of a great illuminated monster bursting out of the sky's darkness with blessings: a Navy blimp roaring over with landing lights spearing the beach and dropping parcels of orange juice and chocolate bars. The elder Clarks and Donald, thus fortified, fought the insects by digging holes in the sand and burying the Clark children and themselves up to their necks. And waiting.

At twenty minutes past one o'clock in the morning, the beam of a Coast Guard patrol boat danced on the sand, a dinghy was rowed to the beach, and five very tired, very bitten, very sandy, relieved and grateful people were borne away to safety.

Speaking of Don McGregor afterward, lawyer Clark had this to say:

"He never showed fear, nor even the slightest concern for his own safety, but was continually swimming and encouraging us to help and directing us to work in the direction of the island. His great courage and optimism kept up our hope when there was little reason to have any."

If this were fiction, any variety of splendid futures might have been imagined for Donald E. McGregor. But while art must simulate truth, truth need not, and only infrequently does, obey the laws of art. The truth does not have to be pleasing to the mind, or symmetrical, or at all in tune with justice. It has no mercy and it stumbles not rarely into the most disspiriting anticlimaxes.

On December 14, 1964, *The Brunswick News,* of Brunswick, Georgia, carried a report concerning Don McGregor, then a college student.

"A 20-year-old Brunswick youth who received the Young American Medal for Bravery from the late President Kennedy (and) on the same day was awarded the Carnegie Hero Medal for a dramatic sea rescue, died here last night of injuries sustained in a wreck on Glynn Avenue . . .

"The car in which the youth was a passenger had been drag-racing shortly before the accident, city police said . . . "

Based on the facts as told in the two segments of Storm, Ice, Wind and Tide, *Vernon P. Bagley won a silver Carnegie Hero Award medal while Sidney A. Guptill and Donald E. McGregor were awarded bronze medals.*

His Arm or His Life?

TO UNDERSTAND THE HORROR which befell Heinrich Wenzel, it is necessary to examine a few facts about deep copper mining.

First there was the mountain, one hump of the Coast Range of western Canada. Arching a mile high near the hamlet of Brittania Beach, British Columbia, about thirty miles north of Vancouver, the mountain was so richly blooded with copper that after forty years of being continuously mined, more could still be torn from it. Like a black worm the ore train popped out several times a day at a hole on the mountain slope. From that exit a horizontal track ran two and a half miles straight in—to Shaft Number 8.

This shaft was deeper than the world's tallest building upside down. It dropped 850 feet, then another 800 feet, to haulage tunnels whose tracks glinted off into the dimness under strings of light bulbs.

If the shaft can be thought of as a tree trunk, the haulage-ways were branches. Blooming out along them like invisible flowers in the stone were the so-called "caves." Not true caves: these were blasted. Regions about 100 feet high and wide and long were split by explosive charges. It was in these cysts of fractured stone that the actual mining took place.

A bee would have admired the method. The ore was block-mined. That is, it was chopped out in uniform sections, about seven feet high, deep, and wide. As this bite was removed, a little house was built: a timber cubicle to hold the roof up. And as these proliferated, they formed extensive "floors" of about 100 cubicles each. At the corners of each cubicle stood log pillars ten inches thick. In the sweep of a miner's headlamp—there being no other light in a cave—the pillars looked like a dead dark grove of blighted trees, uniform and headless. They supported ceilings of six-inch planks. And these in turn became the floors of the cubicles above.

The usual building climbs through air: one doesn't think of the sky opposing its progress. But the floors in the mine could ascend only by hacking out their "sky," block by block. As lower floors were mined out, they would be backfilled with sand and gravel. Up past these buried levels the miners would climb to the working floors on flights of ladders in a narrow, vertical shaft called a manway. The manway was wide enough to contain, also, a wooden rock chute. It was this which conveyed the ore clattering down from the working floors to a rail car in the haulageway.

The logic and wisdom of these arrangements were opposed only, and infrequently, by nature.

For months and years, mining floors would keep checkering upward toward the "dome" of a cave. Theoretically this was an arch of solid rock past the fracturing range of the explosive. But in fact, so much material had been taken out of the mountain—despite backfilling—that the structures which remained labored under thousands of tons of shifting stresses: the weight of rock squeezing in at all times from top and sides.

The earth, on occasion, readjusted to this pressure by a

movement to whose suddenness and vast power for mischief the miners paid the tribute of understatement.

They called it a "bump."

On October 31, 1960, late in the afternoon, Heinrich Wenzel was mining on the 12th floor of one of the caves tributary to Shaft Number 8. The 12th floor was the highest yet reached in that particular cave. All levels up through ten had been already backfilled. The dome of the cave curved only twenty-four feet above the plank ceiling over Wenzel's head.

The working quarters were cramped and a taller miner would have had to stoop. But Wenzel, who stood five feet six, could work without banging his hardhat on the ceiling. Because no inch of progress comes easily underground, he knew—any miner would know—exactly where he was: in the seventh cubicle out from the west wall, the third away from the south wall. Wenzel was the only miner on the 12th floor and his partner, Thomas Archibald, was the only other man in the cave.

A few yards from where he was chopping at the wall of ore, Wenzel had opened some plank flooring. To this opening from time to time with a pneumatic tool he "scraped" large and small chunks of the ore-bearing rock. These rained down to the 11th floor, where Archibald scraped them the rest of the way to a platform at the end of the floor, finally shoveling them into the rock chute.

At 5:45 P.M. Archibald heard a growl in the rock overhead.

He was near the platform. He had time to form the complete, if uncomplicated, thought that a cave-in was about to land on him. With the agility of his twenty-four years he leaped out onto the manway ladder an instant before 2,000 tons of rock (such was the official estimate later recorded) broke from the dome of the cave.

Archibald heard a shuddering roar, the snapping and gnashing of timbers. A cloud of stone and dust puffed out of the floors above his head and sifted around him like dry rain as he scampered down the ladders, while the thunder of the cave-in died away in a crumbly murmur and then silence. Descending, Archibald tensed for a timber or rock to tumble down on him at any moment. But only dust and pebbles pelted his hardhat. He reached the haulageway shaking. He ran to a phone to give the alarm and had trouble keeping from screaming it. A punch of nausea hit him and he sat down by the phone post and took deep breaths till his skin stopped crawling. Never had he been so closely shaved by death.

George J. Preissler felt the cave-in literally as a "bump." It jostled him. He was mining in a similar cave higher and a quarter mile to the east of Wenzel's and Archibald's. When such a shove passes through a mountain, business as usual comes to a halt. Preissler and other miners at once left their posts. Streaming to the scene from all directions, within a few minutes they were huddled around Archibald in the haulageway.

Bits of fine debris still sifted down the manway. But though the men held their breaths to catch the faintest moan, there was no sound from up where the ladders disappeared in dust and darkness.

Company officials received the alarm at their homes. On his way in, superintendent Herbert Shuttleworth picked up veteran miner John Johnson. Johnson, fifty, was a member of the mine rescue squad—and locally famed for an uncanny sense of what men burrowing in stone could and could not perform. John McIntosh, supervisor of first aid at the mine, brought along Dr. Barrie C. Flather, a young physician employed at the clinic under contract to the mining company. With no obligation to go sub-surface, Dr. Flather, twenty-eight, nevertheless felt he might be of some use and he thoughtfully tucked a first aid kit under his arm.

Estimating that it would be a half to three quarters of an hour before any officials arrived, some of the miners felt they ought at least to determine if Heinrich Wenzel was alive, and, if so, whether there was not some quick way to extricate him.

George Preissler and four others climbed the ladders to the platforms at the 10th, 11th, and 12th floors. In the beams of the men's headlamps the floors looked choked with debris. Broken timbers stuck out at crazy angles from a jumble of rocks ranging in size from powder to brickbats to boulders twenty feet long. Could even a mouse have lived under the fall of that?

"Wenzel!" the men shouted, "Wenzel!"

Out of the debris, twisting through its interstices tortuously but clearly, came an unexpected answer: "*Yah, ich bin* here! Help me!"

It was pain which had informed Heinrich Wenzel he was still alive. The voices merely confirmed the fact.

A native of Germany, Wenzel, forty-four, was a dark man with heavy brows and a thin face which at times wore the haunted look of the displaced. He had come to Canada after the war for work; and work he did, stolidly, uncomplainingly, with few words in a language that was foreign to him. When fellow workers casually Anglicized his name to "Henry," he made no objection.

He had had no chance to escape the cave-in. The plank ceiling of his cubicle simply had collapsed under the overwhelming plunge of rock above it. Indeed, the debris smashed through Wenzel's floor, and the 11th floor below it; and jagged timbers had even stabbed in spots into the back-filled 10th floor. As rock fragments and timbers tumbled all about him, a plank in the framing of Wenzel's cubicle socked him near the left ear and hacked into his arm three inches below the shoulder. This drove him down to a seated position in the rubble on his floor. The light died, and he passed out.

Pain woke him. Or was this being awake? It was utterly dark. The blow on his head had knocked off his hardhat, crushing its lamp. There was earth in his mouth. He put out his hand and touched stone a few inches from his face. Stone surrounded him. He was buried—and with the coffin lid closed stupidly on his left arm! How it hurt! He touched the place where the plank had chopped into his left arm, catching it on an anvil of stone beneath. He could feel the hacked bone-end. It was splintery but soft like a green twig. The moist, exposed flesh tingled. It was moist but not sopping wet. Strange there was no blood. Yet his arm was broken open and almost severed. He tugged at it and almost swooned with the pain. Then he heard voices calling his name. His mind snapped into utterly true focus: he must answer. "*Yah!*" he cried out with all his strength. "*Ich bin* here . . . "

A question and answer period followed. Under the circumstances the interrogation was calm and even had, for the trapped man, the auxiliary comfort of being conducted in his native tongue. George Preissler, a younger countryman of his, asked the questions and he, Heinrich Wenzel, answered.

He was buried, he reported, in a cavity only about a foot larger in size than he himself was, seated, crouched slightly forward, held in this position by the debris at his back. Yes, he seemed to be getting air. Air? That meant openings. He felt above his head—but carefully!—so as not to disturb a single pebble. Above, behind and beside him, the rock and timber fragments seemed to have constructed a dome. Only out in front was there some stretching room. He extended his leg. Yes, there was a hole there: a bit more than a foot in diameter. And where had he been working at the time of the bump? Of course, he knew. The seventh block from the manway, the third from the south wall.

What this meant was that Heinrich Wenzel was encapsuled from forty-two to forty-nine feet *in*, and fourteen to twenty-one feet to the left, of his questioners. And in view of the uncertain plunge of the debris, he might be on the 12th, the 11th, possibly as low as the 10th, floor.

Officialdom arrived. An hour had passed. There was a parley of superintendents and a long march up the manway ladders by Shuttleworth and McIntosh, Johnson and ten other miners. While Shuttleworth and Johnson conferred on possible ways of reaching Wenzel, George Preissler began exploring. He found the plank ceiling of the 10th floor, near the platform at least, quite sound.

He thrust his hands deep in under the ceiling in the few inches of air space atop the gravel backfill. Then he began pawing loose gravel out. He remarked that if they kept doing just this, removing loose matter and deepening the space under the 10th floor ceiling, they might be able to dig a good bit closer to Heinrich Wenzel.

There was a conference on it.

Someone remarked that at some point between where they stood and Wenzel, the 10th floor ceiling undoubtedly was punched in by debris, very likely impassably. On the other hand, if the rescuers could penetrate only ten feet, they would be ten feet closer to their man than they were now—and maybe they would chance upon some other interior byway through the debris.

The decision made itself. Short-handed picks and shovels were lifted to the 10th floor platform. Tunneling started shortly after 7 P.M.—one and a quarter hours into the ordeal of Heinrich Wenzel.

Including Preissler and Johnson, twenty miners took turns digging and they were all needed. Up forward, in his trap of rock, Wenzel was getting enough air; but in the tight space under the planking, men grunted with the heat, the stuffiness, the sour stench of their own straining bodies. There was a breeze of forced air in the manway, but the temperature was never below the 80's in the dusty tunnel. The miners' shirts caked with dirt on their backs. They had to control the interval that each man worked at the forward end of the tunnel: a minute or less. The dirt removed was relayed from shovel to shovel, passed back to the platform and down the chute. In order to have at least one solid wall, they burrowed along the south wall of the cave, keeping it at their right hand. They dug four feet down and three feet wide into the gravel backfill.

Their forward progress—per hour—averaged a few inches more than six feet.

Between rasps of their spades and their own audible breathing, the miners tried not to hear the noises Heinrich Wenzel, up ahead in the debris, could not prevent himself now from making. "Won't be long now, Henry! We're getting closer to you every minute!" they shouted in encouragement.

But in his capsule of darkness, Heinrich Wenzel was coming to a resolution.

From the point where the timber had chopped into his arm, great spears seemed to be dashing through his body, while up from the shoulder, along his neck and face, the pain rose like a clinging flame. Only the lower part of his left arm was without feeling. He held his left hand in his right. The fingers were limp: a dead man's hand. From his right trousers pocket he drew a pocket knife and opened the blade with his teeth. While he held the knife in his mouth, he made sure, by examination with his right hand, that the left arm was indeed nearly off. Yes, the bone was cleaved through. There was only an inch thickness of flesh and muscle. The arm was a loss. Only the pain was left to him, and now he would remove that. He took the knife from between his teeth and directed the blade . . .

At 10:45 P.M. a new shift of miners reported for duty. Enough of them volunteered to continue digging, so that all the original group could go home. But Preissler and Johnson remained. Both seemed to have taken hold of the rescue effort as a personal project. For good or ill, they could not bear to have its climactic moments occur while they were home in bed.

Inch by inch the tunnel grew. The first crew of miners had pushed it twenty feet. Now, as it lengthened, more men were needed to relay the removed gravel. The air grew stuffier. Though stretched out longer into the diggings, the men had to be relieved more often.

October 31 passed into November 1. One hour into the new day, a Tuesday, a murmur of dismay passed along the string of miners. Luck had run out. Having dug thirty-five feet, through the fifth cubicle from the platform, they found the ceiling of the sixth cubicle massively penetrated. Heavy chunks of rock and splintered timbers blocked any further progress.

The news was a special blow to Preissler and Johnson. When the other men cleared the tunnel, they crawled forward. In the light of their headlamps they inspected the obstructions. A pair of crossed timbers blocked the way, but it seemed to both men that the timbers were not actually supporting any overburden: their upper ends seemed loose in the plank ceiling. If the blockage were removed, might there not be a hole up into the 11th floor?

Preissler and Johnson crawled out of the tunnel, then went back in with a hand saw. They took turns sawing at the timbers: short turns, only three or four strokes each. Their breath came hard in the cramped, stale space. It was fifteen minutes' labor to saw through the timbers. Gingerly, not unmindful of the dangers of triggering additional collapse, they pulled the chunks of timber out—and nothing fell but a wisp of dust.

A 16-inch black hole gaped up into the 11th floor.

By now Heinrich Wenzel's entrapment had lasted more than seven hours. By supporting the weight of his left arm on his lap, he could slightly relieve the pain; but there was a certain high gleam below which his torment could not be dimmed. He had tried to complete the amputation of his arm, but the knife blade slicing on skin, muscle and ligament had set off such blasts of pain that he had not been able to go through with it. And he was thirsty. The desire for water grew to a fierce, quenchless longing. Why was he being punished like this? "Hurry!" he barked into the stone walls. "Hurry!"

George Preissler decided that he could wriggle through the 16-inch opening up into the 11th floor. An agile six-footer, he weighed only 150 pounds. But more important than the suitability of Preissler's physique, Wenzel seemed to have become his special responsibility. Perhaps it was the bond of language, the familiar inflection of those pleas filtering through the stone. He looked deceptively boyish to be serving as the leading edge of a grim rescue mission. Under a shock of sandy hair, his neat features could break into a truly elfin grin, with merry eyes and a startling flash of sharp white teeth. A man equally at home on top of mountains as inside them, his skiing was so good that he served as an instructor at a United States ski resort in the snow season. Twenty-nine years old, he had worked ten years in Canadian mines after having completed in Germany two years toward a civil engineering degree which he still hoped to obtain one day.

And now this man of wind, light, space, and speed was lying on his belly a third of a mile underground at the closed end of an almost suffocating dirt tunnel.

Preissler extended his arms up into the 11th floor. The light of his headlamp only partially hinted at the shape of the upper cavity. By groping lightly with his hands—he certainly did not want to pluck down any debris—he established the existence of a space at least large enough to admit his arms and shoulders.

And so he gripped with his fingers in the rubbled floor of the cavity; and with the toes of his rubber boots biting in the gravel tunnel behind him, he squirmed upward and slightly to the left, drawing his head, then his shoulders and the upper part of his torso into the opening.

He paused there to reconnoiter.

He appeared to be in a space about eighteen inches wide and

roughly of equal height. In the light of his lamp, as he twisted his head about, he could observe that this space extended some distance upward and to the left. So far, very good: that was the direction in which Wenzel presumably lay. The space reminded him of a digestive tract, an irregular gullet, its walls formed of tumbled planking and rocks.

Preissler understood that critical points of stress might well impinge on small rock fragments. Dislodge one innocent-looking stone and he might bring tons of overburden down on his back. Therefore he could not risk removing any material which might block his path. But if he should get into a spot which wedged him too tightly, so that he could not go forward or back, what then?

And with this question, for the first time in all these hours, George Preissler felt fear for himself. He was not a member of the mine rescue team. He had no *duty* to do what he was doing. Lying full length in the cavity, vividly imagining the sensation of being squashed to death, he felt his heart pounding high in his chest.

There was an impulse to turn back but he accepted it as a goad to go forward. With his fingers ahead and the toes of his boots behind, he dug in and hauled his hips, his thighs, his knees, up into the cavity. The rubble on the floor made painful impressions through his denim shirt and trousers. That was all right. He was content to embrace a rocky floor if he could avoid brushing the walls and ceiling.

The cavity was canted upward and to the left, so Preissler had to climb and twist as well as make "forward" progress. When he had drawn his full length into the cavity, his hands, probing ahead, touched something he did not like at all. It was a place where the vertical clearance squeezed to just fourteen inches. The bottom curve of a boulder bulged down into the roof there. Preissler turned his head sideways as he approached this spot. With extreme caution, he fit his shoulders into it and hunched them through—at the same time, however, thinking that he might not be able to get *back* through such a strait jacket. As he worked his hips up into the ring of rock, he felt that they just about entirely filled the space. He would be able to pass, but first he would rest to regain some strength and control of his breathing. He felt ahead with his outstretched hands meanwhile.

Well, now, this was good! The space ahead felt much bigger—two feet high and a good three feet wide. This cheered him, and he advanced confidently for about a yard before touching more bad news.

It was a rock projecting six inches from the floor of the cavity and extending across it like a curbstone. With his hands Preissler tested the vertical clearance above this step. Finding it about eighteen inches, he decided he probably could move up and over it. He wriggled slightly forward and put his hands over the ledge. Now, gripping some debris beyond it and digging in with his boot toes behind, he slithered up over the projection.

"I'm over here!"

The voice sounded so close it startled him.

Heinrich Wenzel had been listening with almost uncontrollable eagerness to Preissler's struggles in the passage, and at last he had caught a flicker of the rescuer's lamp.

Preissler could not see Wenzel, but the sound of his voice placed him only five or six feet away now. The rescuer squirmed forward about two feet and felt the cavity once again twist upward and to the left. He accommodated his body to this curve, wormed his way another foot or two upward, stretched out his right hand, and touched Heinrich Wenzel's boot.

Both men were startled into a rather formal greeting. Preissler asked Wenzel how he felt; the latter mechanically replied, "All right," as though the two of them were meeting before a sidewalk cafe in their native country, but then Wenzel immediately told of his raging thirst and the throbbing pain in his arm.

By the light of his headlamp Preissler meanwhile noted that the only exit from the trapped man's chamber was the selfsame hole they were speaking through: a roundish opening between jagged halves of a split timber.

It appeared to be only twelve inches across.

Wenzel was pleading for water and something for his pain.

"I will bring it to you," said Preissler, adding with a joviality he did not feel, "Don't worry. We'll get you out now that we have found you." But he was not happy about the tiny size of the opening from Wenzel's chamber.

Preissler, of course, had no room to turn around for his return. He had to wriggle backwards on his belly—feet first—over the course he had crawled to reach Wenzel. Taking extreme care not to dislodge any debris at the critical points of clearance, he made his way back to the gravel tunnel. It was fourteen feet away from Wenzel's outstretched foot.

Word that Preissler had reached the trapped man preceded him to the 10th floor platform. He took grateful breaths of the breeze blowing in the manway as he reported to Shuttleworth and Dr. Flather. The latter gave him a capsule of morphine for Wenzel; Preissler put it in his shirt pocket. Then he took a tin cup full of water and reentered the tunnel.

His second squirming journey up the passage of debris was trickier: he wanted to keep from spilling all the water. What he did was set the cup ahead of him on small level spots, then catch up, and move it farther. A closed canteen would have been easier, but what was available was a tin cup. And he brought it through. With a shaking hand, Wenzel received the water and the pain killer, downed them; and after a minute or so, he was able to talk with a certain calm.

He said he did not believe there was any way for him to get out with his arm as it was. The limb was nothing but a burden now. He had, in fact, tried to cut it off. Should he stay, trapped, clutching a useless arm, or should he rid himself of it and, perhaps, get free? He wished to have a tool to complete the amputation.

Preissler whistled softly. "That is a question for the doctor," he said. He promised to explain to the others how Wenzel felt, and then he backed once more down the passage.

"How can I judge without examining the man?" said Dr. Flather. The facts did not add up. Could an arm be so nearly severed as Preissler described, and yet the victim not bleed to death? But it was nearly eight hours since the accident: grim jest, indeed, if Wenzel's arm were sounder than a delirious man could realize, and yet he were to die of shock.

"I've got to go in there," the doctor said.

"You wouldn't get through the tight spots," said Preissler, frowning at the physician's waistline.

"If you could, I could."

"Don't be too sure. You don't know how cramped it is."

They faced each other just short of belligerence: the boyish but experienced German and the bristling young medical man, plucky but clearly out of his element underground. With crew-cut black hair and dark-rimmed glasses, Flather stood five feet ten and weighed 165 pounds. He was not fond of being called a fat man, or having it insinuated that he did not belong here. Still at the start of his career as a physician and surgeon, he had a curious and frank manner which had enabled him to learn quite a lot about miners, their daily lives, their predictable occupational ailments.

John Johnson, who had been listening to the discussion, had a thought. Johnson stood six feet and weighed 190 pounds; he was at least as ample in silhouette as the doctor. If he, Johnson, could traverse the passage, then it ought to be safe enough, would it not? In short, veteran miner Johnson was volunteering to test the safety of the course for the doctor, with his own body.

Ten minutes later Johnson had his face next to Heinrich Wenzel's boot and was confidently telling him the surgeon soon would follow.

But, in fact, both going up and coming down, Johnson barely scraped through the first critical point of clearance. His report to the superintendent and to Flather was free of any effort to "sell" the doctor. The passage was extremely perilous and restrictive, he said solemnly.

"You *were* able to reach him, though?" Flather insisted.

"I was."

"Then I should be able to," said the doctor, closing the subject.

Not having expected to take part in a rescue that day—not having ever, in fact, been in a mine before!—the physician far from epitomized how the well-equipped mine rescuer should be rigged out. His hardhat was all right—but those street shoes, and shirt and sweater, and flannel trousers! He did carry a useful small kit containing scissors, forceps, bandages, and a roll of cotton.

And he proved to be a skillful squirmer, for a beginner. His hips and waist filled the first point of clearance, however, and pressed with considerable force against the ceiling and floor. It was a tight scrape to get through, but get through he did. He found the second "curbstone" restriction easier. After a crawl of ten minutes, he was examining his patient through the foot-wide circle in the debris, by the light of his headlamp.

The doctor gave a small grunt of astonishment. He would not expect to see too many cases like *this* in his medical career! The upper bone of Heinrich Wenzel's arm was completely severed, to be sure. And the mysterious failure to bleed?

Well, there was the artery—fat as a finger—winking in the headlamp beam like a closed eyelid. The falling timber evidently had pinched it shut, crimped it the way a hot pliers would a plastic tube. If it hadn't, the arm would have simply gushed. Wenzel would have bled to death in three minutes. In any case the trapped man had known what he was talking about. His arm absolutely was a loss.

The doctor asked, "Has the morphine helped, eh?"

"*Yah.*"

"Don't feel much pain there now?"

"Mostly all gone."

"Then we better finish taking that arm off."

"Please," said Wenzel. "Please, yes."

Lying prone in the rubble, Flather removed his surgical scissors, cotton, and bandages from the kit. He saw that he could not reach through the opening as far as Wenzel's arm. "Can you bend down toward me a little closer?"

The miner placed his right hand for leverage on the floor. He lifted himself slightly forward and twisted the upper portion of his body down, so that his left shoulder was opposite the opening in the debris.

From his prone position, Dr. Flather reached through with his scissors, quickly snipped through the flesh, and completed the amputation. Wenzel squeezed his eyelids shut but made no sound.

"Just," said the doctor—and he had to clear his throat—"just hold still a bit longer . . . let me get a bandage on that."

With some help from Wenzel's right hand, Flather worked a crude but effective bandage around the stump of the arm and up over the left shoulder. "That ought to hold long enough," he said. He then wrapped in bandages the amputated arm. He was ready to leave. He had spent a total of about five minutes with the trapped miner. "You feel all right, now?" he said, checking. Wenzel nodded. "Not like you're going to pass out on me?"

Shaking his head, Wenzel managed a wan smile. "No, okay now," he said.

The doctor nodded. "See you out there, then," he said. And he backed away down the passage, drawing after him his kit and Heinrich Wenzel's amputated arm.

But now that he had done his duty by his patient, the perils of the squirming, backwards, return trip truly dawned upon him. It was as though one tide—call it professionalism if not valor—had ebbed out of him, and another tide rolled in, sickening and suffocating. His face rubbed dirt, and the way his backside was scraping the ceiling, he could well bring tons of rock down upon himself. He *was* too fat! And what if he could not get back through the narrowest space? His heart was pounding as he reached the constriction. His hips felt as if he were trying to stuff them down into an iron pipe. He was fighting against panic. He squirmed; he hammered his hips down into the ring of stone. Down! he said to himself, get through! He heaved his breath out, emptied himself of air, and the stone vise slowly passed up over his waist, his chest, his turned head. He pulled his kit and the amputated arm after him. With a relief he dared not give voice to, he felt men's hands behind him, easing his legs down into the gravel tunnel.

The ultimate question remained: could Heinrich Wenzel squeeze through the meager opening out of his cell? Indeed, could any man, even one in strong physical condition—much less someone with a freshly amputated arm?

Seven minutes later, George Preissler was up the passage, trying to talk Wenzel through.

First the injured man tried extending his feet forward into the opening and, from a sitting position, attempted to work his hips down in.

Impossible. Not only did his thighs, as they closed the opening, cut off all light from Preissler's headlamp—leaving Wenzel once more in total darkness—but his hips, supporting his weight, naturally broadened too much to penetrate the tunnel. "No good like this," he said.

He backed away and drew his legs once more up into his cell.

There are a great many household refrigerators larger than the chamber in which Heinrich Wenzel now laboriously began turning himself. He rotated as a physician might attempt to turn a baby from the breech to the head-down position for birth.

Shaped like a funnel, the total space in which Wenzel was trapped was about three and a half feet long and two and a half feet in width and height at the back, but tapering narrowly toward the opening at his feet.

Wenzel drew his legs up and slightly to the left as he bent at the knees. Hunching his torso forward, he put himself into a tight crouch. He extended his right arm through the opening into the passage, while scraping his knees and legs backward to the rear of his chamber.

Now he was prone. He worked his head through the opening. By squirming and twisting, he inserted his good right shoulder; then, very carefully, his bandaged left shoulder. Ironically, the absence of the bulk of his left arm made it possible for him to squeeze out of his trap.

His feet, pushing back against the rear wall of his cell, gave him propulsive force. A few feet ahead of him, George Preissler's headlamp guided him on. No matter the biting of the tight jagged opening in the timber against his waist and hips!—he twisted and turned and scratched and bled them through the neck of the chamber.

And now, head down, blood pounding at his temples, he followed George Preissler's retreating light down the twisting, narrow passage. His good right hand, his only hand now, scratched forward. Preissler's voice was urging him forward, praising and encouraging him. How tight the dark sheath of rock and rubble was. And yet it was releasing him. He was getting through. And panting, bruised, in pain and in joy, Heinrich Wenzel came out, reborn into the outstretched, welcoming hands of men.

Based on the facts as told in His Arm or His Life?, *George J. Preissler was awarded a silver Carnegie Hero Award medal while Dr. Barrie C. Flather and John Johnson earned bronze medals.*